AFRICAN-ASIAN READING GUIDE
for Children and Young Adults

by

Jeanette Hotchkiss

The Scarecrow Press, Inc.
Metuchen, N.J.   1976

Also by Jeanette Hotchkiss:

American Historical Fiction and Biography for Children and Young People (Scarecrow Press, 1973)

European Historical Fiction and Biography for Children and Young People, 2d ed. (Scarecrow Press, 1972).

Library of Congress Cataloging in Publication Data

Hotchkiss, Jeanette.
   African-Asian reading guide for children and young adults.

   Includes indexes.
   1. Eastern hemisphere--Juvenile literature.--Juvenile literature--Bibliography. I. Title.
Z1975.H68   [D891]   016.909'09'811   75-37530
ISBN 0-8108-0886-2

Copyright © 1976 by Jeanette Hotchkiss
Manufactured in the United States of America

TRAVEL

by Robert Louis Stevenson

I should like to rise and go
Where the golden apples grow;--
Where below another sky
Parrot islands anchored lie
And, watched by cockatoos and goats,
Lonely Crusoes building boats;--
Where in sunshine reaching out
Eastern cities, miles about,
Are with mosque and minaret
Among sandy gardens set,
And the rich goods from near and far
Hang for sale in the bazaar;--
Where the Great Wall round China goes
And on one side the desert blows,
And with bell and voice and drum,
Cities on the other hum;--
Where are forests, hot as fire,
Wide as England, tall as a spire,
Full of apes and cocoa-nuts
And the negro hunters' huts;--
Where the knotty crocodile
Lies and blinks in the Nile,
And the red flamingo flies
Hunting fish before his eyes;--
Where in jungles, near and far,

Man-devouring tigers are,
Lying close and giving ear
lest the hunt be drawing near,
Or a comer-by be seen
Swinging in a palanquin;--
Where among the desert sands
Some deserted city stands,
All its children, sweep and prince,
Grown to manhood ages since,
Not a foot in street or house,
Not a stir of child or mouse,
And when kindly falls the night,
In all the town no spark of light.
There I'll come when I'm a man
With a camel caravan;
Light a fire in the gloom
of some dusty dining-room;
See the pictures on the walls,
Heroes, fights and festivals;
And in a corner find the toys
Of the old Egyptian boys.

TABLE OF CONTENTS

Introduction	ix
Note on Symbols and Spellings	xii

Part One: AFRICA, ASIA AND EUROPE
    Non-fiction   1
    Biographies   3
    Folklore and Fiction   4

Part Two: AFRICA
Africa in General   5
    Non-fiction   5
    Biographies   11
    Folklore   14
    Fiction   15
Northeastern Africa (Egypt, Ethiopia, Libya, The Sudan)   16
    Non-fiction   17
    Biographies   21
    Folklore   23
    Fiction--Ancient Egypt   23
    Fiction--Other   27
East Africa (Burundi, Kenya, Rwanda, Somali Republic, Tanzania, Uganda)   29
    Non-fiction   29
    Biographies   33
    Folklore   34
    Fiction   35
Northwestern Africa and the Sahara (Algeria, Mauritania, Morocco, Spanish Sahara, Tunisia)   40
    Non-fiction   40
    Biographies   41
    Folklore   42
    Fiction   43
West Africa (Cameroon, Central African Republic, Chad, Dahomey, Equatorial Africa, Gambia, Ghana, Guinea, Guinea-Bissau, Ivory Coast, Liberia, Mali, Niger, Nigeria, Senegal, Sierra Leone, Togo, Upper Volta)   46

Table of Contents

Non-fiction	47
Biographies	50
Folklore	52
Fiction	55
Central Africa (People's Republic of the Congo, Gabon, Zaïre)	59
Non-fiction	59
Biographies	60
Fiction and Folklore	62
Southern Africa (Angola, Botswana, Lesotho, Malagasy Republic, Malawi, Mauritius, Mozambique, Republic of South Africa, Rhodesia, Namibia/South West Africa, Swaziland, Zambia)	64
Non-fiction	65
Biographies	68
Folklore	69
Fiction	70

Part Three: ASIA

Asia in General	75
Non-fiction	75
Biographies	77
Folklore and Fiction	77
Turkey	78
Non-fiction	78
Biographies	80
Folklore	81
Fiction	82
The Middle East (Afghanistan, Iran, Iraq, Israel, Jordan, Kuwait, Lebanon, Muscat and Oman, Palestine, Saudi Arabia, Syria, United Arab Emirates)	84
Non-fiction	84
Biographies	93
Folklore	96
Fiction--Biblical	98
Fiction--Historical	102
Fiction--Contemporary	104
The Soviet Union in Asia	111
Non-Fiction	112
Biographies	113
Folklore	113
Fiction	114
India and Neighboring Countries (Bangladesh, Bhutan, Burma, Nepal, Pakistan, Sikkim, Sri Lanka [Ceylon])	117
Non-fiction	117

Biographies	121
Folklore	124
Fiction	127
China and Neighboring Countries (Hong Kong, Manchuria, Mongolia, Taiwan, Tibet)	138
Non-fiction	139
Biographies	145
Folklore	149
Fiction	151
Japan and Korea	161
Non-fiction	162
Biographies	167
Folklore	168
Fiction	171
Southeast Asia (Cambodia, Indonesia, Laos, Malaysia, the Philippines, Singapore, Thailand, Vietnam)	179
Non-fiction	180
Biographies	185
Folklore	185
Fiction	186

Part Four: AUSTRALASIA AND OCEANIA
(Australia, Borneo, New Guinea, New Zealand, Tasmania)

Non-fiction	191
Biographies	197
Folklore	199
Fiction	200

Part Five: PICTURE BOOKS

Africa	215
Australia	217
China and Hong Kong	218
India	220
Japan	221
Middle East and Bible Stories	224
Mongolia	225
Southeast Asia	225
Turkey	226

INDEXES

Author	229
Title	239
Illustrator	262
Biographical	268

INTRODUCTION

Dear Young Readers of the Western Hemisphere:

You are hereby cordially invited to take passage on a voyage through the <u>eastern</u> hemisphere, to visit Africa, Asia, Australia, and the South Seas; to be transported by books, with a library card as your round-trip ticket. The purpose of the trip will be to acquire a sense of familiarity with, and deepening understanding of, the lands and peoples on the other side of the world.

As your guide, I shall not be dictatorial as to where you should go or how long you should stay in any one area of reading. You may be so intrigued by one in particular that you won't want to leave it and will want to pursue your reading beyond the books suggested here. Works of fiction, non-fiction, and biography (including autobiographical works, memoirs, etc.) are included; the sub-heading "Folklore" should be understood to contain myths and legends as well.

I have purposely refrained from starring any titles as being better or more important than others. Each has its own merit or it would not have been included but in books as in other matters there is no accounting for tastes, and I leave it up to readers to make their own judgments and choices. I often think of long-ago days when my younger brother, George, and I were growing up, very close, yet strongly disagreeing about books. We finally had to abstain from giving each other literary birthday presents.

As tastes differ, so do reading abilities and interests --too widely, indeed, for strict age classification. Just think how quickly the picture book set grow up to go to school, intermediates become young adults, and junior highschoolers go into senior high and then to college. So as to reader age, this is an integrated guide in which elementary books often share pages with adult novels. Many of the titles listed here may provide suggestions for family enjoyment, for reading aloud or lively discussions. I like to imagine grandparents (being one myself) sharing with one of the younger generation an amusing folktale or scary story.

As you start on this reading voyage, I strongly recommend having an atlas at hand (as up to date as possible) but I realize that this is not always practical, so I have arranged the guidebook in geographical "chunks," introducing each section with the old and new names of the included countries and stating briefly the present, and immediately preceding, governmental status of each. This will, I hope, aid readers in visualizing the relative geographical setting of a book they wish to read. Many books of fiction as well as non-fiction contain maps and diagrams.

Books that are sequels to another or are part of a trilogy or other series are arranged under author by their order within the series, as a convenience to the browser.

So bon voyage, my young fellow readers. You are in for an exciting and richly rewarding trip.

SOURCES AND ACKNOWLEDGMENTS

The sources of this book were manifold: my own memories of reading enjoyment, conversations with family and friends of various ages, and reading the shelves in libraries, not only, though mainly, in childrens' rooms, but also in the general stacks (particularly in the travel category). Then, with suggestions alphabetically listed from these sources, and from those listed below, I searched out the books I wanted to see and read. Serendipity played an important part in my research as it often happened that seeking one particular book in vain, I came upon another of which I had never heard but which suited my purpose remarkably well.

As is always the case in compiling a bibliography, the author regrets the deserving books that have been missed, but it has been my steadfast principle to read, or at the very least scan, every book that goes into my book.

Below is a short list of principal published sources:

<u>Africa: An Annotated List of Printed Materials Suitable for Children</u>; Information Center on Childrens' Cultures, 1968.

The Near East and North Africa: An Annotated List of Materials for Children; Information Center on Childrens' Cultures, 1970.
(The above two are both publications of the United States Committee for UNICEF.)

Asia: A Guide to Books for Children. The Asia Society, 1966.

Eakin, Mary K. Good Books for Children, 3d ed. Chicago: University of Chicago Press, 1966. A selection of outstanding children's books published 1950-65.

Sutherland, Zena. The Best in Childrens' Books, 1966-72. Chicago: University of Chicago Press, 1973.

The Horn Book Magazine, The New York Times (Sunday) Book Review section, Publishers Weekly, World Almanac and Book of Facts 1975 (published by the Chicago Tribune), and other catalogues and publications too numerous to list.

"There is always something new out of Africa," wrote Pliny the Elder, way back in the first century A.D., and this is certainly true in the twentieth. I am most grateful for the help given me in respect to the African section of my book by Mr. Christopher Mojekwu of Lake Forest College, and Mr. Hans Panofsky, the curator of the Library of African Studies at Northwestern University, Evanston, Illinois. My thanks also to the librarians in my home town of Highland Park, Illinois, and the neighboring towns of Waukegan, Lake Forest, Glencoe, Winnetka, Wilmette and Evanston, who made me feel so warmly welcome in their children's rooms and shared my enjoyment and excitement in this project.

Jeanette Kennan Hotchkiss

Highland Park, Illinois
January 1975

NOTE ON SYMBOLS AND SPELLINGS

The following symbols designate approximate reading and interest levels:

PB   Picture Books

E   Elementary from kindergarten through 2d grade

I   Intermediate, to junior high school

I up   Intermediate to senior high school

YA   Young Adult, mainly junior high school

YA up   Junior and senior high school

A   Adult, mainly college preparatory, but sometimes suitable for various or all ages.

The spelling of proper or place names is given as used by the authors and vary in some cases--e.g. "Ghengis" and "Genghis" Khan; "Bagdad" and "Baghdad"; "Mohammed" and "Muhammad"; "Shaka" and "Chaka," and numerous others.

Part One

AFRICA, ASIA, AND EUROPE

This short section includes books dealing with Africa, Asia, and, in the case of those about the Moslem Empire, with Europe as well.

Alexander of Macedon's empire spread over much of Asia but also dipped into Egypt. Vasco da Gama sailed around the Cape of Good Hope and visited African ports before he arrived in India and set up a marble pillar as a mark of Portuguese conquest. Intrepid 19th-century women explored the mysterious East from Central Africa to the Arctic. And the present newly-rich oil countries are situated in both Africa and Asia.

NON-FICTION

1 Ellis, Harry B. The Arabs. Ill. by Leonard Everett Fisher. World, 1968. A book about the Arabian peoples and culture in many countries of Asia and Africa and Europe. Also a history of Islam and the Bedouin nomads. Appended is a chart correlating Arabian history from A.D. 500 with other world events of importance. Even though it is not up to date, it is good background for current events in Arab countries. YA
2 Falls, C. B. The First 3,000 Years. Ill. by the author. Viking, 1960. A handsome book about the ancient civilizations of the valleys of the Tigris and Euphrates, and the Nile, and shores of the Mediterranean Sea. I, YA
3 Lengyel, Emil. The Oil Countries of the Middle East. Ill. with a map and photographs. Franklin Watts, 1973. An invaluable book for furthering understanding of current events in the Mideast, especially in consideration of the world oil crisis of the 1970s. The countries, with descriptions of their governments, economies and people are: Algeria, Libya, Iraq, Iran, Saudi Arabia, Kuwait, and Qatar. YA up

4 Price, Christine. The Story of Moslem Art. Ill. with photographs and drawings by the author. Dutton, 1974. This highly informative book is divided by chapters into regions and countries, and includes, aside from the usual art forms, carpet-making and mosque architecture. YA

5 Ruskin, Ariane. Prehistoric Art and Ancient Art of the Near East. Ill. with reproductions of cave paintings, carvings, jewelry, architecture and paintings. McGraw-Hill, 1971. An excellent book about prehistoric art in Africa and Europe and ancient art of Egypt and Mesopotamia. A relative index. YA up

6 Shippen, Katharine B. Portals to the Past; The Story of Archaeology. Ill. with stone lithographs by Mel Silverman. Viking, 1963. Most of the exciting stories of archaeological discoveries in this comprehensive and pleasantly readable book pertain to the African-Asian world of antiquity: Egypt, Mesopotamia, Assyria, Troy, Crete and new areas of exploration: the lost cities along the Indus River and stone age paintings in the Sahara desert. I, YA

7 Stewart, Desmond and the Editors of Life. The Arab World. Ill. with maps and photographs. Time Inc., 1962. A comprehensive book of Arabian history, culture, and conditions and politics as of 1962. An excellent reference book, for appended are the following lists and charts: historical dates, further reading suggestions, famous figures and works in Arab culture, and political units in the Arab world. The units listed with their population figures, areas, capitals and governments are: Aden (colony) Aden (protectorate), Algeria, Bahrain, Iraq, Jordan, Kuwait, Lebanon, Libya, Morocco, Muscat and Oman, Qatar, Saudi Arabia, Syria, the Sudan, the United Arab Emirates, Tunisia, Egypt and Yemen. In 1962 Egypt and Syria were for a short time the United Arab Republic. YA up

8 Suskind, Richard. The Sword of the Prophet, The Story of the Moslem Empire. Ill. by Enrico Arno. Grosset and Dunlap, 1972. In this handsomely illustrated book the author has managed to compress in 86 pages the entire history of Islam, beginning with Mohammad's revelations in Arabia (now Saudi Arabia) in the 7th century B.C.; through the wars, civil and foreign, which finally led to the formation of an empire even more extensive than the Roman one and which resulted in a religion practiced today by more than 500 million followers. YA up

Africa, Asia, Europe 3

BIOGRAPHIES

9   Fitch, Florence Mary. <u>Allah: the God of Islam, Moslem Life and Worship.</u> Ill. with photographs selected by Beatrice Creighton and the author. Lothrop, 1950. The story of the life of Mohammad (570?-632) and of Islam from the 7th century to the mid 20th. Most of its million followers are in the eastern world but there are many in Europe and the Americas also. Appended is a list of the 139 photographs and their sources, and an index. I, YA

10 Gunther, John. <u>Alexander the Great.</u> Ill. by Isa Barnett. Random, 1953 (a Landmark book). A biography of the King of Macedon who created an empire extending from the Greek states through Persia to India and into Egypt (356-323 B.C.). I

11 Mercer, Charles and the Editors of Horizon magazine. <u>Alexander the Great</u> (consultant, Cornelius Mermeuls III). Ill. with many paintings, mosaics, sculptures and maps of the period. American Heritage Pub. Co. 1962. A Horizon Caravel Book. A beautiful pictorial story of Alexander's life (356-323 B.C.) and his conquests. I, YA

12 Rittenhouse, Mignon. <u>Seven Women Explorers.</u> J. B. Lippincott, 1964. Seven brief and exciting biographies of the following women: Alexine Tinné (19th-century Africa), Florence Van Sass Baker (19th-century Africa), Delia J. Denning Akeley (19th- and 20th-century Africa), Fanny Bullock Workman (the Himalayas at the turn of the 20th century), Kathleen M. Kenyon (20th-century Jordan), Louise Arner Boyd (19th-century Arctic), and Lucy Bird Bishop (19th-century world traveler). YA up

13 Robinson, Charles Alexander Jr. <u>Alexander the Great, Conqueror and Creator of a New World.</u> Franklin Watts, 1963. A fine factual biography in which, though there are many details of military strategy and tactics, Alexander emerges as a man with a dream of world solidarity and the brotherhood of man. A chronological summary of the principal events of Alexander's life, and a map of Alexander's empire, 334-323 B.C. are useful additions to the book. YA

14 Suggs, Robert C. <u>Alexander the Great: Scientist-King.</u> Ill. by Leonard Everett Fisher. Macmillan, 1964 (Science Story Library). In this short biography (356-323 B.C.) we are shown a side of the great

conqueror, sometimes overlooked, as we see him at his studies under Aristotle and later as a king who believed in "one world" and whose dreams of empire were nearly fulfilled when he died at the early age of 33. I

15 Syme, Ronald. <u>Vasco da Gama; Sailor Toward the Sunrise.</u> Ill. by William Stobbs. Morrow, 1959. A biography of the man who first sailed from Portugal to India around the Cape of Good Hope (1497-99) and whose serious diplomatic mistakes in his relations with the Arabs, caused long enmity between them and the Portuguese. I

FOLKLORE AND FICTION

16 Andrews, Mary Evans. <u>Hostage to Alexander.</u> Ill. by Avery Johnson. <u>Longmans Green, 1961.</u> A story of Alexander the Great as narrated by a fictional young hostage from Rome, with a postscript identifying the historical figures, giving sources, and a map of Alexander's conquests. I

17 Baumann, Hans. <u>The Stolen Fire, Legends of Heroes and Rebels from Around the World.</u> Ill. by Herbert Holzing, translated by Stella Humphries. Pantheon Books, 1974. A collection of ancient legends about men and women who were faced with threats to their lives and freedom and who met the challenges either by their wits or with their physical strength. All the tales are from the eastern hemisphere except for four from North America, two from South America, and one from Mexico. I, YA

18 Fon Eisen, Anthony. <u>The Prince of Omeya.</u> World, 1964. An introduction sets the stage for this novel in the 8th-century Moslem world of Syria, Egypt and Africa, though its climax comes in Cordoba, Spain. It is about the thrilling escape from the Caliph of a rival house, of the last of the Ommiad dynasty of Syria, a subject suggested to the author by Washington Irving's "Spanish Papers." YA

Part Two

AFRICA

AFRICA IN GENERAL

The continent of Africa is so large and contains such varieties of topography, climate, peoples and cultures that it has seemed advisable for the purposes of this book to divide it into geographical sections: Northeast, East, Northwest, West, Central, and Southern. Each of these has divisions of its own, and the dividing lines are not longitudinally nor latitudinally exact, but this arrangement makes it possible to follow a map fairly easily, and even to visualize a map of the continent.

This section is for books about Africa as a whole, books that do not conveniently fit into the arbitrary divisions mentioned above; non-fiction books pertaining to the whole continent, or most of it, and stories with indefinite African settings. Also there are biographies of explorers who penetrated many parts of Africa.

NON-FICTION

19 Addison, John. Ancient Africa. Ill. with photographs. John Day, 1970 (The Young Historians' Books). A book about the centuries before the interior of Africa was opened up by explorers and missionaries, and before it was divided into colonies by the Europeans. It tells of the ancient states of Ghana, Mali and Songhai, Guinea, Benín, Oyo and Ashanti and we recognize some of those names once more in use. It also tells of such ancient rulers as Mansa Musa of Mali, Askia Mohammed of Songhai, Idris Alooma of Kanem-Bornu and Alfonso of Kongo. YA up

20 Allen, Samuel. Poems from Africa. Ill. by Romare Beorden. Thomas Y. Crowell, 1973. A book to own, if possible, for dipping into and rereading. Mr.

Allen, who selected these poems, speaks in his introduction about the twofold loss "in reducing the living word, whether spoken or sung, to the printed page" and "in translating it from the language in which it first was uttered" but he seems to have overcome both difficulties successfully as far as this general reader could determine. There are paragraph biographies of 24 poets, an index of poets and one of the origins of oral poems, and an index of the translators. YA up

21 Bayliss, John. Exploits in Africa. New York Graphic Society, 1964. Thirteen short stories, some amusing ones about animals, some terrifying tales about snake and crocodile hunting, and one about a 1936 air race to Johannesburg in a single-seat, open cockpit, second-hand Miles Hawk plane. The stories are excerpted from books by A. E. Clauston, Michaela Denis, Charles Lagus, Gerald Durrell, John Gunther, Alan Wyker, Paul L. Patus, Wynant D. Hubbard, Alexander Fullerton, J. A. Hunter, Alan Moorehead, and Attilio Gatti. Each story will tempt you to read the whole book from which it was taken. I up

22 Beebe, B. F. African Lions and Cats. Ill. by James Ralph Johnson. David Mckay, 1969. For those who have enjoyed the adventure stories of Willard Price, this small book will support the authenticity of his animal lore. I, YA

23 Bernheim, Marc and Evelyne. From Bush to City, A Look at the New Africa. Ill. with photographs. Harcourt, Brace and World, 1966. Generously illustrated with photographs, this is a lively objective story of the rapid change and progress in Africa (mainly south of the Sahara) in the fields of politics, religion, education, status of women, and the arts. YA up

24 Brooks, Lester. Great Civilizations of Ancient Africa. Ill. with many photographs of African artifacts, maps by Irmgard Lochner, designed by Lucy Bitzer. Four Winds Press, 1971. A well arranged book, scholarly and lively, including an invaluable time chart as well as bibliography and index. A book for thoughtful reading and reference and well worth older adults' attention. YA up

25 Chu, Daniel and Skinner, Elliott. A Glorious Age in Africa; The Story of Three African Empires. Ill. by Moneta Barnett. Zenith Books, Doubleday, 1965. A fascinating history of Central Africa from the 8th

Africa in General

to the 16th century and the successive rise of three great Sudanese empires--Ghana, Mali, and Songhay. YA up

26 Coughlin, Robert and the Editors of Life. Tropical Africa. Ill. in color, and black and white photographs. Time, Inc., 1962. A handsome and enlightening book about "Black Africa," invaluable for its historical content up to the time of publication. Since then many of these nations have become independent, and political situations have changed. I up

27 Davidson, Basil. African Kingdoms. Ill. with color photographs, and reproductions of paintings, sculpture and other works of art. Time-Life, 1966. A colorful, pictorial book about the great ancient kingdoms. YA up

28 _____. A Guide to African History. Ill. by Robin Jaques, Rev. and ed. by Haskell Frankell. Doubleday, 1965. A remarkable little book which somehow manages to compress into 112 pages a "satellite's view" of the great mysterious continent. True it is almost impossible to keep up with name changes, but that is of minor consequence, as we quickly and easily grasp the main historic periods and follow the illustrations and maps. I up

29 Glubok, Shirley. The Art of Africa. Ill. with special photography by Alfred H. Tamarin, designed by Gerard Nook. Harper, 1965. All of Miss Glubok's "Art of" books are outstanding for text, illustrations and design, but this one is particularly exciting, because African art has only fairly recently been recognized and pictured. I up

30 Hoff, Rhoda. Africa: Adventures in Eyewitness History. Henry Z. Walck, 1963. A collection of firsthand stories of Africa, by 45 writers, covering the history of the continent from the 5th century B.C. (Herodotus), through A.D. 1816. YA up

31 Kaula, Edna Mason. The Bantu Africans. Ill. with photographs and a map. Franklin Watts, 1968. Bantu is a name given to millions of Africans of many different countries. Here the author takes up briefly the recent history of the following countries: Tanzania, the Democratic Republic of the Congo, Uganda, Kenya, Malawi, Zambia, Republic of South Africa, Botswana, Lesotho, Swaziland, Angola and Mozambique. YA up

32 Kimble, George H. T. and Steel, Ronald. Tropical Africa Today. Ill. with photographs, maps and charts.

McGraw-Hill, 1966. An adaptation of the Twentieth Century Fund study of tropical Africa--the countries south of the Sahara and north of the Republic of South Africa. YA up

33 Lens, Sidney. Africa, Awakening Giant. Ill. with photographs and a map of the countries and islands of Africa. G. P. Putnam's, 1962. A good readable history, primarily about people rather than economics and geography. YA

34 McDowell, Robert E. and Lavitt, Edward. Third World Voices for Children. Ill. by Barbara Kohn Isaac. The Third Press, 1971 (Odarkai Books). A collection of stories, folktales and poems by Africans, many of whose traditions were carried by slaves into the Caribbean islands and the United States. I up

35 McGregor-Hastie, Roy. Africa-Background for Today. Ill. with photographs and maps. Criterion, 1967. A well-organized basic book in which the author has covered an amazing number of subjects: colonization, exploration, slave trade, development of resources, and rebellions. There are also sketches of prominent African leaders, White and Black. YA up

36 McKown, Robin. The Colonial Conquest of Africa. Ill. with prints and photographs and maps by George Buctel. Franklin Watts, 1971. A concise, readable book on the subject of colonization, with clearly drawn maps of the various territories: one of "Africa 1938" when Liberia, Egypt, and South Africa were the only independent countries (although Ethiopia had been since B.C. until conquered by the Italians in the 1930's), and one of "Today" (meaning 1971). A good chart, at the end, of present-day Africa and its colonial background. YA

37 Murphy, E. Jefferson. Understanding Africa. Ill. by Louise E. Jefferson. Thomas Y. Crowell, 1969. An attractively made book, with explicitly informative maps and cleanly drawn illustrations, its authoritative text written by the executive vice-president of the African-American Institute. YA up

38 Neurath, Marie and Worboys, Evelyn. They Lived Like This in Ancient Africa. Ill. by Evelyn Worboys. Isotype Institute and, Franklin Watts, 1967. What a pleasant way to learn a good deal about ancient Africa in a very short time. E, I

39 Nickel, Helmut. Arms and Armor in Africa. Ill. with photographs and drawings by the author and map. Atheneum, 1971. Facts about the cultures of the

peoples whose armaments are here described, divided into the following regions: West Africa, the Sudan, the Congo, East Africa, North Africa and South Africa. I, YA

40 Nolan, Barbara. Africa Is People: First Hand Accounts from Contemporary Africa. Ill. with photographs; with an introduction by Dr. Mercer Cook. E. P. Dutton, 1967. The accounts are by the following authors: Camara Laye, Mbonu Ojike, Jomo Kenyatta, Robert Wellesley Cole, Noni Jabavu, Baba of Karo, Laurens van der Post, Colin Turnbull, Chief Kabongo, David Reed, Alan Moorehead, Anne Putnam, Barbara Hall, Esther Warner, Leopold Sédar Senghor, André Malraux, W. W. C. Echezona, Father Trevor Huddleston, Norman Cousins, Louis B. Leakey, Chinua Achebe, Robert Collis, Peter Abrahams, Ulli Beir, Legson Kayira, Garry Fullerton, David Hapgood, Nancy Scott, Julius Nyerere, Mary Benson, and Cunduzu K. Chisiza. The selections are presented under three headings, The Way of the Ancestors, Currents and Cross Currents, and The Wind of Change. Appended are suggestions for further reading and at the beginning is a map accompanied by a key to the areas represented by the selections, an editor's note, and the introduction by Dr. Cook, former U.S. Ambassador to Niger, Gambia and Senegal. YA up

41 Ojigbo, A. Okion. (What It Means to Be) Young and Black in Africa. Ill. with photographs. Random, 1971. With an introductory note by the compiler, Mr. Ojigbo. Dramatic episodes from their own lives are related by eight Africans: Prince Modupe (Guinea), Olandah Equiano (Nigeria), Charity Waciumba (Kenya), Peter Abrahams (South Africa), Francis Selormey (Ghana), R. Mugo Gatheru (Kenya), Babs Fafuna (Nigeria), and Legson Kayira (Malawi). YA up

42 Olden, Sam. Getting to Know Africa's French Community. Ill. by Harris Petie. Coward McCann, 1961. An introduction to the sister republics having special ties with each other and with France, as of 1961 (names and ties change quickly these days): the Central African Republic, the Gabon Republic, Islamic Republic of Mauritania, the Malagasy Republic, the Republic of Chad, the Republic of the Congo, the Republic of Dahomey, the Republic of the Ivory Coast, the Republic of the Niger, the Republic of Senegal,

the Republic of the Upper Volta, and the Republic of the Sudan. I
43 Pine, Tillie S. and Levine, Joseph. The Africans Knew. Ill. by Anne Grifalconi. McGraw-Hill, 1967. A book about some of the wonderful things Africans knew and did long, long ago, and how we can perform experiments that will help us to understand their ancient ways, such as making musical instruments like theirs. Good ideas for fun on a rainy day. E, I
44 Price, Christine. Talking Drums of Africa. Ill. with photographs and drawings by the author. Scribner's, 1973. A discussion of the place of talking drums in the lives of the Yoruba and Ashanti tribes, a description of how the drums are made, and of the skills needed by the drummers.
45 Savage, Katherine. The Story of Africa South of the Sahara. Ill. with photographs and maps. Henry Z. Walck, 1961. Accounts of explorers and missionaries and colonizers of the dark continent. YA
46 Sterling, Thomas and the Editors of Horizon Magazine. Explorations of Africa. Ill. with paintings, drawings, and maps of the period. American Heritage, 1963. A rich, colorful book of famous explorers and their explorations. The drawings made by members of the exploring parties and the well-written text make for pleasurable as well as instructive reading. YA
47 Sutton, Felix. The Illustrated Book about Africa. Ill. by H. B. Vestal, created and designed by Archie Bennett; introd. by Stuart Cloete. Grosset and Dunlap, 1959. It is hard to imagine a finer introduction to this land of mystery. As Cloete says, in his introduction, "The story is not an easy one to tell between the covers of one book. Felix Sutton is to be congratulated upon having done it so well." all ages
48 Thompson, Elizabeth Bartlett. Africa, Past and Present. Ill. with photographs and maps. Houghton Mifflin, 1966. The organization, chapter titles, and narrative style of the writing provide a panorama of the vast continent which helps the reader comprehend the sweep of its history. Included are biographies of some of the men who have had an important impact on the land and its people. YA up
49 Turnbull, Colin. The Peoples of Africa. Ill. by Richard M. Powers. World, 1962. Here is not only a handsomely illustrated and well-told story of African cultures, but an invaluable reference book because of its

Africa in General

appended "Chronological Chart of Africa and World Events." YA up

50 Vlahos, Olivia. African Beginnings. Ill. by George Ford. Viking, 1967. A well organized, informative and interestingly written book, describing folk and tribal patterns from the earliest organized social life and kingdoms and sociological systems, with a long, divided bibliography and good index. YA up

BIOGRAPHIES

51 Alter, Robert Edmond. Henry M. Stanley, The Man from Africa. Maps by Steele Savage. G. P. Putnam's, 1967. Henry Stanley, whose real name was John Rowlands, was born in northern Wales in 1841 and died in England in 1904. He spent some time in the United States where he was an unwilling soldier in the Confederate army, but the most important years of his life were spent in Africa. A good lively narrative of an always exciting life. I, YA

52 Benét, Laura. Stanley, Invincible Explorer. Dodd Mead, 1960. A full length biography (1841-1904) but necessarily a selective one because of the mass of material available. The author has chosen the most striking episodes in Stanley's exciting and dramatic life. Too many people only know of him as the man who discovered Livingstone in the African jungle, but there is much much more to know. His childhood and youth were most unusual and very harsh--even his name was that by adoption--and his expeditions, aside from the one in search of Livingstone, opened up what was to become the Belgian Congo. YA up

53 Crane, Louise. Ms. Africa: Profiles of Modern African Women. Ill. with photographs of the subjects. Lippincott, 1973. The remarkable women whose stories are told in this book are Annie Jiagge (Ghana)--and the Women Who Went Before Her: Julia Barbara de Lima Sedode and Henrietta Louise Baeta; Efira Sutherland (Ghana); Angie Brooks (Liberia); Irene Ighodaro (Nigeria); Margaret Kenyatta (Kenya); Gwendoline Komi (Zambia), Rahantavololona Andriamanjato (Madagascar); and, from South Africa, Joyce Sikhakane, Winnie Mandela, Brigilia Bam, and Miriam Makeba. The careers of these outstanding women have been in the fields of the law, the ministry, literature and music, engineering, social work, and,

especially the South African women, the struggle for freedom and civil rights, but all have distinguished themselves in many ways while maintaining their essential womanliness. YA up

54 Dobler, Lavinia and Brown, William A. Great Rulers of the African Past. Ill. by Yvonne Johnson. Doubleday, 1965 (Zenith Books). A short, well-made, readable book, with a map of the territory ruled preceding each chapter. The chosen subjects are: Mansa Musa (1312-37); Sunni Ali Ben, the Conqueror (1464-92); Askia Muhammed (1493-1528); Afonso I (1506-45); Idris Alooma (1580-1617). A guide to pronounciation is appended. I

55 Eaton, Jeanette. David Livingstone, Foe of Darkness. Ill. by Ralph Ray. Morrow, 1947 (Morrow Junior Books). A fictionalized biography of the explorer-missionary-scientist (1813-73) who was born in Scotland and died in the Africa to which he was dedicated, showing his courage and idealism. The perils he faced and the suffering he endured in his persistent explorations and missionary work were inspired by his will to counteract the evils of slavery and tribal warfare. YA

56 Hall-Quest, Olga. With Stanley in Africa. Map by Rus Anderson. E. P. Dutton, 1961. A biography of the intrepid explorer (1841-1904) born in England, American by adoption, and African by vocation, whose quest for Dr. Livingstone was only the beginning of his exciting adventures on that continent. I, YA

57 Hennessy, Maurice and Sauter, Edwin Jr. Soldier of Africa. Ives Washburn, 1965 (Men of Africa Series). A dramatized biography of Charley Maigumeri, a Nigerian soldier, who first, when fighting with the German army in Africa in World War I, was captured by the British and served that country with such distinction in both World Wars, that he was decorated by Queen Elizabeth II when Nigeria became an independent republic and member of the British Commonwealth in 1960. Written by a man who actually knew Charley and found him to be not only a great soldier but a great man in every way. YA

58 Kaula, Edna Mason. Leaders of the New Africa. Ill. by the author. World, 1966. A collective biography, with a short history of each of the emerging nations from which these leaders spring. There are 37 brief biographies with many more names mentioned, too many to list here. An interesting black and white

Africa in General

map of Africa has below it a key to the names of the countries outlined--at least as of the date of publication. Some have changed since 1966. YA up

59 Mitchison, Naomi. African Heroes. Ill. by William Stobbs. Farrar, Straus & Giroux, 1968. Accounts of eleven African heroes, their backgrounds covering all of Africa south of the Sahara, and their periods spanning the centuries from 1300 to 1900: Sundiata, Mai Idris, Maru Kongo, Okomfor Anoyke, Ja Ja, Shaka, Moshesh, Kgamanyane, Lobengula, Khama, Cetshwayo. YA up

60 Purton, Rowland W. Doctor Livingstone. Ill. by Alan Gilham. McGraw-Hill, 1968. An exceptionally well arranged and vivid biography of the missionary-explorer with many maps and drawings, particularly a geographical note for those who may like to trace Livingstone's travels on a large contemporary map, giving place name changes since his time (1813-73). Appended is a list of important dates and a glossary. I, YA

61 Smith, Fredrica Shumway. Stanley, African Explorer. Ill. by Charles Moser and with a map. Rand McNally, 1968. A biography of Henry Morton Stanley, born John Rowland in England in 1841, but adopted by an American who gave him his name, and the stories of his three strenuous, dangerous expeditions into darkest Africa: the Livingstone expedition, 1871; the Congo expedition, 1874-77; the Emir Pasha expedition, 1887-89. I, YA

62 Syme, Ronald. African Traveler, The Story of Mary Kingsley. Ill. by Jacqueline Tomes. Morrow Jr. Books, 1962. Mary Kingsley was born in England in 1862 and died in 1900 while nursing in a Boer prison camp. When she was 31, she began her career as an explorer in southwest Africa, making three perilous jungle journeys, decorously clad in ankle-length skirt and long-sleeved blouse, wearing a flowered bonnet and armed only with an umbrella. She spoke sternly to cannibals, leopards and gorillas and bopped a hungry crocodile on the snout. As Rudyard Kipling wrote, "Being human, Mary Kingsley must have been afraid of something, but one never found out what it was." Syme says of her, "one of the greatest, perhaps the greatest Englishwoman of her age." I up

FOLKLORE

63 Aardema, Verna. <u>Otwe.</u> Ill. by Elton Fax. Coward McCann, 1960. A tale, based on "The Man and the Snake" by Ray Huffman, about a man who could hear animals talk and of how his wife wormed the secret out of him. E

64 ———. <u>Tales for the Third Ear from Equatorial Africa.</u> Ill. by Ib Ohlsson. E. P. Dutton, 1969. Nine folktales, several of which are about Ananse the spider, a familiar feature of African folklore. Two pages of notes give the sources of the tales. E, I

65 ———. <u>Tales from the Story Hat, African Folk Tales.</u> Ill. by Elton Fax. Introduction by Augusta Baker. Coward-McCann, 1960. Nine stories from various parts of Africa, with notes and a bibliography and glossary. E, I

66 Achebe, Chinua and Iroaganach, John. <u>How the Leopard Got His Claws</u> (with <u>The Lament of the Deer</u> by Christopher Okigbo). Ill. by Per Christianson. Third Press, 1973 (Odarkai Books). A story about conflicts in the animal kingdom. E

67 Arnott, Kathleen. <u>African Myths and Legends.</u> Ill. by Joan Kiddell-Monroe. Henry Z. Walck, 1963. Thirty-four tales of African folklore from south of the Sahara, their sources identified in the table of contents. Entertaining for children and of interest to older students of African history and culture. I up

68 Bryan, Ashley. <u>The Ox of the Wonderful Horns and Other African Folktales.</u> Ill. by the author. Atheneum, 1971. Four amusing short tales and one longer one from various sources, listed in the front of the book. In one, Anansi the spider plays his usual mischievous part. E, I

69 Carpenter, Frances. <u>African Wonder Tales.</u> Ill. by Joseph Escourido. Doubleday, 1963. A book brimming with fun, containing twenty-four tales from West Africa, Egypt, Central Africa, Nigeria, Liberia, the Sudan, the Kafir country, Madagascar, Basutoland, Algeria, the Gold Coast, Senegal, South Africa and Morocco. I

70 Chetin, Helen. <u>Tales from an African Drum.</u> Ill. by Charles Robinson. Harcourt Brace Jovanovich, 1970. Eleven original tales with the folk flavor, about a great chief training his grandson to lead his tribe after he, the grandfather, dies. I

71 Courlander, Harold. <u>The King's Drum and Other African</u>

Africa in General 15

        Stories. Ill. by Enrico Arno. Harcourt, Brace and World, 1962. A collection of folktales from many peoples and regions, but mainly south of the Sahara. The notes on the stories are particularly interesting for students of African cultures. I up

72 Guillot, René. René Guillot's African Folk Tales, sel. and trans. by Gwen March, 1st Amer. ed. Ill. by William Pappas. Franklin Watts, 1964. Tales of the jungle, including the African story of creation and a wide variety of fables and nonsense tales. I

73 Kipling, Rudyard. Just So Stories (1902), Anniv. ed., large size. Ill. by Etienne Delessert; foreword by Nelson Doubleday, 1948. Doubleday, 1972. There are many fine and interesting editions of this perennial favorite. The twelve stories of the "long-ago time, when the world was new and all" have worldwide settings, but the best known and remembered is probably "The Elephant's Child" set in Africa on the "Great Gray-green Greasy Limpopo River" where the young elephant because of his "satiable curiosity" acquired his trunk. E, I

FICTION

74 Baumann, Hans. The Barque of the Brothers, trans. by Isabel and Florence McHugh. Ill. by Ulrich Schramm. Walck, 1958. A novel of the period of Henry the Navigator in Spain in the 15th century, in particular the disastrous expedition against Tangiers and the Moors in Africa in 1436. A chronology of historical events from 1328 to A.D. 1460. YA

75 Catherall, Arthur. A Zebra Came to Drink. Ill. by John Schoenherr. E. P. Dutton, 1967. An animal story of a mother zebra who was lying beside her new foal by the water hole when suddenly all the other animals fled, and she was left alone to fend off a hungry lioness, hyenas and jackals, and finally the cruelest enemy of all, the poachers. I

76 Coatsworth, Elizabeth. Ronnie and the Chief's Son. Ill. by Stefan Martin. Macmillan, 1962. A story set in the "Africa of the imagination" of a white boy who is captured by a black chief and held to be sacrificed at the next new moon. I

77 Fechter, Alyce Shinn. M'Toto, Adventures of a Baby Elephant. Ill. by Bernard Garbutt. McGraw-Hill, 1965. M'Toto is a prince whose youthful adventures

cause considerable disturbance to the elephants of his tribe and even danger to his mother the Queen. Strangely enough it takes a little dik dik to make M'Toto more responsible and, indeed, to save the herd from disastrous fire and flood. Good story with good elephant lore. E, I

78 London, Carolyn. Zarga's Shadow, An African Adventure. Ill. by George Wilson. Duell, Sloan and Pearce, 1966. A novel of the conflict of pagan and Christian beliefs in which an African boy tries to seek revenge for the death of his father before adopting the "Jesus ways" of a white missionary. I, YA

79 Stevens, Eden Vale. Abba. Ill. by Anthony Stevens. Atheneum, 1962. A short, poetic, allegorical tale about a young boy elephant who finds a girl elephant held captive by hunters and who must seek the help of others to free her. E, I

NORTHEASTERN AFRICA
(Egypt, Ethiopia, Libya, and the Sudan)

The ancient history of Egypt, revealed by the study of tombs, their contents and decorations, and the discovery, in 1882, of the key to Egyptian hieroglyphics, is so remarkably complete that I have subdivided the fiction in this section into two lists: one of stories of ancient Egypt and the other of those of contemporary Egypt and other countries in northeastern Africa. Previously a protectorate of Britain, Egypt was recognized by the British as a sovereign state in 1922.

In 1956 the Sudan obtained its independence from an Anglo-Egyptian condominium. The kingdom of Libya, having been held by Italy from 1911 to World War II, was, in 1951, the first country to obtain independence through direct United Nations action.

Ethiopia, like Egypt, has a long known history, with the earlier name of Abyssinia. It has recently been prominent in the news because of the revolution in process there and the deposing, imprisonment and death of Haile Selassie, "The Lion of Judah," who came to the throne in 1928 and of whom it is claimed that he was a descendant of King Solomon and the Queen of Sheba.

Northeastern Africa   17

NON-FICTION

80 Barnett, Correlli. The Battle of El Alamein, Decision
    in the Desert. Ill. with photographs and maps.
    Macmillan, 1964. A story of desert warfare in World
    War II, and the decisive battle in northern Egypt in
    which the British, under Montgomery, defeated the
    Germans under Rommel, November 1 and 2, 1942.
    YA up
81 Burchell, S. C. Getting to Know the Suez Canal. Ill.
    by Michael Hampshire. Coward, McCann and
    Geoghegan, 1971. The dramatic story of a much
    fought-over waterway: the history of east-west com-
    merce before its building and the story of its actual
    construction and the problems caused by its great
    commercial value. I
82 Copeland, Paul W. The Land and People of Libya. Ill.
    with photographs and a map. J. B. Lippincott, Por-
    traits of the Nations Series, 1967. A history of this
    kingdom from 8000 B.C. when the first inhabitants
    probably arrived from Central Africa; through the in-
    vasions and occupations by Phoenicians, Greeks, Ro-
    mans, Arabs and Italians until it achieved indepen-
    dence in 1951, and thereafter. YA up
83 Cottrell, Leonard. Land of the Pharaohs. Ill. by
    Richard M. Powers. World, 1960. About Egypt in
    the 14th century B.C. the time of King Tutankhamen
    whose unspoiled tomb was discovered by the English-
    man, Howard Carter in 1922. The story is told
    through the life and experiences of an imaginary
    young scribe of that time. Appended is a chrono-
    logical chart of ancient Egyptian history and corres-
    ponding world events, a list of books for further
    reading, glossary and index. YA up
84 _____. Secrets of Tutankahmen's Tomb. Ill. by Ray-
    mond Cruz. New York Graphic Society, 1964. The
    hero of this book is the young English Egyptologist,
    Howard Carter (1873-1939) who, when his sponsor
    was about to give up his support, pursuaded him to
    finance one more search for a tomb intact--a search
    so thrillingly rewarded. YA
85 Englebert, Victor. Camera on Africa; The World of an
    Ethiopian Boy. Ill. with photographs. Harcourt,
    1970. How Christmas and the Epiphany are cele-
    brated by an Ethiopian boy, home for the holidays. I
86 Glubok, Shirley. The Art of Ancient Egypt. Ill. with
    photographs of many art forms. Designed by Gerard

Nook. Atheneum, 1962. A simple visual history of ancient Egypt with text on the same or facing page as the illustrations. I up

87   Hawkes, Jacquetta and the Editors of Horizon Magazine. Pharaohs of Egypt. Ill. with reliefs, sculptures, wall paintings and monuments of Ancient Egypt--consultant: Bernard V. Bothmer--American Heritage, A Horizon Caravel Book. 1965 YA

88   Henderson, Larry. Egypt and the Sudan, Countries of the Nile. Ill. with photographs. Thomas Nelson, 1971. An eminently readable history of these two countries which were, for a brief time, joined in the United Arab Republic; interspersed with accounts of current conditions and written with fairness toward all the various peoples involved in mideastern problems: Arabs, Egyptians, Sudanese tribes, white explorers, colonizers and missionaries. Special attention is given to General Gordon and Gamel Abdel Nassar. Appended are chronologies of both countries' histories, a bibliography, index and map. YA up

89   Heuer, Kenneth. City of Stargazers; The Rise and Fall of Ancient Alexandria. Ill. with photographs and drawings. Charles Scribner's Sons, 1972. A romantic story, told in scholarly detail, about the city founded in 332 B.C. by Alexander the Great and destroyed in A.D. 346. Emphasis is on the great astronomers of the city, but readers of this beautifully designed book may be particularly interested in accounts of the two great libraries, and saddened to think of their destruction. Appended are a chronology, glossary, bibliography and name index. YA up

90   James, T. G. H. The Archaeology of Ancient Egypt. Ill. with photographs and maps and drawings by Rosamonde Nairac. Henry Z. Walck, 1972. No aspiring archaeologist should miss this beautiful book, and it may well inspire some young readers to consider archaeology as a career. YA up

91. Kaula, Edna Mason. The Land and People of Ethiopia. Ill. with photographs and a map. J. B. Lippincott, Portraits of the Nations Series, 1965. As the source of the Blue Nile; as an island of Christianity (Coptic) since the 7th century; and as the empire of Haile Selassie (the only recently deposed "Lion of Judah," self-proclaimed descendent of Solomon and the Queen of Sheba), Ethiopia's story is one of a country "out of this world." Once called Abyssinia, its known

Northeastern Africa

history is the second oldest in Africa, only that of Egypt being more ancient. YA up

92 Keith, Agnes Newton. Children of Allah, Between the Sea and Sahara. Ill. with sketches by the author. Little Brown, 1966. The author lived for nine years in Libya where her husband was chief of the F.A.O. Mission of the United Nations. The Keiths moved from Tripoli to Benghazi and back again, and Mrs. Keith went with her husband on field trips into the Sahara. Classed as a travel book, it is so much more than that, as she made many friends with Libyans of both sexes and various social and economic levels and fell in love with the land and its people. A comprehensive book written with unfailing humor and passion about the country fought over so fiercely during World War II, struggling against great odds to recover from its wounds, and suddenly becoming prominent because of oil. A

93 Mahmoud, Zaki Naguib. The Land and People of Egypt, rev. ed. Ill. with photographs. J. B. Lippincott, 1972 (Portraits of the Nations Series). This follows the design of all the other books in this series, but, written by an Egyptian it is particularly important for its comment on recent mideast tensions and the 1967 war. YA up

94 Meadowcroft, Enid LaMonte. The Gift of the River. Ill. by Katherine Dewey, from Egyptian sources. Thomas Y. Crowell, 1937. A short concise readable history of Egypt.

95 Naden, Corinne J. The Nile River. Ill. with photographs. Map by Walter Hortens. Franklin Watts, 1972 (a First Book). A factual background book with attractive illustrations. I up

96 Ochsenschlager, Edward. The Egyptians in the Middle Kingdom. Ill. by Shane Miller. Coward McCann, 1963. A very fine book indeed, with text and pictures complementing each other, about the period extending from 2134 to 1570 B.C. Appended are: Significant Dates in the Middle Kingdom; Suggestions for Further Reading; List of Egyptian gods, and a partially annotated index. I, YA

97 Pace, Mildred Mastin. Wrapped for Eternity. Ill. with line drawings by Tom Huffmann. McGraw-Hill, 1974. Egyptologist and content consultant, Kenneth Jay Lister. Have you ever wondered just how the ancient Egyptians went about preserving bodies in such a way that three or four thousand years later they can be

carefully unwrapped and displayed in museums as very real characters? Well the answers are given graphically, and somewhat gruesomely, in the first part of this fascinating book. There are also chapters on the burial customs of the ancient Egyptians, tomb robberies, the wanton destruction of thousands of mummies, archaeological methods, and the trials and thrills of archaeology as a career. The book ends with this inspiring thought for those who wonder if there are any "finds" left to be found: "One official in the department of Antiquities in Cairo said there was still so much treasure to be found that if he could he would invite all the young archaeologists in the world to come to Egypt and dig." I up

98 Price, Christine. Made in Ancient Egypt. Ill. with photographs and drawings. E. P. Dutton, 1970. A readable and pictorial combination of history and art, the period covered being from about 3100 to 1200 B.C. Of aid in tracing the time lines involved are two pages listing the dynasties of ancient Egypt, and a map. YA up

99 Scott, Joseph and Lenore. Egyptian Hieroglyphs for Everyone. Ill. with diagrams, a map and some identifying pictures of Egyptian deities. Funk and Wagnalls, 1968. The title is misleading, for this subject is not everyone's dish, by any means. But anyone at all interested in Egyptology will enjoy skimming the book, and it will be an interesting challenge for those with strong curiosity to read about the deciphering of the Rosetta numbers and the subjects of Egyptian writing. A chronology is appended. YA up

100 Silverberg, Robert. Before the Sphinx: Early Egypt. Ill. with photographs. Thomas Nelson, 1971. An exciting story of archaeological sleuthing into the span of history from 3200 to 2270 B.C. covering three dynasties. For when the sphinx was new, Egypt was already ancient. YA up

101 Wallace, John A. Getting to Know Egypt, U.A.R. Ill. by Haris Petie. Coward McCann, 1961. When this book was published Egypt called itself the United Arab Republic, but after Syria seceded from the federation, the name was changed again to the Republic of Egypt. I

102 Warren, Ruth. The Nile: The Story of Pharaohs, Farmers and Explorers. Ill. by Victor Lazzaro and with photographs. McGraw-Hill, 1968. The impressionistic drawings are an intriguing addition to the

informative and romantic story of this longest river in Africa--4,132 miles, the basin of which includes the countries of Burundi, Rwanda, Republic of the Congo, Tanzania, Kenya, Uganda and Ethiopia. YA up

103 Watson, Jane Werner. Egypt, Child of the Nile. Ill. by Egyptian artists: Samiha Hassanein, Mohammad Tohani, Dr. Abdel Maquid Wafi, and with photographs. Garrard, 1967. With these illustrations by Egyptians and by introducing people--boys and girls, parents and grandparents--this book of Egyptian history and contemporary life makes exceptionally pleasant reading. I

104 _____. Ethiopia, Mountain Kingdom. Ill. by Ethiopian artists: Afework Tekle, Tesfaye, and Wallace Tong. Garrard, 1966. Written in enjoyable narrative style, the history, geography, religion and present conditions of Ethiopia are woven into an absorbing story of the uniquely Christian country ruled, until very recently, by Emperor Haile Selassie, "King of Kings, Elect of God and Conquering Lion of Judah." The book includes legends of his descent from King Solomon and the Queen of Sheba and the disappearance of the tablets containing the Ten Commandments. I

105 Weingarten, Violet. The Nile, Lifeline of Egypt. Ill. by Ronnie Solbert. Maps by Fred Kleim. Garrard, 1964. The story of the longest river in Africa and the second longest in the world, giving the history of ancient Egypt as learned from archaeological findings, and telling of the explorers of the Nile valley in search of its source: James Bruce in the 18th century, Richard Francis Burton, John Speke and Sir Samuel Baker and his wife in the 19th century. I

BIOGRAPHIES

106 Cottrell, Leonard. Five Queens of Ancient Egypt. Ill. with photographs. Bobbs-Merrill, 1969. An excellent and utterly fascinating book about the queens and great ladies of the New Kingdom, 1550 to 1200 B.C. showing how in many ways they resembled women of today. The five of the title are: Hashepsowe, Tiye, Nefertiti, Ankhesnamun, and Nefertari. The lives and times of these alluring ladies have been reconstructed by the author "from the shreds and patches"

of Egyptian history. YA up
107 Davis, Jean (Enid Meadowcroft). Cleopatra's Egypt. Ill. with reproductions of paintings etc. and map. Grosset and Dunlop, 1963. A biography of Cleopatra and an account of her first century B.C. world. I, YA
108 Gorham, Charles. The Lion of Judah; A Life of Haile Selassie I, Emperor of Ethiopia. Farrar Straus and Giroux, 1966. A biography of the Lion of Judah (1891-) and portrait and history of Ethiopia, written when, as of the summer of 1973, he was still ruling but soon to be deposed. YA up
109 Hornblow, Leonora. Cleopatra of Egypt. Ill. by W. T. Mars. Random Landmark, 1961. A fictional biography, containing a good measure of Roman history of the 1st century B.C. YA
110 Johnson, E. Harper. Piankhy the Great. Ill. by the author with a foreword by William Leo Hansberry. Thomas Nelson and Sons, 1962. The story, with striking illustrations by the author, based on the "Conquest Stele" discovered in 1862, of a great man who ruled over the Land of Kush (called Ethiopia by the Greeks) in the Nubian Valley of the Nile, from 744 to 712 B.C. and of how, in the 21st year of his reign, he invaded and conquered Egypt. YA
111 Leighton, Margaret. Cleopatra, Sister of the Moon. Farrar Straus and Giroux, 1969. An excellent biography of the lady of "infinite variety" and a good history of Roman conquests in Egypt and of Rome at the time when Cleopatra was married to Julius Caesar. YA
112 Noble, Iris. Egypt's Queen, Cleopatra. Messner, 1963. A fairly long biographical novel about Cleopatra, Julius Caesar, Brutus and Mark Antony. YA
113 Orrmont, Arthur. Chinese Gordon, Hero of Khartoum. Ill. with maps. G. P. Putnam's Sons, 1966. A biography of the Englishman (1833-85) whose adventurous career involved him in internal conflicts in China, the Equatorial Province, and the Sudan. The history of that period in those parts of the world is not easy to follow, but according to his epitaph, "He saved an Empire by his warlike genius, he ruled vast provinces with justice, wisdom and power." YA up
114 Silverberg, Robert. Bruce of the Blue Nile. Ill. with a map and photographs. Holt, Rinehart and Winston, 1969. The exciting life story of the tall Scot, James Bruce, 1730-1794 and the account of his adventures in

Northeastern Africa   23

>   getting to Ethiopia and, indeed, in getting out. YA
>   up

FOLKLORE

115 Courlander, Harold. The Fire on the Mountain and Other Ethiopian Stories. Ill. by Robert Kane. Henry Holt, 1950. Twenty-five stories of great variety, from ancient sources, with excellent notes and a glossary and pronunciation guide appended. I up
116 _____. The Son of the Leopard. Ill. by Rocco Negri. Crown, 1974. An original tale told in the tradition of heroic lore of the nomadic peoples of northern Africa, based on the legend of Wolde Nebri, Son of the Leopard, believed to be the reincarnation of an exceptionally cruel (and that must have been pretty terrible) ruler. I, YA
117 Green, Roger Lancelyn. Tales of Ancient Egypt. Ill. by Elaine Raphael. Henry Z. Walck, 1968. A book divided into three sections: Tales of the Gods, Tales of Magic, and Tales of Adventure. Among the adventure tales are "The Girl with the Rose Red Slippers," which is possibly the earliest version of the Cinderella story, and an Egyptian story of the Trojan War. I up
118 Howard, Alice Woodbury. Sokar and the Crocodile; A Fairy Story of Egypt. Ill. by Coleman Kubinyi. Macmillan, 1928, 1954. The drawings and decorations are an integral part of this story which is set in the times of the great Pharaohs ("12th printing, 1954"). E, I
119 Mozley, Charles. Tales of Ancient Egypt (The First Book of). Ill. by the reteller. Franklin Watts, 1960. Seven classic stories vividly illustrated. I

FICTION--ANCIENT EGYPT

120 Baumann, Hans. The World of the Pharaohs. Ill. with line drawings by Hans Peter Renner. Color photographs by Albert Burges. Translated by Richard and Clara Winston. Pantheon, 1960. Megdi, the 13-year-old son of an Egyptian archaeologist, tries his luck at making a "find" on his own and is saved from disaster only by an old man who has long been associated with archaeologists and who hopes to make one

out of Megdi. As the boy learns about tombs and
hieroglyphics and the pyramids, we learn with him
in a very personal way, and rejoice with him when,
at the end, he does succeed in a discovery. Appended are: the dynasties of the pharaohs; a glossary,
author's note and map. I, YA

121 Berry, Erick (Allena Best). Honey of the Nile. Ill.
by the author. Viking, 1938, revised, 1963. An
exciting novel about King Tutankhaman and his young
queen, and what the author imagines might have become of her after young King Tut's death (nothing is
actually known). A preface, "Before the Story Opens,"
explains the conflict between the young pharaoh and
his queen in the matter of religion. She believed in
one god, and the king's priests believed in several.
YA

122 Bruckner, Karl. The Golden Pharaoh. Ill. by Hans
Thomas. Translated by Frances Lobb. Pantheon,
1959. A novel in three parts but with a continuous
narrative thread about the tomb of King Tut; the first
being a reconstruction by the author of a 14th century
B.C. robbery of the tomb; the second about the time
when Napoleon's armies in Egypt found the Rosetta
stone and the key to its decipherment was discovered
by a young French genius; and finally, the rediscovery of the tomb itself by the English archaeologist,
Howard Carter. A list of Egyptian gods and the diagrams and drawings add greatly to reading enjoyment and understanding of that period in Egyptian
history. YA up

123 Coolidge, Olivia E. Egyptian Adventures. Ill. by
Joseph Low. Houghton Mifflin, 1954. Through these
well-constructed short stories of the New Kingdom
(1600-1100 B.C.) the reader meets all sorts and
classes of Egyptians in a wide variety of settings:
the slums, workshops, and tombs. YA

124 Harris, Rosemary. The Moon in the Cloud. Macmillan, 1968. What fun! A rare combination of fable,
fantasy, adventure and delicious humor as Reuben,
a neighbor of Noah, goes on a mission to Egypt to
obtain some animals for the Ark, then in the building
stage. While he is gone, Ham makes advances to
Reuben's wife, telling her that her husband is dead.
So off goes the wife to find Reuben. YA up

125 _____. The Shadow on the Sun. Macmillan, 1970.
The second in a trilogy, beginning with "The Moon
in the Cloud" and followed by "The Bright and Morn-

Northeastern Africa   25

ing Star." Now the Biblical floodwaters have gone down, and Reuben and his lovely wife have been made Prince and Princess of Canaan by Noah who has been behaving rather badly since the end of the flood. Reuben wants to see how his friends in Egypt survived the Flood, if it went that far, so most of the story is set there (Kemi, they call it). There Reuben becomes embroiled in a contest of wills between the young king of Kemi and the daughter of his Court Chamberlain, and horrendous adventures ensue. YA up

126 _____. The Bright and Morning Star. Macmillan, 1972. The third of the trilogy of Egypt, ca. 2600 B.C. in which Reuben's wife seeks help for her afflicted son in Kemi and becomes involved in court intrigues there. The heroine is the daughter of the king and queen of the preceding novels. YA up

127 Jones, Ruth Fosdick. Boy of the Pyramids; A Mystery of Ancient Egypt. Ill. by Dorothy Bayley Morse. Random, 1952. A story of two children in the time of Cheops, 2650-2630 B.C., who watch the pyramids being built and become involved with some tomb robbers. I

128 Lownsbery, Eloise. A Camel for a Throne. Ill. by Elizabeth Tyler Wolcott. Houghton Mifflin, 1941. Woven through and around an absorbing story line is a vivid description of ancient Egypt and Nubia during the reign of Pharaoh Amenemhet, the founder of the great 12th dynasty of the Middle Kingdom, about 2000 B.C. Neferta, supposedly the niece of this pharaoh, runs away from her cruel Mother-Nurse, and is almost devoured by a crocodile. Saved by a young Nubian boy, she and he travel on her camel all the way up the Nile into Nubia. A map shows their journey, and a glossary is appended. I, YA

129 McGraw, Eloise. Mara, Daughter of the Nile. Ill. by Jack Myers. Coward McCann, 1953. A romantic spy story of the time of the female pharaoh, Queen Hatshepsut. The beautiful blue-eyed, reckless slave, Mara, finds herself in a very hot spot indeed as a spy for the Queen's interests and also those of the revolutionists, particularly their handsome young leader. All this against a well researched background of 15th century B.C. Egypt. YA up

130 _____. The Golden Goblet. Coward McCann, 1961. A novel of the time of Queen Tiy, 14th century B.C., whose parents' tombs were being robbed. She was

the mother-in-law of the beautiful Nefertiti, but the story is mainly about the young boy Ranofer who tries to uncover his cruel half-brother's thefts. Interesting material concerning the craft of ancient Egyptian goldsmiths is incorporated in the plot. YA

131 Meadowcroft, Enid LaMonte. Scarab for Luck. Ill. by Leonard Weisgard. Thomas Y. Crowell, 1964. A lively exciting story about tomb robbers during the reign of Thutmos III in the 15th century B.C. in which a young boy running away from home because of trouble at school has some harrowing adventures but also meets Prince Amenhotep who gives him a "scarab for luck." I, YA

132 Mitchison, Naomi. Sun and Moon. Ill. by Barry Wilkinson. Thomas Nelson, 1973. The story of the twin children of Cleopatra: Sun, a boy, and Moon, a girl. It is mainly the story of little Moon who wanted so very much to go to the island of Pharos and see its remarkable lighthouse. Because he was a boy, Sun was finally allowed to go there, but Moon had to contrive a way to get there, and that she did. The story is humorously told and contains much interesting information about Alexandria, Pharos, and the lives of royal children in 1st Century B.C. Egypt. E, I

133 Morrison, Lucile. The Lost Queen of Egypt. Ill. by Frank Gentz. Frontispiece in color by Winifred Brunton. J. B. Lippincott, 1937. A novel about Ankhsenpaaten, the child bride and queen of Tutankhamen, and the daughter of the beautiful Nefertiti. The story of this young queen is based on thorough research and authenticated by the secretary of the Egyptian Exploration Fund (in 1937). It is set in the latter part of the 18th dynasty (1580-1350) and has appended a glossary and a table of the seasons and months of the Sacred Year of the Egyptians. YA up

134 Neavles, Janet. The Mystery of the Pharaoh's Treasure. Ill. by Luciana Roselli. J. B. Lippincott, 1963. A novel of tomb robbery in the time of the woman Pharaoh, Hatshepsut, in which a young archer from Bubastis is falsely accused of that crime. His brother, Kamosi, visiting Thebes for the first time, is determined to clear the young man's name and is greatly aided by the children of the man who is painting in the Queen's new temple, especially by the painter's daughter, Neferti who is, indeed, the heroine of the story. I, YA

135 Palmer, Myron Tim. The Egyptian Necklace. Ill. by

the author. Houghton Mifflin, 1961. A tale of mystery and danger in 15th century B.C. Egypt, in which Ar and his friend, Pta, are captured and sealed into a Pharaoh's burial chamber, thereby learning of danger to Ar's father, the Pharaoh's chief architect. Now take it from there. I, YA

136 Patterson, Emma L. Sun-Queen, Nefertiti. David McKay, 1967. A novel about the Egyptian queen whose sculptured head is so familiar and beautiful. Very little is actually known about this wife of King Aknaton, so the writer could give free reign to her imagination, while, nevertheless, basing her guesses on sound research about a place and period (14th century B.C.). YA

137 Schlein, Miriam. Amuny, Boy of Old Egypt. Ill. by Thea Dupays. Abelard Schuman, 1961. A simple story of the day-to-day life of an Egyptian boy, living near Memphis in the days of pyramid building around 3000 B.C. The yearly flooding of the Nile, the planting of crops, the plague of locusts, the problem of high taxes, are all routine in Amuny's life, but a new and exciting experience is in learning to write, as he copies his brother's hieroglyphs. I

138 Shakespeare, William. Antony and Cleopatra. 1608? What can one say about a play by Shakespeare except that what it may lack in historical authenticity it more than makes up in poetry. A

FICTION--OTHER

139 Bradley, Duane. Meeting With a Stranger. A story of changing ways in contemporary Ethiopia and the resistance to scientific sheep care and breeding being introduced by a young white American. Teffera, his Ethiopian friend shows great courage, but not always wisdom, in testing the new methods. I, YA

140 Coatsworth, Elizabeth. Bess and the Sphinx. Ill. by Bernice Loewenstein. Macmillan, 1967. An autobiographical story of a timid, awkward little girl named Bess who later became Betty and, still later, the Elizabeth Coatsworth who has written so many enchanting books about foreign and domestic places. In 1898 she set off, with her Father, Mother, Grandmother and brother for seven months of foreign travel, and while in Egypt, her brother frightened Bess terribly with stories about a crocodile. However,

after she made friends with the Sphinx she became a little braver, less awkward, and more sure of herself. E, I

141 _____. The Princess and the Lion. Ill. by Evaline Ness. Pantheon, 1963. A tale of high adventure for a young Abyssinian princess, in 18th century Ethiopia (then called Abyssinia) when she endeavors to prevent her brother from trying to escape from the Prison of Princes, as she knows he is planning to do. Events have suddenly made his escape unnecessary and particularly dangerous, but he does not know this, and it is nearly impossible for her to get near enough to tell him. I

142 Eastwick, Ivy. A Camel for Saida. Ill. by Peggy Fortnum. Roy, 1961. A story of the Libyan Sahara. Ali, age 11, is going with his father to Kufra, a three-week camel trip away and he is tremendously excited at the prospect, only regretting that his little friend, Saida cannot go with them. To solace her disappointment, Ali promises to bring her a little white camel--a promise which could only be fulfilled by a miracle. After many exciting meetings and adventures in the desert, however, anything can happen and does. I

143 Latimer, John. The Last Pharaoh. Thomas Nelson, 1970. A fantastic adventure story in which three 19th century scientists in search of dinosaurs fall from their balloon into the isolated jungle kingdom of "the last pharaoh" who is quite mad and planning to have his whole domain destroyed after his death. Can the three enslaved men rescue themselves and the people of this weird country? Well, as one of the characters says, "there are things that folks like you wouldn't half believe, hidden in them jungles." YA

144 Silverberg, Robert. Mask of Akhnaten. The fictional story of a contemporary discovery of the tomb of King Akhnaten of ancient Egypt. The author's note indicates the point in the story where "fancy" enters in and makes for an exciting plot. The factual part of the novel, however, is rich in archaeological matter and the combination of fact and fancy produces an absorbing story about an American boy and his young journalist uncle seeking archaeological treasure before the Aswan dam shall flood a certain little village in Nubia. I, YA

145 Snyder, Zilpha Keatley. The Egypt Game. Ill. by

Northeastern Africa 29

Alton Raible. Atheneum, 1967 (an Aladdin Book paperback). A murder mystery, set in California in the mid 20th century. The "game" is invented by "boys and girls of every size, style and color," in the apartment in which April--deserted by her Mother--is living with her grandmother, and is built on what she knows about ancient Egypt. The humor is the chuckly kind, the dialogue contemporary, and there is a message at the end about how long any game can be played. I up

146 Williams, Jay and Abrashkin, Raymond. Danny Dunn and the Swamp Monster. Ill. by Paul Sagsoorian. G. K. Hall Sightsaving Book, 1973. A most entertaining story about a search in the Nile valley in the Sudan, for a legendary animal, the "lau." Or is it legendary? And who is the stranger in the white suit who follows Danny and Professor Bullfinch, the eccentric millionaire zoologist, into the swampland south of Khartoum? I

EAST AFRICA
(Burundi, Kenya, Rwanda,
Somali Republic, Tanzania, Uganda)

Before 1962 when both Burundi and Rwanda became independent, they were part of the Belgian-administered U.N. Trust Territory of Burundi-Rwanda. Kenya was a British colony and protectorate before independence in 1963. The Somali Republic, in 1963, combined the former Italian-administered U.N. Trust Territory of Somalia and British Somaliland. The United Republic of Tanzania combined, in 1961, the British-administered U.N. Trust Territory of Tanganyika and the protectorate of Zanzibar. Uganda, a former British protectorate, gained its independence in 1962.

NON-FICTION

147 Adamson, Joy. Born Free. Ill. with photographs. Pantheon, 1960. When George Adamson was forced to kill a lioness in self-defense, he and his wife adopted her three cubs and decided to rear one, Elsa, as a pet, yet still training her to kill and fend for

herself. A beautiful story of the happy, affectionate relationship between Elsa and her foster parents, the Adamsons. A

148 _____. Living Free; The Story of Elsa and Her Cubs. Illus. with 64 pages of photographs and with an introduction by Julian Huxley. Harcourt Brace and World, 1961 (A Helen and Kurt Wolf Book). A sequel to Born Free. A

149 _____. Forever Free. Ill. with 60 pages of photographs and maps. Harcourt, Brace and World, 1962 (A Helen and Kurt Wolf Book). The final story of a rare personal relationship between lions and humans, in which Elsa dies and her cubs must be deported. A

150 Bleeker, Sonia. The Masai, Herders of East Africa. Ill. by Kisa N. Sasaki. Morrow Jr. Books, 1963. This short book is about one of the most exciting tribal groups in Africa. I

151 Burton, Jane. Animals of the African Year; Ecology of East Africa. Ill. with photographs and maps and diagrams. Holt Rinehart and Winston, 1972. A finely illustrated and narrated study of the wild life of East Africa, its behavior, and the ecology of its territory. YA up

152 Carpenter, Allen and Delany, Milan. Enchantment of Africa--Kenya. Ill. with photographs and maps. Children's Press, 1973. Like the other "Enchantment" books this begins with a story "to set the scene" and ends with the Handy Reference Section containing "Instant Facts" and a chronology. Kenya became independent in 1963. I, YA

153 _____ and Hughes, James. Enchantment of Africa--Uganda. Consulting ed., John Rowe, Ph.D. Ill. with map and photographs. Children's Press, 1973. Uganda, a landlocked East African nation, became independent in 1962, except for the kingdom of Buganda which only became part of the unified country in 1966. I, YA

154 _____ and Maginnis, Matthew. Enchantment of Africa--Burundi. Consulting ed., John Rowe, Ph.D. Ill. with map and photographs. Children's Press, 1973. An introduction to one of the smallest countries of Africa, which gained its independence in 1962. All the Children's Press attractive "Enchantment" books have a map, a Handy Reference Section, historical outline, and index, and cover such subjects as geography, people, history, culture and many others. Burundi, a little mountain country is often called

East Africa

155 "The Switzerland of Africa. I, YA
_____ and _____. Enchantment of Africa--Rwanda.
Consulting ed., Ethel M. Albert. Ill. with map and
photographs. Children's Press, 1973. Completely
landlocked by Uganda on the north, Tanzania on the
east, Burundi, south, and Zaïre, west, this, like
Burundi, one of the smallest countries in all Africa,
won its independence in 1962. The usual outstanding
organization of material characteristic of the Enchantment series. I, YA

156 Fellows, Lawrence. East Africa. Ill. with photographs.
Macmillan, 1972. An outstanding portrait of Kenya,
Uganda and Tanzania, three countries set apart from
the rest of the continent by the Great Rift Valley and
all (Zanzibar included in Tanzania) having become independent by 1964. A book of special importance for
its appraisal of the current problems of these countries. YA up

157 Ingalls, Leonard. Getting to Know Kenya. Ill. by Don
Lambo. Coward McCann, 1963. A brief profile of
this fascinating East African country. Appended are:
a pronunciation list and an historical chronology up
to the time of independence in 1963. I

158 Joy, Charles R. Getting to Know Tanzania. Ill. by
Shannon Stirnweis. Coward McCann, revised edition,
1966. An attractive book about a country possibly
best known in the west for its Mt. Kilimanjaro and
lakes and wild life. Tanzania (which now includes
Zanzibar), is bordered by Kenya, Uganda, Ruanda,
Burundi, Zaïre, Zambia, Malawi, and Mozambique.
Appended are: an outline of Tanzanian history, a
pronunciation list of foreign words and a few expressions in Swahili. I, YA

159 Kaula, Edna Mason. The Land and People of Kenya.
Ill. with photographs and a map. Portraits of the
Nations Series, J. B. Lippincott, 1968. The story
of the beautiful and exciting country which gained its
independence in 1963, including the many subjects
such as history, geography, religion etc. which are
to be found in all the books in this series. YA

160 _____. The Land and People of Tanzania. Ill. with
photographs and map by the author. Portraits of the
Nations Series, J. B. Lippincott, 1972. The history,
geography and culture of the United Republic of Tanzania, formed in 1964 from the independent republics
of Tanganyika and Zanzibar. YA

161 Kenworthy, Leonard S. Profile of Kenya. Ill. with

map and photographs. Doubleday, 1963. Always keeping in mind the constant changes in African states, this book gives a concise, easily comprehended history of the former British Crown Colony, and will, it is hoped, be updated before long. I, YA

162 Lobsenz, Norman M. The First Book of East Africa; Kenya, Uganda, Tanganyika and Zanzibar. Ill. with photographs. Franklin Watts, 1964. This book was obviously written shortly before Tanganyika and Zanzibar were united, in 1964, under the name of Tanzania. Of special interest are chapters on the fossil beds of East Africa and the various tribes and wild life. A list of over 50 Swahili words, with their pronunciation and meaning in English is appended. I

163 Miller, Charles. The Lunatic Express; An Entertainment in Imperialism. Ill. with historical pictures and maps. Macmillan, 1971. A massive book about how the white man changed East Africa in many ways but particularly, as here narrated, by the building of the railway from Mombasa to Lake Victoria. A book as long and thick (but never heavy) as this one may seem out of place in a guide for young readers, but it simply couldn't be left out, and even if few may be able to read it from cover to cover, it is well worth taking from the library to dip into and skim, and would be most valuable to own for its lively style and sound historical and biographical material pertaining to East Africa. To quote from the jacket, it is: "the saga of the turbulent international race for the mastery and development of an immense region ... the gripping narrative of the building of the railway itself.... It is also a diorama of an earlier Africa of slave and ivory empires; of sultans and tribal monarchs and the vast lands they ruled."

164 Perl, Lila. East Africa: Kenya, Tanzania, Uganda. Ill. with photographs. William Morrow, 1973. A fact-filled book, exploring East Africa as a whole: its geography, people and history in the first chapters, and, in the later ones, its present day politics, economy and social conditions. YA up

165 Wenner, Kate. Shamba Letu; An American Girl's Adventure in a Communal Village in Tanzania. Ill. with maps. Houghton Mifflin, 1970. Kate Wenner had just finished her freshman year at Radcliffe College when she went to Africa to spend a year in the small village of Litowa in Tanzania, not as a Peace

Corps volunteer but as a member of a small program called "Teachers for Africa." Modestly and sensitively written, her courage and persistence shine through the account, and her growth in understanding: of the village people, their problems and values, of her own country in America as well, and most important, perhaps, of herself. YA up

BIOGRAPHIES

166 Archer, Jules. African Firebrand, Kenyatta of Kenya. Julian Messner, 1969. A biography of the African born in 1890, who rose from being a shepherd boy, son of a tribal farmer, to become the "George Washington" of Kenya. Here is the story of that eventful and hazardous rise and also an account of colonial suppression of the natives, of rivalries between the many tribes of Kenya, of the brutality of the Mau Maus (toward their own black brothers as well as to whites), of Kenyatta's resistance to both Western and Soviet domination, and, finally, of the emergence of Kenya as a republic and the many problems facing Kenyatta in governing it. YA up

167 Dinesen, Isak. Out of Africa. Random, 1937 (facsimile paperback, 1970). Through this classic of Africa, the author, who lived from 1914 to 1931 on a coffee plantation in Kenya, recreates for the reader the very essence of the land, its people and their way of life. A

168 _____. Shadows on the Grass. Ill. with a frontispiece portrait by Cecil Beaton and several portraits painted by the author. Random, 1961. Four stories about the author's relations with her servants and neighbors during her years as hunter and farmer in Kenya in the first third of the 20th century; written in retrospect after 25 years' absence from Africa. Her sensitivity and literary style make her books unforgettable. A

169 Huxley, Elspeth. The Flame Trees of Thika; Memories of an African Childhood. William Morrow, 1959. More like entrancing fiction than autobiography, this book takes us into British colonial Kenya in the early years of the 20th century, where Elspeth, exceptionally perceptive at the age of six, lived for a few years with her intrepid mother and improvident father. Her clear childhood impressions are recalled with her

later mature understanding. A
170 Mulvey, Mina White. Digging Up Adam; The Story of L. S. B. Leakey. Ill. with photographs and map by Rus Anderson. David McKay, 1969. A dual biography of a remarkable and dedicated man (1903-72) and his equally dedicated wife, Mary, and the story of their adventures in the Olduvai Gorge in Tanzania, as they dug for ancient forms of life (the science of paleontology). It was Mary Leakey who, in 1959, uncovered a fossil hominid, given the scientific name, "zinjanthropus." YA up

FOLKLORE

171 Harmon, Humphrey. Tales Told Near a Crocodile; Stories from Nyanza. Ill. by George Ford. Viking, 1962. Ten tales from the regions surrounding Lake Victoria; the coastlines of Kenya, Uganda, and Tanzania; stories from tribes named Abaluya, Kisii, Samiu, Nandi, and Masai. I
172 Heady, Eleanor B. Jambo Sungura; Folk Tales from East Africa. Ill. by Robert Frankenberg. W. W. Norton, 1965. These tales of Sungura the Hare, may well be the origin of our American "Br'er Rabbit" stories. Mrs. Heady has selected the best known and best liked of many versions of Sungura lore. E, I
173 _____. Safiri the Singer: East African Folk Tales. Ill. by Harold James. Follett, 1972. The Safiri (traveling minstrels) spread these amusing stories over a wide expanse of East Africa, to the accompaniment of a gambusi, gourd, or two- or three-string violins. E, I
174 _____. When the Stones Were Soft; East African Fireside Tales. Ill. by Tom Feelings. Funk and Wagnalls, 1968. Sixteen "how and why" stories from Kenya, Tanzania, and Uganda, told against their separate backgrounds, each with a preface in which Mama Semamingi gathers the children around the fire for a story time. I
175 Serwadda, W. Moses. Songs and Stories from Uganda. Transcribed and ed. by Hewitt Pantaleoni. Ill. by Leo and Diane Dillon. Thomas Y. Crowell, 1974. In his introductory note, the author of this unique, intriguing book says, "For a long time I had had a desire to see that Americans and Europeans under-

stand our music and learn to sing or play it.... Although I wrote this small book for children of school age, it has been written with care so that it can be useful to those who are studying African history and culture as well as African music. I know there is a lot that can be learned about Africa through its songs." With the help of the page on how to pronounce words in Luganda (the language of the peoples in southern Uganda) children can sing the songs with African words and dance or act them with African rhythms. I up

FICTION

176 Arundel, Jocelyn. <u>Simba of the White Mane.</u> Ill. by Wesley Dennis. Whittlesey House, 1958. Toki, a small Tanzanian boy who has become lost from the safari on which he was working comes upon a wounded lion, and recognizes it as the great Simba who, the Masai believe, brings good days to their tribe when he "speaks beneath the crescent moon." But to Mr. Pike, the hunter, Simba is only valuable as a trophy. How Toki saves Simba's life and shows up Mr. Pike's cowardice, makes an exciting story. I

177 Bothwell, Jean. <u>African Herdboy; A Story of the Masai.</u> Ill. by Carl Owens. Harcourt Brace Jovanovich, 1970. A story of the conflict, in Kenya and Tanzania, between the old and new ways, focusing on a young Masai boy whose father clings to tradition, while his mother is forward-looking. I

178 Cavanna, Betty (Headley). <u>Mystery on Safari.</u> Ill. by Joseph Cellini. Morrow Jr. Books, 1970. Almost as good as going on an east African safari to Amboseli, Kilaguni, Manyara, and Serengeti, is the reading of this mystery novel in which 17-year-old Kim, and her grandmother become involved, along with an English youth, in the detection of a gang of leopard poachers. YA

179 Child, Fay. <u>Wacheera, Child of Africa.</u> Ill. by Richard Lewis. Criterion, 1965. Another story of the conflict between parents and children, old and new ways. Wacheera who lives near Mt. Kenya, desperately wants to go to school and learn to become a nurse, but her father resists her pleas and tries to appease her with beads and leg coils and a new hoe. Many

folk tales and legends are woven through the story.
I, YA

180 Christopher, John. <u>Dom and Va.</u> Macmillan, 1973.
In this novel the popular writer of science fiction has turned back to the dim dark past, possibly five hundred thousand years ago, basing his story on bones found in the Olduvai Gorge in Tanzania and surmising from them a clash of two cultures at that time: one is that of a warlike hunting tribe; the other a peaceful agrarian one. Dom and Va, exemplifying the two cultures finally, after many vicissitudes which create the action and suspense of the novel, start a new union of cultures in their mating. YA

181 Clifford, Mary Louise. <u>Bisha of Burundi.</u> Ill. by Trevor Stubley. Thomas Crowell, 1973. The story of a young Tutsi girl of Burundi, a Belgian colony until 1962 when its king was overthrown and it became a republic. Bisha's problem in this rapidly changing world lay in avoiding early marriage and overcoming her parents' objections to continuing her education, while continuing to show them her love and respect. The book contains interesting sidelights on Catholic missions, the old and new agricultural methods, and particularly the changing position of women in general. A list of the African names of Bisha's family and their meaning is given and a foreword about Burundi: its location, history and people. I, YA

182 Dineen, Betty. <u>A Lurk of Leopards.</u> Ill. by Charles Robinson. Henry Z. Walck, 1972. A 12-year-old English girl living in colonial Kenya, yearns for a wild animal pet, and when she finds leopard footprints outside her window, sets off to track them. She is not sure that they are leopard prints until she suddenly confronts the animal who made them, fortunately a well-fed female which ignores Karen. Later, however, when her neighbor's precious dachshund disappears, Karen, with her friend Richard and two boy visitors, goes in search, and there is another close confrontation with a leopard, and a much more perilous one. A book full of animal lore, not only about leopards, but about bees, ants, turtles, and other small but often extremely dangerous creatures.
I, YA

183 Donna, Natalie. <u>Boy of the Masai.</u> Ill. with photographs by Peter Larson. Dodd Mead, 1964. Supati is a Masai boy living in the big city of Nairobi in

Kenya, and this is the story of how, when he becomes nine, his uncle takes him to visit his tribal village. Through these fine photographs, we too may visit a Masai village and even watch the famous dance of the Masai warriors. E, I

184 Fenner, Carol. Gorilla, Gorilla. Ill. by Symeon Shimin. Random, 1973. A story about a gorilla from his babyhood to his full strength; about his capture and caged travel to a zoo; his refusal to eat and his gradual adjustment, and his refusal to perform for zoo visitors until a young female gorilla is brought into the cage next to him at which he once again asserts his gorillahood. A beautiful story graphically told about an animal rarely considered beautiful in any way. All ages

185 Goetz, Lee Garrett. A Camel in the Sea. Ill. by Paul Galdone. McGraw-Hill, 1966. Mohammed Hassan Ali, living in a Somali village on the Indian Ocean, loved to go swimming but when he became ten, he was made to help his father, a shipbuilder and had no time for swimming and playing. He was lonely for a playmate and happy when he was given a baby camel to care for and play with. When the village was plagued, first by locusts, and then by drought, an old man was heard to say that rain would come when a camel went into the sea, but as camels abhor the sea this did not provide much comfort until 10-year-old Mohammed and his camel gave the villagers a surprise. E, I

186 Harmon, Humphrey. African Samson. Viking, 1965. A legendary novel about how the Nanci tribe discovered the secret of Magere the Stone. What is especially remarkable and intriguing about this story is its similarity to the story of the Biblical Samson, yet the author insists in an epilogue that it is based on a purely African legend. YA

187 Johnson, E. Harper. Kenny. Ill. by the author. Henry Holt, 1957. Eleven-year-old Kenny, the son of a Black American engineer, goes to Uganda with his father who is to work on a special project there. Though this is the land of his ancestors, Kenny does not feel comfortable in Africa and finds more rapport with a white boy than with the native boy, Akeke. However, when the three boys are lost in the jungle, Kenny learns to appreciate African talents and values. I

188 Kessel, Joseph. The Lion. Ill. by Harper Johnson.

Tr. from French by Peter Green. Alfred A. Knopf, 1962. First Borzoi illustrated edition prepared by the author from his full-length novel originally published in French in 1958. The relationship of humans to animals and of humans to other humans, are dramatized in this novel of a little girl, the daughter of a former white hunter who is now a game warden, and a neurotic mother, who has a strange absolute power of control over a large lion she has raised from a cub. She also believes that she can control a Masai who is threatening her lion, King. A powerful yet delicate and poignant novel, skillfully abridged. YA up

189 Lousada, Audrey. Poachers in the Serengeti. Ill. by Stuart Tresilian. Walker, 1965. It is good to know that the author of this exciting story (all of which, she says, could have happened) is contributing a percentage of her royalties to the World Wild Life Fund. The setting is colonial Tanganyika, now independent Tanzania, where, unhappily, poaching is still going on. Three intrepid youngsters--two 14-year-old boys and the younger sister of one, are the adventurous characters of the story, and between them and an elephant, the poachers get their just deserts. I

190 Nagenda, John. Mukasa. Ill. by Charles Lilly. Macmillan, 1973. Constructed from this Ugandan author's loving memory of his own childhood, this is an appealing, poetically written story of a goat boy, back in the early 1940s, adapting first to school, and then readapting to goat herding, and finding friends in both worlds. In essence it is conflict between youth and age, progress and tradition. I up

191 Nagenda, Musa. Dogs of Fear. Ill. by Floyd Sowell. Holt Rinehart and Winston, 1972. The exciting story of a 13-year-old boy in rapidly changing Uganda who is facing the "rites of manhood" for which warrior skills are prerequisite and yet have not been taught in the school which Kabana has just left. I, YA

192 Price, Willard. Elephant Adventure. John Day, 1964. The second of a series of adventure stories (and wild ones, believe me) featuring the Hunt brothers: Hal, age 19, and Roger, age 13, and their incredible adventures while trying to capture a white elephant in the Mountains of the Moon in Uganda. While the yarn is obviously completely fictional, all the factual matter is authentic--about the Watusi and the Pygmies and the ways of elephants, and in the vivid

descriptions of those wild weird mountains with their giant flora and fauna. I, YA

193 _____. Lion Adventure. John Day, 1967. A fourth book in the African adventure series in which Hal and Roger go after a man-eating lion which has already killed several men, women and children. In support of his claim to authenticity, Mr. Price introduces into one of the most horrendous crises of the story, three actual and well-known people: Dr. Louis Leakey, Joy Adamson, and Michael Grzimek (or, rather, his monument). I, YA

194 _____. Safari Adventure. John Day, 1966. A third book about Hal and Roger Hunt, beginning as they start out to capture certain wild animals in Kenya for zoos in America. They soon become involved with black poachers under the leadership of a white hunter called Blackbeard. Their adventures are purely fictional, but the animal lore and native customs are authentic, and there is much to be learned as we follow Hal and Roger on their reckless endeavors to rescue wild animals from the poachers who cruelly slaughter them for trophies and trinkets for wealthy tourists. I, YA

195 Stevenson, William. The Bushbabies. Ill. by Victor Ambrus. Houghton Mifflin, 1965. Thirteen-year-old Jackie, her beloved bushbaby named Kamau (and there really was a Kamau, a tiny tarsier, a species of monkey), and an old African named Tembo, make a harrowing trek from Mombasa to the Place of the Hippopotamus where Jackie intends to release her pet which she can't take with her when leaving Africa. Along the way, the threesome run into elephants, lions, a leopard, a Masai, and Pygmies who shoot poisoned arrows; also fire and flood. There is a lot to be learned about Kenya in this book. I, YA

196 Van Stockum, Hilda. Mogo's Flute. Ill. by Robin Jaques. Viking, 1966. A story of a frail Kikuyu boy of Kenya who is considered to be "under a spell" and therefore unable to even make an effort to be strong and well until his sister seeks help for him from a wise man of the tribe, and Mogo learns that his flute playing is actually an escape from physical exertion.

NORTHWESTERN AFRICA AND THE SAHARA
(Algeria, Mauritania, Morocco,
Spanish Sahara, Tunisia)

All of these countries, excluding Spanish Sahara, were, before achieving independence, either French protectorates, part of French West Africa, or, in the case of Algeria, juridically an integral part of France. Their independence dates were: Algeria, 1962; Mauritania, 1960; Morocco, 1956; and Tunisia, 1956.

The history of these Mediterranean coast countries is closely related to that of Europe, especially in the case of ancient Carthage, founded about 814-813 B.C. and finally destroyed by the Arabs in A.D. 698. You will consequently find in this section several biographies and stories of Hannibal, the great military genius, and of the Punic Wars. The ruins of Carthage may still be visited in Tunisia.

NON-FICTION

197 Bleeker, Sonia. The Tuareg, Nomads and Warriors of the Sahara. Ill. by Kisa N. Sasaki. William Morrow, 1964. A most interesting small book about the people of the blue veils, the Moslem Berbers. I
198 Carpenter, Allan and Chourou, Bechir. Enchantment of Africa--Tunisia. Ill. with map and photographs. Consulting ed. Prof. Ivor G. Wilks. Children's Press, 1973. An introduction to the North African country which gained its independence from the French in 1956, with a colorful history of many cultures: Greek, Roman, Islamic, French. There is the usual fine organization and readability that is to be found in all the Enchantment books and a Handy Reference Section, historical outline and index.
199 Gunther, John and Epstein, Beryl. Meet North Africa. Ill. by Grisha. Harper and Row, 1957. This is the first of Gunther's famous "Inside" books to be adapted for young readers in collaboration with Epstein, and even though it is not up to date it is valuable for its detailed descriptions of four countries in transition: Morocco, Tunisia, Algeria and Libya. Egypt is not included as being more closely associated with the mideast than with north Africa. At the time the book was written, Algeria had not achieved independence

Northwestern Africa

and would not until 1962, while Libya had just received her's, in which Tripolitania, Cyrenaica, and Fezzan were united. YA up

200 Joy, Charles R. Getting to Know the Sahara. Ill. by Haris Petie. Coward McCann, 1963. Deserts hold a special fascination for most of us, and particularly the great and mysterious Sahara. This short book tells of some of the early explorations and modern developments in that area. I

201 Sears, Stephen W. and the Editors of Horizon Magazine. Desert War in North Africa. Ill. with photographs, paintings, drawings and maps. Consultant: Maj. Gen. I. S. O. Playfair. American Heritage, 1967. The North African desert was the scene of one of World War II's most dramatic and decisive campaigns, graphically illustrated and narrated in this book. YA up

202 Spencer, William. The Land and People of Algeria. Ill. with photographs and a map. J. B. Lippincott, 1969 (Portraits of the Nations Series). A French dependency from 1832 to 1962, Algeria won its independence only after an eight-year civil war. Geography, history, peoples, politics, economy, culture are among the subjects treated in this excellent book. YA up

203 _____. The Land and People of Morocco. Ill. with photographs and a map. J. B. Lippincott, 1965 (Portraits of the Nations Series). The Kingdom of Morocco became independent in 1956, with young King Hassan II as its ruler. This is the story of its ancient and modern history, geography, economy and people. YA up

204 _____. The Land and People of Tunisia. Ill. with photographs. J. B. Lippincott, 1967 (Portraits of the Nations Series). An introduction to the history, geography and people of Tunisia where, for centuries, the historic city of Carthage was the gateway to the African continent, and which gained its independence from France in 1956, largely through the statesmanship of Habib Bourguiba who became the first president. YA up

BIOGRAPHIES

205 DeBeer, Sir Gavin. Hannibal, Challenging Rome's Supremacy. Ill. with 206 black and white illustrations,

16 in color, and 10 maps and diagrams. Viking, 1969 (a Studio Book). A handsome, definitive biography of the great Carthaginian general (247-183 B.C.), with magnificent photographs of the terrain over which he led his troops (and elephants) as well as of African art and artifacts.

206 Hansel, Robert R. The Life of Saint Augustine. Franklin Watts, 1969 (Immortals of Philosophy and Religion). Augustine was born in North Africa in the year A.D. 354, and died in 430, just before the Vandals destroyed the City of Hippo where he was Bishop. This biography is based largely on his own voluminous writings, especially, his "Confessions," now available in many editions including paperback. The changing times in which he lived make this book particularly relevant to the changing times of the mid and latter 20th century, and non-Christians as well as Christians will find meaning in the story of his life. YA up

207 Jacobs, William J. Hannibal, An African Hero. Ill. with maps. McGraw-Hill, 1973. Starting with a review of Phoenician and Roman history and the rise of Carthage as background, this is the story of Hannibal's brilliant military strategy and his powerful, and often humorous, personality. It is the story of an African general who, in the estimation of some, surpassed Alexander and Napoleon as a tactician, and whose tactics are still studied by military historians and used in modern guerrilla warfare. There is also a summary of the three Punic Wars, and the story of the total destruction of Carthage at the end of the third, in B.C. 146. A list of suggested reading is appended. YA up

FOLKLORE

208 Benson, Harold. Why the Jackal Won't Speak to the Hedgehog; A Tunisian Folktale. Ill. by the author. Seabury, 1969. The jackal didn't realize that some crops grow in the ground and some above it. And so ... E

209 Gilstrap, Robert and Estabrook, Irene. The Sultan's Fool and Other North African Tales. Ill. by Robert Greco. Henry Holt, 1958. Eleven entertaining stories often with surprise endings. E, I

210 Ridge, Antonia. Never Run from a Lion and Another

Story. Ill. by the author. Henry Z. Walck, 1958.
Two amusing tales with some meaty thoughts about
fear and courage. As told by an Algerian story-
teller and retold by Antonia Ridge. I

FICTION

211 Baumann, Hans. I Marched with Hannibal. Ill. by
Ulrick Schramm. Tr. by Katherine Potts. Walck,
1962. A novel based on the life and times of Hanni-
bal, with a map of his route and a chronology of
Carthaginian history, Hannibal's life, and the Punic
Wars. YA

212 Catherall, Arthur. Camel Caravan. Ill. by Joseph
Papin. Seabury, 1968. A story of the Sahara,
about a young boy, his little sister, and a new-born
camel and their perilous adventures after being cut
off from their caravan carrying salt to Timbuktu. I

213 Cavanna, Betty (Headley). Mystery in Marakech. Morrow Jr. Books, 1968. An exotic adventure story involving a kidnapping and a terrifying auto pursuit
across the Atlas mountains by the brother and a
friend of the kidnapped girl. The medieval atmosphere of the city of Marakech and the Atlas mountains give the reader a sense of their wild history
and present. YA

214 Coatsworth, Elizabeth. The White Horse. Ill. by Helen
Sewell. Macmillan, 1942. I wish I could have found
some of the earlier books about this remarkable and
intrepid little Sally who, in this one, is captured by
pirates, from her uncle's ship in the Mediterranean
and taken into the harem of the terrible Sultan Mou-
lay Isamil (an actual person) as a slave to the White
Lalla (a Sultana) in the time of the Barbary pirates
in the late 17th or early 18th century. Apparently
Sally has appeared in three proceeding books, Away
Goes Sally, Five Bushel Farm, and The Fair American. I

215 Frost, Kelman. Exiles in the Sahara. Ill. by Anne
Linton. Abelard Schuman, 1964. A splendid historical novel about the warring tribes of 11th century
North Africa; about the peace-loving Ibadites driven
by the fiery Malikites into that part of the Sahara
now known as the M'Zab and how a young Ibadite boy,
his blind friend, and his devilish black goat rescue
the fleeing tribe. YA

216 Houghton, Eric. The White Wall. Ill. by Robin Jaques. McGraw-Hill, 1961. A suspenseful novel about Hannibal's crossing of the Alps, based on Alps and Elephants by Sir Gavin DeBeer, with an explanatory note. YA

217 Kaufmann, Herbert. Adventure in the Desert. Ill. by Eugene Karlin, tr. by Stella Humphries. Ivan Obolensky, 1961 (an Astor Book). A fascinating novel of the Tamaschek tribe of the northern Sahara, popularly known as the Tuareg--the people of the blue veils. There is Med-e-Med, the wandering troubadour; the outlaw with whom he becomes involved; Red Moon, the proud young prince of the desert; and High Summer, the beautiful daughter of the marabout. An interesting account of the Tamaschek, their language, social organization etc. is appended. YA up

218 _____. The Lost Sahara Trail. Ill. by M. Richter, tr. by Isabel and Florence McHugh. Ivan Obolensky, 1962. Captain Gevert, an officer in the French desert forces, has dreamt for a long time of locating an ancient trail that was used for driving sheep from Timbuktu to Ain Salah in the northern Sahara, and finally his dream comes true as he sets out on a 45-day "baraka" with only two companions. An exciting adventure novel of men, camels, thirst and sand. YA

219 Kellogg, Jean. The Rod and the Rose. Reilly and Lee, 1964. A novel about Hannibal's son, Hamilcar, based on the histories of Carthage by Roman Livy and Greek Polybus. It needs a map for clarification. A

220 Kent, Louise Andrews. He Went with Hannibal. Ill. by W. T. Mars. Houghton Mifflin, 1964. A good combination of fiction and history, with a list of Hannibal's important campaigns. YA

221 L'Engle, Madeleine. Dance in the Desert. Ill. by Symeon Shimin. Farrar, Straus and Giroux, 1969. A fantasy of the Sahara, long long ago, and a miraculous infant boy just learning to walk, who, with his young parents, is allowed to join a rich caravan on its way to Egypt, though some of its members were against burdening themselves with an infant. I

222 Lezia, Giggy. Mechido, Aziza and Ahmed. Ill. by Nancy Seligsohn. Atheneum, 1969. Three humorous short stories set in contemporary Morocco. Mechido is a bread boy who gets into all kinds of comical misadventures with his bakery goods; Aziza is a little girl who is supposed to be learning to be a lady; and Ahmed, a dull shy boy, is sent to his uncle, the

bean merchant, in order to develop character and personality. I

223 Martin, Dahris. Adventure in Tunisia. Ill. by Flora Nash Demuth. Julian Messner, 1946 (Junior Literary Guild). A jolly, colorful story about Allee, a boy who simply couldn't keep from painting in spite of his father's trying every which way to keep him from it, wanting him to become a successful merchant instead of a painter. The small Tunisian village is in a flurry of excitement over a great Fair to be held there which the Bey himself will attend, and Allee designs a rug for his cousin Breeka to weave for it, with happy consequences. I

224 Merrill, Leigh. Prisoners of Hannibal. Nelson, 1958. A story about the great Carthaginian general, after the Battle of Canai, narrated by a fictional young prisoner of war who had been taken at that time (216 B.C.) Map. YA

225 Powers, Alfred. Hannibal's Elephants. Ill. by James Reid. Longmans Green, 1944. A particularly appealing story of one particular old elephant among Hannibal's troops. YA

226 Seufert, Karl Rolf. Caravan in Peril. Pantheon Books, 1963. The absorbing true story, in fictional form, of the dangers and ordeals of three men: James Richardson, a young Englishman, and two Germans, Dr. Adolph Overweg, and Dr. Heinrich Barth, who set out in 1850 from Tripoli to cross and map the still unexplored Sahara. The story is based on their diaries, published in five volumes in 1857, and fantastic as many of the adventures seem, they are not imaginary. Those Tuareg and Bedouin tribesmen were truly fearsome people. YA up

227 Stinetorf, Louise A. Musa the Shoemaker. Ill. by Harper Johnson. J. B. Lippincott, 1959. Arabian Musa was born with a deformed foot which prevented his being an acrobat like all the other boys and men of his little village in the Atlas Mountains of Algeria. How he travels by caravan to Oran for hospital treatment and returns to bring glory to his village in an unexpected way, presents a vivid picture of the Arabian desert, with a universal lesson about the importance of fully using one's uniquely individual gifts. I

228 Worthington, Marjorie. Bouboukar, Child of the Sahara. Ill. by Douglas Gorsline. Little, Brown, 1962. A poor, dirty Arabian orphan (who knows his age?) is

suddenly given some French money and a toy soldier by a rather sentimental American lady traveling with her husband who is exploring for oil in the Sahara. Naturally, when the boy spends the money, he is accused of stealing it, and the Americans are hard to find for proof of his innocence. There are humorous details of Arabian bargaining, and all turns out happily. A glossary of Arabic words is appended. I

229 Wren, Percival. Beau Geste. Frederick A. Stokes, 1925. An exciting romance of the French Foreign Legion and three English brothers who enlist in it for purposes which seem quixotic by present-day standards. The typically British humor of these brothers contrasting sharply with that of two American legionnaires who become their buddies, and the mystery of Lady Brandon's priceless gem are some of the ingredients of this perennially popular novel. A

WEST AFRICA

Because there are so many countries in the western bulge of Africa I have charted them as follows:

name	year of independence	pre-independence status
Fed. Rep. of Cameroon	1960	U.N. Trust Terr. under French (east) and British (west) administration
Central African Rep.	1960	Part of French Equatorial Africa
Chad	1960	Part of French Equatorial Africa
Dahomey	1960	Part of French West Africa
Equatorial Africa	1968	Spanish island of Fernando Po and mainland territory of Rio Muni
Gambia	1965	British protectorate
Ghana	1957	British Gold Coast Colony

West Africa   47

Guinea	1958	Part of French West Africa
Guinea-Bissau	1974	Portuguese colony
Ivory Coast	1960	Part of French West Africa
Liberia	1847	Founded by freed American slaves
Mali	1960	As French Sudan, part of French West Africa
Niger	1960	Part of French West Africa
Nigeria	1960	British colony and protectorate
Senegal	1960	Part of French West Africa
Sierra Leone	1961	British colony and protectorate
Togo	1960	French administered trust territory
Upper Volta	1960	Part of French West Africa

NON-FICTION

230   Bernheim, Marc and Evelyne. <u>African Success Story--
      The Ivory Coast.</u> Ill. with photographs by the authors.
      Harcourt Brace and World, 1970. The history of the
      Ivory Coast before its independence from France,
      1960, and since under the leadership of its first
      president, Felix Houphouët-Boigny. A companion volume to the equally well written and illustrated <u>From
      Bush to City: A Look at New Africa.</u> The Bernheim's enthusiasm for the Ivory Coast is infectious.
      YA
231   <u>   . The Drums Speak--The Story of Kofi, Boy of
      West Africa.</u> Ill. in color. Harcourt Brace Jovanovich, 1971. A beautiful book about West Africa in
      general. E, I
232   <u>   . A Week in Aya's World.</u> Ill. with photographs. Macmillan, 1969. A delightful way to learn
      about the Ivory Coast by visiting an urban child there
      for a week. E
233   Bleeker, Sonia. <u>The Ashanti of Ghana.</u> Ill. by Edith
      Singer. Morrow Jr. Books, 1966. A book with detailed drawings, about the history, folklore and present condition of the leading tribal group of Ghana. I

234 _____. The Ibo of Biafra. Ill. by Edith Singer. Morrow Jr. Books, 1969. A description of the Ibo's way of life around 1925 and their later history up to 1969. I

235 Clifford, Mary Louise. The Land and People of Liberia. Ill. with photographs and a map. J. B. Lippincott, 1971 (Portraits of the Nations Series). All about the country, founded in 1822 by an American philanthropic society as a colony for freed slaves from the United States. It became a free Republic, the first Negro one on the African continent, in 1847. A very solid book of factual material. YA up

236 Darbois, Dominique. Agossou, Boy of Africa. Ill. by the author. Follett, 1962. Almost a picture book. E

237 Davis, Russell and Ashabranner, Brent. Land in the Sun; The Story of West Africa. Ill. by Robert William Hinds. Little Brown, 1963. A brightly illustrated background book, covering the independent countries of Ghana, Guinea, Cameroon, Togo, Dahomey, Niger, Upper Volta, Ivory Coast, Senegal, Mali, Nigeria, Mauritania, and Sierra Leone, all of which have achieved independence since World War II, plus Liberia, founded for returning slaves before the American Civil War. While dealing almost entirely with contemporary West Africa (as of 1963) it also describes conditions which existed centuries ago in the villages of the Rain Forest. I

238 Dihoff, Gretchen. Katsina, Profile of a Nigerian City. Ill. with photographs and a map. Praeger, 1970. The writer who lived in Katsina for two years, takes her readers on an intimate visit to a city which, on the whole resists industrialization, clinging to a 14th century economic system. YA up

239 Englebert, Victor. Camera on Ghana; The World of a Young Fisherman. Ill. with photographs. Harcourt, 1971. About the life of a chief's son in a Ghanaian fishing village. I

240 Forman, Brenda-Lu and Harrison. The Land and People of Nigeria. Ill. with photographs and a map. J. B. Lippincott, 1972 (Portraits of the Nations Series). The geography, history and complex politics of one of the largest African countries, and the most heavily populated, which obtained its independence in 1960. Its amazing diversity (12 ethnically-based states) and consequent problems resulted in the terrible civil war of 1967, in which secessionist

Biafra was defeated and retained within the Federation of Nigeria.   YA up

241 Freville, Nicholas and Caldwell, John C.   Let's Visit Nigeria.   Ill. with photographs.   John Day, 1970.
A book about city life and also tribal life and customs that provides excellent background for the fiction and folklore of the country.   I

242 Gidal, Sonia and Tim.   My Village in Ghana.   Ill. with photographs, map and chart of the village.   Pantheon, 1969.   As in all of their "My Village" books, the Gidals make it possible for us to enter into the life of the place, not as a tourist but as a welcome friend.   I

243 Kenworthy, Leonard.   Profile of Nigeria.   Ill. with photographs.   Doubleday, 1960.   A clear, simply told, well-illustrated story of Nigeria in 1961, with chapters on its history and government.   I

244 Larson, Peter and Elaine.   Boy of Dahomey.   Ill. with photographs by Peter Larson.   Dodd Mead, 1970.
How little most of us know about the country of Dahomey, lying between Nigeria and Togo in West Africa, and what better way to learn more than by reading about a boy who lives there.   E

245 Naylor, Penelope.   Black Images; The Art of West Africa.   Photography by Lisa Little.   Doubleday, 1973.
African art is an intrinsic part of the African people, not simply a decoration, and this beautiful book reveals more of West African thought and spirit than can possibly be conveyed in the usual "background books."   All ages

246 Rice, Justus B.   My Number Two Wife; A Young Doctor's African Adventure.   Hawthorne, 1968.   The author, doctor for an American company in West Africa shortly before World War II, made a visit to a remote hill tribe for the purpose of engaging labor for his company.   While there he was feasted, plied with fermented palm juice, and involved in a "head bumping" ceremonial dance which he only later learned was equivalent to marriage rites.   As a result he discovered that he had acquired a 14-year-old native wife named Somba, who was to return with him to the camp where his beautiful red-haired wife, Helen, was awaiting him.   This is the very laughable, yet tender, story of Somba, the doctor's Number Two Wife.   Some names of people, places and tribes have been changed, but in essence it is an appealing true story.   A

247 Sale, J. Kirk. The Land and People of Ghana. Ill. with map and photographs. Rev. ed. J. B. Lippincott, 1972. The story of the former "Gold Coast," the first Black nation to win its independence in the 20th century (1957), and especially interesting for its ancient history, its cultural traditions, and its emergence, largely through the efforts of Kwame Nkrumah, into the modern world. YA up

248 Schloat, G. Warren Jr. Duee, A Boy of Liberia. Ill. with photographs. Alfred A. Knopf, 1962. Liberia, the oldest republic in Africa, is situated on the southern tip of the bulge of West Africa. This is the story of a tree as well as Duee's story, and here you will read about and see the many various uses of the Jungle Palm. E, I

249 Spencer, Sue. African Creeks I Have Been Up. David McKay, 1963. Letters to her college-age daughter in the United States from her mother who, "with a mining engineer and three male minors" goes on four tours of duty in the Sierra Leone bush. Written with contagious humor, the letters are also full of honest and unprejudiced information about the country, its wild life and, especially, its people. There are laughs in every letter, but as much at the writer herself and her three small sons, as at the Africans. Toward the latter she shows no condescension, only a warm interest. A

250 Trupin, James E. West Africa; From Ancient Kingdoms to Modern Times. Ill. with maps by Don Pitcher and photographs, Introd. by Steven Jervis. Parents' Magazine Press, 1971. A rich background book about a part of Africa largely free from white settlement, colonialism and tourism, containing a list of the tribes of West Africa and the nations they inhabit, and lists of and notes on West Africa's new states. YA up

BIOGRAPHIES

251 Ames, Sophia Ripley. Nkrumah of Ghana. Ill. with photographs and maps. Rand McNally, 1961. A biography of Kwame Nkrumah (1909-72), president of Ghana from 1960 to 1966 and, in many ways, the "father of his country" (formerly the Gold Coast); certainly a personality worthy of the biographer's careful research, and the reader's sustained attention. YA up

West Africa 51

252 Feelings, Tom. Black Pilgrimage. Ill. by the author. Lothrop Lee and Shepard. The autobiography of the black artist whose experiences during a stay in Ghana, working for a government publishing house, persuaded him to return to Africa. Though the book is addressed to "children of African descent and African soul" he welcomes young white readers as well to share his insights into Black consciousness. YA up

253 Hennessy, Maurice and Sauter, Edwin Jr. A Crown for Thomas Peters. Ives Washburn, 1964 (Men of Africa Series). A biographical novel about a young Negro captured by the British in the early 18th century and sold into slavery in Charleston, North Carolina. After his escape by the underground railroad, he returned to Sierra Leone as a leader of fugative slaves. YA

254 ———. Sword of the Hausas. Ives Washburn, 1964 (Men of Africa Series). A biographical novel of a British naval officer, John Hawley Glover, who led a life of danger and adventure (1829-85). When in command of a loyal regiment of African Hausas, he wiped out the brutal "Leopard Men" who were murdering natives as well as white men. Later, after a peaceful interlude in England, he was called back to Nigeria and his faithful Hausas to vanquish the Ashanti army and capture their barbarous king. YA up

255 McKown, Robin. Nkrumah; A Biography. Doubleday, 1973. At the time of Kwame Nkrumah's birth in 1909, what is now known as Ghana was the British Crown Colony of the Gold Coast. He led the country to independence in 1957 and was its first Prime Minister. In 1960 Ghana became a republic, with Nkrumah as President. But his life and that of his country were turbulent. He was exiled to Guinea after a military coup, and died in a Rumanian hospital in 1972, having been denied the right to spend his last months in Ghana. YA up

256 Modupe, Prince. I Was a Savage. Ill. by Rosemary Grimble, Foreword by Elspeth Huxley. Museum Press (England), 1958. The reminiscences of a man who grew up in a truly primitive society in French Guinea in the early 20th century and who, after many adventures, some tragic, left Africa for good and came to America.

FOLKLORE

257 Aardema, Verna. The Na of Wa. Ill. by Elton C. Fax. Coward McCann, 1960. An amusing story of a boy who spent all the money his Mother gave him on a dog, a cat, and a dove, and what good investments they proved to be. Based on a story from R. S. Rattray's Akan-Ashanti Folk Tales (Clarendon Press, 1930). E

258 Arkhurst, Joyce Cooper. The Adventures of Spider. Ill. by Jerry Pinkney. Little Brown, 1964. Spider is a favorite folk character in West Africa, and here are six of many many stories about him which were told to the "reteller" in Ghana. E

259 Bertol, Roland. Sundiata; The Epic of the Lion King. Ill. by Gregorio Prestopino. Thomas Y. Crowell, 1970. In the 13th century, in the country now called Mali, there was a great king, named Sundiata, about whom the legends recounted here have grown through the centuries into an epic. The story is the eternal one of man's struggle against the powers of darkness, and a saga of the once powerful land of Mali. YA up

260 Courlander, Harold and Eshugboy, Ezekiel A. Olode the Hunter and Other Tales From Nigeria (with Ezekiel A. Eshugboy). Ill. by Enrico Arno. Harcourt Brace and World, 1968. Stories mainly from the Yoruba people of western Nigeria, with some from the Ibo and Hausa groups. The notes, glossary, and pronounciation guide will especially interest older students of African folklore. I up

261 _____ and Herzog, George. The Cow-Tail Switch and Other West African Stories. Ill. by Madye Lee Chastain. Holt Rinehart and Winston, 1961. "Africa is many things" we read in the introduction to this collection of tales of humor and folkways and traditional spiritual and moral values. E, I

262 _____ and Prempeh, Albert Kofi. The Hat-Shaking Dance and Other Tales from the Gold Coast (with Albert Kofi Prempeh). Ill. by Enrico Arno. Harcourt Brace, 1957. Ashanti stories, many about the spider, Anansi, who was sometimes a hero, and sometimes a scoundrel, sometimes very very shrewd, and, at other times, extremely stupid. I

263 Dorliae, Peter. Animals Mourn for Da Leopard and Other West African Tales. Ill. by Irein Wangbaje. Bobbs-Merrill, 1970. The teller of these fables and proverbs of West Africa is Paramount Chief of the

Yarwin-Mehnsonah Chiefdom, Lower Nuruba County, Liberia. I

264 Fuja, Abayomi. Fourteen Hundred Cowries and Other African Folk Tales. Ill. by Ademola Olugebefola. With an Introd. by Anne Pellowski. Oxford, 1962; Lothrop Lee and Shepard, 1971. Thirty-two traditional Yoruba tales, mainly from western Nigeria and connected with ancient tribal beliefs. I

265 Gerson, Mary-Joan. Why the Sky Is Far Away; A Folktale from Nigeria. Ill. by Hope Meryman. Harcourt Brace and World, 1974. A story first told in Bini, the language of the Bini tribe of Nigeria, retold and strikingly illustrated. E, I

266 Gleason, Judith. Orisha: The Gods of Yorubaland. Art by Aduni Olorisa. Atheneum, 1971. Accounts of ancient beliefs of the Yoruba of Nigeria, collected and arranged by a woman who studied the Yoruba language in Harlem and spent several weeks in a Nigerian village, talking with priests and priestesses of the Yoruban faith and tradition; decorated by a Yoruban priestess. The Orisha are not really gods, but close to gods and have no counterpart in western mythology. YA up

267 Graham, Lorenz. David He No Fear. Ill. by Ann Grifalconi. Thomas Y. Crowell, 1971. This story, like the three listed below, is taken from the author's "How God Fix Jonah," a collection of Bible stories retold in Liberian dialect, "in the idiom of Africans newly come to the English speech" and in rhythmic, poetic form. This is a single-story edition based on that of David and Goliath. E, I

268 ———. Every Man Heart Lay Down. Ill. by Colleen Browning. T. Y. Crowell, 1970. The Nativity story in Liberian dialect. E. I

269 ———. Hongry Catch the Foolish Boy. Ill. by James Brown Jr. T. Y. Crowell, 1973. The story of Jonah and the whale, told in Liberian dialect. E, I

270 ———. A Road Down in the Sea. Ill. by Gregorio Prestopino. T. Y. Crowell, 1970. The story of the exodus from Egypt, told in Liberian dialect. E, I

271 Jablow, Alta. Gassire's Lute; A West African Epic. Ill. by Leo and Diane Dillon. E. P. Dutton, 1971. An example of the relatively unknown oral literature of Africa, this is an epic tale of wars and heroes, translated and adapted by Alta Jablow. The introduction explains its origins and how the author found it,

and a glossary is appended. YA up

272 McDermott, Gerald. <u>Anansi the Spider; A Tale from the Ashanti.</u> Ill. by the author. Landmark Production, 1972. Of the many stories of this mythical spider, this is one of the most striking and unusual in its illustrations. E

273 Robinson, Adjai. <u>Femi and the Old Grandaddie.</u> Ill. by Jerry Pinkney. Coward McCann, 1972. A tale, told to the author by his grandmother in Sierra Leone, about a boy whose parents had been swept away by a river in flood. Femi bravely decides to stay by the river, nevertheless and cultivate a casava patch of his own. His plans to trap a ground pig who was destroying his crop are frustrated by an old grandaddie who begs for the bait Femi had planned to use, and Femi is too kindhearted to refuse. E, I

274 _____. <u>Singing Tales of Africa.</u> Ill. by Christine Price. Scribner's, 1974. An enchanting book of West African folk tales with the words and musical lines of the songs as integral parts of the stories; notes about the origins of the singing tales are included. The collector is a native of Sierra Leone, but the tales come from various west African countries, and one, "Leave It There" is told even in Kenya. E, I

275 Sturton, Hugh. <u>Zomo the Rabbit.</u> Ill. by Peter Warner. Atheneum, 1966. Among the slaves brought from Africa to America, were the Hausa people of Nigeria who brought with them stories they had heard around their home fires. Zomo the rabbit is thought by many to have become the familiar Br'er Rabbit of Uncle Remus stories. These tales about him are retold in fresh, amusing, slangy style. I

276 Walker, Barbara. <u>The Dancing Palm Tree and Other Nigerian Folk Tales.</u> Ill. with woodcuts by Helen Siegl. Parents' Magazine Press, 1968. Eleven traditional tales, told to Barbara Walker by Olowale Idewu, a Nigerian student in an American college-- stories with a moral or human truth shown through the happenings. The illuminating glossary appended will interest folklore readers of all ages. I

277 _____ and Walker, Warren S. <u>Nigerian Folk Tales</u> (told to and ed. by ...). Ill. by Margaret Barbour. Rutgers University Press, 1961. Tales told to the editors by Olawale Idewu and Omotayo Adu, arranged in five sections: Tales of Demon Lovers; Pourquoi Stories; Moral Fables; Trickster Tales; Fertility

West Africa 55

Tales; with an introduction and notes of interest to students of the folk genre. A

FICTION

278 Achebe, Chinua. Things Fall Apart; The Story of a Strong Man. McDowell Obolensky, 1959. A sensitive novel, written by an African, of the westernization of a Nigerian village in the late 19th century; about the life and customs of a West African tribe before the invasion of the white man and the "falling apart" afterward, exemplified by the experience of the principal character, Okonkwo, a successful self-made man. The novel also contains the universal theme of a man causing some of his own problems and of his loss of prestige as he ages. A

279 Barnes, Gregory Allen. A Wind of Change. Lothrop Lee and Shepard, 1968. Some reckless students in an African government school decide to set some of its dormitories afire as a protest against their shabbiness. Joseph Konda knows of the plans and tries to warn the American teacher who has befriended him and encouraged his love of learning, but the fire is set, and he is faced with a dilemma: to betray the ringleaders and be allowed to continue his education, or to abide by tribal tradition and be expelled from school. YA

280 Buckley, Peter. Okolo of Nigeria. Ill. with photographs. Simon and Schuster, 1962. The story of a small Ibo boy desperately seeking to earn money for continued education so that he can become a teacher. I

281 Davis, Norman. Picken's Great Adventure. Ill. by Winslade. Oxford, 1949. Picken, a little boy of Gambia has more than one adventure. He encounters bush-cats and deadly snakes before he embarks on catching robbers. E, I

282 Davis, Russell and Ashabranner, Brent. Strangers in Africa. McGraw-Hill, 1963. A novel of two young Americans, one black and one white, in northern Nigeria, where they have come to work on a tsetsefly eradication program. Each has a particular quest of his own in addition and as they pursue their work and purposes, the reader learns a great deal about northern Nigeria and its people, and about racial attitudes in both America and Africa, and about the

drawbacks and benefits of foreign aid to underdeveloped areas of the world. YA

283 Graham, Lorenz. I, Momolu. Ill. by John Biggers. Thomas Crowell, 1966. Momolu is a boy of the Liberian bush country who has never seen a city until there is trouble with the soldiers of the government. Momolu's father shoots one of them and Momolu takes the blame. It is a story of the conflict between the bush people and the Liberian government and between old and new cultures. I

284 Guillot, René. Elephant Road. Ill. by Don Higgins, tr. by Richard Graves. Criterion, 1959. A mystery-adventure story set in the French Sudan and Ivory Coast in which a boy named Serge, being trained for a part in a jungle adventure film, meets a white boy named Francis and becomes involved in a mystery having to do with the disappearance of Francis' father. Like all of Guillot's African stories (see below) there is a fascinating background of jungle lore, in this book built around the moving of the elephant herds from the Ivory Coast to their own "kingdoms." YA

285 ———. Fofana. Ill. by Victor Ambrus, tr. by Barbara Seccombe. Criterion, 1962. Jean-Luc, at 14, is flown from France to the Ivory Coast to join his father who lives in the Lobi country with his huge chimpanzee, Ounogo and his "boy," Tembla. At school Jean-Luc meets Fofana, a young chieftain of the wild Lobi tribe, who knows all the age-old secrets of the jungle and who becomes so close a friend that he and the French boy achieve a mystical sense of identification with each other. A strong novel of brotherhood and of communication between humans and animals. YA

286 ———. Fonabio and the Lion. Ill. by W. F. Phillips and J. P. Ariel, tr. by Sarah Chokla Gross. Franklin Watts, 1966. The story of a warm friendship between a young African boy and a lion which he had saved and nursed as a cub after its mother was killed; it is also the story of Fonabio's love for and hero-worship of Marlow, the Great White Man of Kotokro. YA

287 ———. Mokokambo, The Lost Land. Ill. by B. L. Driscoll, tr. by John Marshall. Criterion, 1961. Just as the past and present seem all of a piece in many of Rene Guillot's books, so do fantasy and realism blend, and the interrelations of humans and

animals seem credible. In this story the element of
fantasy is dominant. A turtle is dropped by parachute
into the "forbidden land" in the French Sudan and his
young French owner follows him and sees that which
must forever remain secret. I

288 _____. Pascal and the Lioness. Ill. by Barry
Wilkinson, tr. and adapted by Christina Holyoak.
McGraw-Hill, 1965. An exciting story of the African jungle and a little boy whose best friend, a
lioness, has to leave him, after the death of the lion
king, to take up her duties as Queen. Pascal is
heartbroken but eventually a new friend comes to
comfort him. E, I

289 _____. Riders of the Wind. Ill. by Richard Kennedy, tr. by George H. Bell. Rand McNally, 1961.
A mixture of fantasy and reality. Calvi, from
Nantes, France, is "won" in a game of chance by a
sea captain and taken to Africa where his fantastic
adventures begin and end. A mystical novel of rivers and deserts and winds. YA up

290 _____. Sama. Ill. by Joan Kiddell-Monroe, tr. by
Gwen Marsh. Criterion, 1961. This is principally
an animal story, for Sama is a princess of the elephants in the African Ivory Coast, but we again meet
Marlow, of other books, the Great White Man of Kotokro, and, we identify, as he does, with the elephants and the filed-tooth natives of Lobi Land.
Warning! This novel may be dangerous for your
enjoyment of zoos and circuses. YA

291 _____. Sirga, Queen of the African Bush. Ill. by
Joan Kiddell-Monroe. Criterion, 1959. A novel
about a young lioness born to be queen of the kingdom of the lions, and about Ulé, the son of an African chief, born to lead his tribe. The two share
childhood, but suddenly the lions go away and Ulé is
captured by hostile horsemen who make him a slave.
How he escapes and finds his "sister" Sirga again,
is a story of jungle mystery and fantastic beauty.
YA

292 _____. Tom-Toms in Kotokro. Ill. by A. Douthwaite, tr. by Brian Rhys. Criterion, 1957. One of
Guillot's spell-binding novels of the pointed-teeth natives of Lobi Land in the Ivory Coast. Janek and
his father, a leading atomic scientist, have been
forced to flee from their native Poland to Africa to
avoid capture by the Nazis, the time being just before the onset of World War II. In Africa Janek

becomes a blood brother of a Lobi boy, Yago, and learns from him many secrets of the jungle, and with him, becomes a close friend of a monkey, a panther, and a young elephant. The plot builds up to a meeting between Janek's father and a Nazi pursuer and the beginning of World War II. YA

293 Levy, Mimi. Caravan from Timbuktu. Ill. by Frederick T. Chapman. Viking, 1961. A novel of a 14th century boy's perilous adventures with the caravan of which his father was camel master when the great emperor, Mansa Musa of Mali, made a pilgrimage to Mecca. The facts on which this suspense story is constructed, are that Mansa, the great ruler of Mali, did make such a pilgrimage to the holy city of Mecca in the year A.D. 1324. YA

294 O'Brien, Brian. Ivory, Apes and Jimibel. Ill. by Grisha Dotzenko. E. P. Dutton, 1960. Another exciting story of the animals and peoples of the bush of French Equatorial Africa, specifically on the adjoining borders of the Cameroon, Spanish Guinea and Gabon when the French were still administering that area. Jimibel was the name given by an African companion to the 14-year-old son of a bush trader father, but his real name was Jim Bell, and the book is based on actual happenings. I, YA

295 Schatz, Letta. Bola and the Oba's Drummers. Ill. by Tom Feelings. McGraw-Hill, 1967. A story of the Yoruba drummers in Nigeria and a small boy, son of a farmer, who aspires to be one. I

296. _____. Taiwo and Her Twin. Ill. by Elton Fax. McGraw-Hill, 1964. In the new Africa, schooling for girls is still apt to lag behind that for boys, especially when there is little money for fees. This poses a problem for a pair of Nigerian twins who had always done everything together. When a fine new school is being built in the village, the boy twin is signed up as one of the first pupils to attend it, but the twins' father insists that it isn't important enough for a girl to be educated to spend the money needed for clothes and books. Taiwo's mother urges the little girl to be patient, but patience is not one of her virtues, so she sets about in various ways to earn money. However, when she finally does succeed in going to school, her objective is achieved in a surprising way. I

297 Wellman, Alice. Tatu and the Honey Bird; A Story of the Woodlands in Angola, West Africa. Ill. by Dale

Payson. G. P. Putnam's. 1972. The story of a
boy and girl who follow the honey bee, a remarkable
insect that helps humans find honey. The author
grew up in Portuguese Angola and learned the speech
of that area even before English. E, I

CENTRAL AFRICA
(People's Republic of the Congo, Gabon, Zaïre)

Two of these three countries of central Africa are confusing in name. The People's Republic of the Congo (also and formerly called Congo-Brazzaville upon obtaining independence in 1960), was formerly the (French) Moyen-Congo, part of French Equatorial Africa. Zaïre, also becoming independent in 1960, was newly after independence called the Democratic Republic of the Congo, or often simply Congo-Kinshasa. It was formerly a Belgian colony. As for Gabon, it was part of French Equatorial Africa before its independence in 1960.

NON-FICTION

298 Bleeker, Sonia. The Pygmies, Africans of the Congo Forest. Ill. by Edith G. Singer. Morrow Junior Books, 1968. In the Iturbi Forest of Zaïre, are possibly about 150,000 of these small people, living in much the same way as their ancestors lived for thousands of years. This small book provides a most interesting introduction to their strange culture. I

299 Crane, Louise. The Land and People of the Congo. Ill. with photographs and a map. J. B. Lippincott, 1971 (Portraits of the Nations Series). The various names, and their changes, of the countries of the Congo are most bewildering. What was once called the Congo (Brazzaville), is now the People's Republic of the Congo, while the former Congo (Kinshasa), which became the Democratic Republic of the Congo, is now Zaïre Republic.

300 Kittler, Glen D. Central Africa, The New World of Tomorrow. Ill. with photographs. Nelson, 1971 (World Neighbors Series). A revision of Equatorial

Africa. This book covers a much larger territory than we have included in our Central Africa division, so it is extremely comprehensive and valuable as a reference book. It contains biographical material on Livingstone, Stanley, certainly Peace Corps volunteers, Schweitzer, and members of the White Fathers and of the Blacks: Kenyatta, Mboya, Odinga, Nyere, Oboto Tshombe, Lamumba, Kasavubu, Mobutu. Appended are map, bibliography and index and "Historical Highlights" of each of the following countries: the People's Republic of the Congo (Brazzaville), Zaïre, Gabon, Central African Republic, Chad, Rwanda, Burundi, Uganda, Kenya, and Tanzania. YA up

301 Lauber, Patricia. The Congo, River into Central Africa. Ill. by Ted Schroeder, maps by Fred Kliem. Garrard, 1964. The story of the great river itself which, with its tributaries and lakes, makes up over 8000 miles of water highways. Also the story of its explorers, particularly Stanley and Livingstone. I

302 McKown, Robin. The Congo, River of Mystery. Ill. by Tom Feelings. McGraw-Hill, 1968. A book of history, geography, biography, and the "agonizing birth pangs of independence" of the countries now known (1974) as the People's Republic of the Congo (Brazzaville Congo) and Zaïre (Kinshasa Congo). An absorbing narrative, with sensitive drawings, of the river, 2716 miles long, and the countries in its basin, including what was until recently Portuguese Angola. YA up

303 _____. The Republic of Zaïre. Ill. with prints and photographs. Franklin Watts, 1972 (a First Book). In 1960 when independence came to the Belgian Congo, the country chose a new name: the Democratic Republic of the Congo, and in 1971 the name was changed again to Zaïre. Each transition was accompanied by violence. Prominent figures in the book are: Patrice Lumumba, Joseph Mobutu, Joseph Kasavubu and Moise Tshombe. YA up

BIOGRAPHIES

304 Carbonnier, Jeanne. Congo Explorer, Pierre Savorgnan de Brazza. Ill. with photographs and a map. Scribner's, 1960. Like most stories of African explorers and colonizers, this is one of almost incredible dedication, endurance, and courage (also frustration), but

Central Africa

unlike many it is a story of human kindness and understanding and fierce hatred of slavery. De Brazza was Italian born but always loyal to the country of his adoption, France. He was born in 1852 and died in Dakar in 1905, having obtained for France a large part of the Congolese territory. YA up

305 Daniel, Anita. The Story of Albert Schweitzer. Ill. with photographs by Erica Anderson. Drawings by W. T. Mars. Random House, 1957 (a Landmark Book). A well written, easily readable biography (1875-1965) with an inspiring concluding chapter outlining the many aspects of Schweitzer's greatness. I

306 Exman, Eugene. The World of Albert Schweitzer; A Book of Photographs by Erica Anderson. Harper, 1955. The "Introduction to Albert Schweitzer" at the beginning of this book of 169 splendid photographs, and the short texts accompanying them supply a biography of the man (1875-1965) and also express much of his thought and philosophy. I up

307 Gollomb, Joseph. Albert Schweitzer, Genius in the Jungle. Vanguard, 1949. A warm, pleasantly readable biography of the Nobel Prize winner (1952) who built his jungle hospital at Lambaréné in 1913 and continued to serve the people there until his death, at 90, in 1965. YA

308 McKown, Robin. Lumumba; A Biography. Doubleday, 1969. A biography of the dynamic leader of the struggle for independence who was brutally assasinated in 1960 at the age of 35, giving the violent history of the Congo's emergence into the political realities of the 20th century. Map, extensive bibliography and index. YA up

309 Manton, Jo. Albert Schweitzer. Ill. by Astrid Walford. Abelard Schuman, 1955. A biography "to be read as a story" of the Alsatian musician, philosopher, missionary, and medical doctor (1875-1965) who founded a jungle hospital in Lambaréné in Gabon (then part of French Equatorial Africa). The book only covers his life until he was seventy-five. I, YA

310 Simon, Charlie May. All Men Are Brothers; A Portrait of Albert Schweitzer. Ill. with photographs by Erica Anderson. E. P. Dutton, 1956. An especially endearing biography of the great jungle doctor (1875-1965) by one who was twice privileged to visit him in Lambaréné. YA

FICTION AND FOLKLORE

311 Bambote. Daba's Travels, from Ouadda to Bangui. Translated from the French by John Buchanan-Brown. Pantheon, 1970. A story written by an African, born and brought up in the Central African Republic, based on his boyhood memories, of a boy's boarding school years in Bomban; his exciting vacations with his schoolmates in the wilds of the bush, plains and rivers; his correspondence with a French pen pal who comes to visit him, and finally his obtaining a scholarship for study in France, and his take-off. I

312 Booth, Esma Rideout. Kalena. Ill. by E. Harper Johnson. Longmans Green, 1958. A novel set in the Belgian Congo, before independence as the Democratic Republic of the Congo, and now Zaïre. Kalena is a young girl whose marriage has been long delayed because of her Mother's illness. At last, however, the bride gifts are sent by the Chief whose son she is to marry. But with them comes a message that the bridegroom-to-be has grown restless after repeated postponements and has taken off for the city to find work and excitement. In the meantime he wants Kalena to go to school and learn to cook and sew. Since that is just what Kalena wants to do (except that she looks for more than cooking and sewing lessons) she uses some of the "bride gift" to pay for education. What a dilemma then when she falls in love with a young medical student and finds that she no longer wishes to marry the Chief's son. YA

313 _____. Kalena and Sana. Ill. by E. Harper Johnson. McKay, 1962. A sequel to "Kalena" in which Kalena and Sana are married. While her husband is gaining medical experience at the clinic, Kalena starts teaching her little neighbors to read and begins a career in radio, telling stories to children. YA

314 Burton, W. F. P. The Magic Drum--Tales from Central Africa. Ill. by Ralph Thompson. Criterion, 1961. Thirty-eight authentic folk tales from the Congo as they were told to Burton who was a missionary there for over forty-five years, with a preface that will interest older readers as well as children. I

315 Carlson, Dale. The Human Apes. Ill. by Al Carlson. Atheneum, 1973. Wow! Here's a whizz of a science fiction novel, set in Central Africa. It starts out with three young people who, just before entering col-

lege, join their fathers in an expedition to study the gorillas near the Virunga volcanoes of Central Africa. The three had grown up together and were close friends, but it is only one, Todd, who discovers the human apes. And it is only Todd whom the human apes want as one of their group. YA

316 Clair, Andrée. Bemba, An African Adventure. Tr. from French by Marie Ponset. Harcourt Brace and World, 1962. This exciting adventure story is set in what was, before 1960, the Middle Congo of French Equatorial Africa with its capital at Brazzaville, and the time setting is in the late 1950s, just before independence. Because of the skullduggery of the old village witch doctor, disgruntled because he is being shown up as a fraud, the village lands are being bought up for a pittance by white colonials. Bemba, not yet ten, braves evil spirits by going into a tabboo cave, and makes a discovery that brings new hope and pride to the villagers. Excellent plot and characterizations. I, YA

317 Elting, Mary and McKown, Robin. A Mongo Homecoming. Ill. by Moneta Barnett. Evans, 1969. The story of a girl of the Mongo people of the Congo (now Zaïre) and her visit to her grandmother's village where there is still a traditional way of life. I

318 Fleming, Elizabeth P. The Takula Tree. Ill. by Robert L. Jefferson. Westminster, 1964. Paul Manship, an American missionary's son is suddenly confronted, for the first time in his life, with the violent face of hatred. The white plantation owners show hatred toward the missionaries because they encourage the natives to educate themselves for independence, and the inflammatory Blacks exhibit hatred for all Whites. Caught in the middle of pre-independence violence in the Congo, Paul and his family experience many perilous adventures. I, YA

319 Franck, Frederick. My Friend in Africa. Ill. by the author. Bobbs-Merrill, 1960. A story about Dr. Schweitzer's jungle hospital at Lambaréné in Gabon, told by a boy patient who hates to leave it. E

320 Price, Willard. African Adventure. Endpapers by Charles Geer. John Day, 1963. The first book in a series of the incredible adventures of the Hunt boys and their father while seeking to take wild animals alive to sell to zoos around the world. The recklessness of the boys, the stupidity of a self-named "white hunter" in their midst, and the villainy of one of their

trackers, are the stuff of which tall tales are made, but the author, who has led expeditions for the National Geographic Society and the American Museum of Natural History, introduces throughout the adventure story authentic facts about wild life in Central Africa. I, YA

321 _____. Gorilla Adventure. Endpapers by Charles Geer. John Day, 1969. The fifth book of the adventures in Africa of the Hunt boys, Roger and Hal, in which they are principally after a giant mountain gorilla for their Father's collection. They manage to snare a lively variety of other creatures, including a black panther, a white python, and a spitting cobra. In their usual foolhardy way they take along a self-acknowledged guide who causes no end of trouble. Their knowledge of animal nature seems to be much sounder than their understanding of human nature. Between the first and fifth books are three adventure stories set in East Africa (see that section of the Reading Guide). I, YA

322 Waldeck, Theodore J. Jamba the Elephant. Ill. by Kurt Wiese. Viking, 1942. The viewpoint in this story, set in the Belgian Congo in the early 20th century, alternates between that of Jamba, a young elephant being trained to carry ebony logs, and that of Bomi, his young trainer. I

SOUTHERN AFRICA
(Angola, Botswana, Lesotho, Malagasy Republic, Malawi, Mauritius, Mozambique, Republic of South Africa, Rhodesia, Namibia/South West Africa, Swaziland, Zambia)

Following is a chart of the independent countries:

name	year of independence	pre-independence status
Angola*	1975	Portuguese colony
Botswana	1966	British protectorate (and High Commission Territory of Bechuanaland)

Southern Africa 65

Lesotho	1966	British High Commission of Basutoland
Malagasy Republic (Madagascar)	1960	French protectorate
Malawi	1964	British protectorate of Nyasaland: member of Federation of Rhodesia
Mauritius	1968	British colony
Mozambique*	1975	Portuguese colony
Republic of South Africa	1910	Four British colonies of Transvaal, Orange Free State, Cape Colony, Natal
Rhodesia†	1965	British Colony (self-governing)
Swaziland	1968	British High Commission Territory
Zambia	1964	British protectorate of Northern Rhodesia; member of Federation of Rhodesia and Nyasaland.

*The governments of Portugal and Angola and Mozambique have agreed on an orderly changeover in late 1975.
†The former Southern Rhodesia unilaterally declared its independence in 1965, an act to which Britain did not accede, and established itself as a republic in 1970. The black native name for the country is Zimbabwe.

Namibia (the African name adopted in 1968 by the United Nations for South West Africa), a German protectorate surrendered to South Africa in 1915 and administered by South Africa as an international territory under a League of Nations, then a U.N. mandate, became the object of international dispute beginning in 1966, centering about South Africa's refusal to grant the country independence. Its status is still undetermined.

NON-FICTION

323 Bleeker, Sonia. The Zulu of South Africa, Cattlemen, Farmers and Warriors. Ill. by Kisa N. Sasaki. William Morrow, 1970. The strange story of the

African tribesmen of South Africa, some three million, known as the Zulu or Southern Bantu, who live in the province of Natal in the Republic of South Africa; and of their great warrior king, Shaka (1787-1828) and of their present sad conditions under the apartheid system. I

324 Carpenter, Allan and Balow, Tom. <u>Enchantment of Africa--Botswana.</u> Ill. with photographs. Children's Press, 1973. A book about the land, history, economy, wild life, culture, and people, of the country formerly called Bechuanaland, which gained its independence from Britain in 1966. A map of Africa in the front of the book places Botswana in relation to its neighbors. There are also short biographies of Khama the Great, Chief in the mid 870s, and Seretse Khama, the first President of independent Botswana, and married to a white woman. Handy reference section. I, YA

325 _____ and Ragin, Lynn. <u>Enchantment of Africa--Zambia.</u> Ill. with photographs. Children's Press, 1973. This book, like others of its series covers many subjects (see above) and is an attractive introduction to the country, formerly Northern Rhodesia, which obtained its independence in 1964, with Kenneth Kaunda as its first president. The handy reference section at the end includes political and geographical data, population figures, and principal cities. "Date with History" (included in all the Enchantment series books) gives a complete chronology, and the map at the beginning places the country in the context of Africa as a whole. I, YA

326 Hopkinson, Tom. <u>South Africa.</u> Ill. in color and black and white photographs. Time, Inc., 1964. Like other Time-Life books, this is a pictorial story of this part of Africa, and though already outdated in matters of political boundaries and name changes, still portrays the lands and peoples as they now are and describes racial tensions which seem to be constantly increasing. YA up

327 McKown, Robin. <u>Crisis in South Africa.</u> G. P. Putnam's Sons, 1972. A book about the shocking state of affairs in the Republic of South Africa, largely because of its policy of apartheid (apart-Hate); about a beautiful and rich country but one where the inhumanity of Whites toward Blacks seems almost unbelievable. The historical background of the present turmoil is clearly presented, beginning with the Time

of Troubles (late 18th and early 19th centuries) when there was horrendous tribal warfare during the reign of King Shaka and his successor. There was also discord among the white settlers in the 19th century, culminating in the Boer War (1899-1902). Chapters on the U.S. and foreign boycotts and Black heroes and White sympathizers show all too clearly how all efforts to liberalize racial policies have been frustrated. An extensive bibliography is appended. YA

328 Marshall, Anthony. The Malagasy Republic (Madagascar). Ill. with photographs. Franklin Watts, 1972 (a First Book). A book in which the pictures are more significant than the somewhat pedestrian text, because few of us have any mental pictures of this large island (some think it a continent) formerly called Madagascar. When it received its independence in 1960 it renamed itself the Malagasy Republic. I up

329 Mertens, Alice. Children of the Kalahari. Ill. with photographs. Bobbs-Merrill, 1966. The life of the Bushmen of this South African desert is almost incomprehensible to outsiders, but through the story of a little boy named Unkra in this book we can at least learn something of the lives of the children there. E, I

330 Newman, Bernard and Caldwell, John C. Let's Visit South Africa. Ill. with maps and photographs. John Day, 1968. A short book about a large country, the Republic of South Africa, covering briefly but adequately its geography, history, culture, and policy of apartheid. There is a particularly interesting section on its wild life. I, YA

331 Paton, Alan. The Land and People of South Africa, rev. ed. Ill. with photographs. J. B. Lippincott, 1972 (Portraits of the Nations Series). Written by a white South African, born there and dedicated to the cause of the Blacks in that country of apartheid. He is the author of the novel, "Cry the Beloved Country," which you will find noted with the fiction in this section. YA up

332 Perkins, Carol Morse and Marlin. "I Saw You from Afar"; A Visit to the Bushmen of the Kalihari Desert. Ill. with photographs and endpaper maps of Africa. Atheneum, 1965. An illuminating and appealing story of the Bushmen. The title comes from their typical greeting which implies that the visitor is so big that he can be seen from afar. The Bushmen themselves

are seldom taller than five feet and often shorter. I
333 Stein, Mini. Majola, A Zulu Boy. Ill. with photographs
by Duncan G. Greaves. Julian Messner, 1969. A
simple pictorial story of the daily life of a Zulu boy
living in Natal, a province of South Africa. E, I

BIOGRAPHIES

334 Cohen, Daniel. Shaka, King of the Zulus. Ill. with
prints and cover maps. Doubleday, 1973. There
can be no question of Shaka's place in history. His
forging of one Zulu nation out of many scattered
tribes, and his military and political genius, place
him in the top ranks of world military leaders.
There can, however be a question as to whether he
was a madman, or simply completely ruthless in his
personal ambition. We have had recent examples of
this same fine line between insanity and ruthlessness,
and the bombing of civilians in recent wars must
give us pause in our judgment of this great African
leader (1787-1828). A glossary of Zulu and South
African terms is appended. YA up

335 Keating, Bern. Chaka, King of the Zulus. G. P. Put-
nams Sons, 1968. The name of this African king is
spelled in various ways, because of the difficulty of
translating Zulu sounds. This is a story of a most
bloodthirsty military leader, interestingly related to
corresponding world history. For instance the year
that Chaka was born was the year of the Constitutional Convention in the American states, and the Napo-
leonic Wars were going on during his time of conquest. YA

336 Legum, Colin and Margaret. The Bitter Choice; Eight
South Africans' Resistance to Tyranny. Ill. with
photographs of the subjects. Excaliber Book, World,
1968. The eight subjects of these brief biographies
are: Alan Paton, Albert Lutuli, Nelson Mandela,
Robert Mangaliso Sobukwe, C. F. Beyers Naude,
Dennis Brutus, Michael Scott. The first two chapters of this sober, highly informative book discuss
the general situation of apartheid and the dilemma
of South Africa, and the last deals with the choice
of weapons against this desperate situation. Appended are a chronology and a list of the writings of the
eight men. YA up

337 Polatnick, F. T. and Saletan. Zambia's President,

Kenneth Kaunda. Messner, 1972. A biography of a great leader, born in 1924 in northern Rhodesia, who rose from extreme poverty and endured prison and exile in his struggle against racism and apartheid and in his insistence on the use of non-violent means to achieve independence for the new country of Zambia. Also, it is a history of Rhodesia, north and south, and the problems caused by Rhodesia's rebellion against British control. YA

338 Seed, Jenny. The Voice of the Great Elephant. Pantheon, 1968. A biographical novel of the powerful and barbaric King Shaka, based largely on the writings of the first white traders who settled around Durban Bay. A novel of violence in early 19th century Natal. I up

FOLKLORE

339 Aardema, Verna. Behind the Back of the Mountain; Black Folktales from Southern Africa. Ill. by Leo and Diane Dillon. Dial, 1973. Ten stories, their sources indicated by the reteller-adapter, many of which are amusing trickery tales, but some having universal themes. E, I

340 Berger, Terry. Black Fairy Tales. Ill. by David Omar White. Atheneum, 1969. Ten tales adapted from Fairy Tales from South Africa by E. J. Bourhill and J. B. Drake. Included are seven Swazi tales, two Shangani stories and one 'Msuto story, and the collector explains that the book was prepared "especially for Black children who have never read Black fairy tales." I

341 Helfman, Elizabeth S. The Bushmen and Their Stories. Ill. by Richard Cuffari. Seabury Press, 1971. Besides the 17 folk stories, most collected by a German scholar, Dr. Wilhelm H. I. Bleek during the second half of the 19th century, there is a chapter on the history of the Bushmen and one about the source of the tales which include creation stories, and many tales of the Bushman God, Mantis, and the members of his animal family. I

342 Savory, Phyllis. Zulu Fireside Tales. Ill. by Sylvia Baxter. Hastings House, 1961. A collection of stories told to the author by a little Zulu girl and her Mother. The reteller has tried, successfully, I feel, "To tell the stories from the point of view of

the Zulu people." I up

FICTION

343   Buchan, John. Prester John (1910). Houghton Mifflin, 1938 (Popular Library Edition). The Prester John of this wildly adventurous mystery novel is not the legendary king of the 12th century in the heart of Asia. This one is a purely fictional Abyssinian king, who possessed, at one time, a fabulous "necklace of evil." Young Crawfurt, the narrator in this novel, has been sent from England to become a trader and storekeeper in the Zulu country of southern Africa, and from the time he leaves England his life becomes entangled with that of a black giant of a man, John Laputa, who is believed to be the heir of the Ethiopian king, Prester John, and the possessor of the evil treasure. Young Crawfurt recklessly tries to thwart Laputa's planned conquest of the white men in those parts, namely the Boers, and the plot thickens into a real stew. A

344   Haggard, Rider. King Solomon's Mines (1885). Ill. by A. R. Whitear. E. P. Dutton, 1963. A suspenseful novel, in late 19th century style, of a hunt for diamonds in the deserts and mountains of South Africa, written by a great story-teller with a "fine, weird imagination," and dedicated to "all the big and little boys who read it." He should have added "girls." YA, A

345   McKown, Robin. The Boy Who Woke Up in Madagascar. Ill. by Robert Quackenbush. G. P. Putnam's, 1967. A truly fantastic novel and, at the same time, a remarkably informative one about this fourth largest island in the world, once called Madagascar but, since 1960, the Malagasy Republic. When Peter went to sleep he was in New York, but when he woke up, as the title tells us, he found himself in a remote African country in its early days of independence, a place where magic and sorcery were used against the new government. The blend of fact and fancy is nicely made, the facts supported by an appendix chapter: "Some Facts About Madagascar" which includes a glossary, a list of major rulers of the island, and a list of the 18 major tribes and the six major provinces. YA

346   Manzi, Alberto. White Boy. Ill. by Charles Molina.

Macmillan, 1963. An historical novel set in South
Africa in the early years of the 19th century when
Swazis were fighting the Bushmen of the Kalihari
Desert and Zulus, under the fearsome King Chaka,
were attacking both the Bushmen and the white Boers
who were led by Andries Pretorius. Isa is a white
boy who, as an orphan, was brought up by the Swazis
but never really accepted by them. Befriended by
Bushmen he is returned to his own white people, but
they reject him because of his friendship with the
people of the desert. It is only after many harrowing adventures that he discovers a love that knows no
skin color. YA

347 Mirsky, Reba Paeff. Thirty-one Brothers and Sisters.
Ill. by W. T. Mars. Follett, 1952. An engaging
story, set in the province of Natal in the Republic
of South Africa, of Nomusa, the young daughter of a
Zulu chief who is the husband of six wives and father of 31 children. Nomusa yearns to live the life
that boys live, and dreams wistfully of going on an
elephant hunt. This is the first of three books about
Nomusa and readers will grow up with her as she
enters the world of the 20th century. I, YA

348 _____. Seven Grandmothers. Ill. by W. T. Mars.
Follett, 1955. In this sequel to Thirty-one Brothers
and Sisters about the chief's daughter Nomusa, the
modern world begins to infringe on the primitive one
of Zululand, exemplified by the conflicting ideas of
a witch doctor and a nurse, a young native woman
who has studied in Durban. Nomusa begins to feel
that the new ways in medicine are best, but also
feels guilty about rejecting the methods of the witch
doctor. Her dearest wish, however, is to study
nursing. I, YA

349 _____. Nomusa and the New Magic. Ill. by W. T.
Mars. Follett, 1962. A sequel to Seven Grandmothers
in which Nomusa, the Zulu Chief's daughter, goes away
from home to start school to learn to read and write before taking up nurse's training. However, back in
her village tension continues to mount in the conflict
between modern medical methods and those of the
witch doctor, but after the latter's trial for sorcery,
Nomusa's father gently shows her that there is some
good to be had from both the old and the new ways.
I, YA

350 Mitchison, Naomi. The Family at Kitlabeng. Farrar,
Straus and Girous, 1969 (an Ariel Book). The author,

an adopted member of the Bakgatta tribe in Botswana, gives a very vivid depiction of the ordeals of the people there in time of drought. When Masaye's father has to go to South Africa to work for meager wages in the mines, the girl loses all prospects of going away to learn to improve her skill in pottery making. Even when the rains finally come, she has very little hope until suddenly she has a visitor. I, YA

351 _____. Friends and Enemies. Ill. by Anne Grifalconi. John Day, 1968. When boundaries were drawn in 1966 between the Republic of South Africa and Bechuanaland (now Botswana), no consideration was given to tribal units. In this novel a boy whose brother has been imprisoned "below the line" escapes from South Africa to the freedom and near starvation to be found in Botswana, in order to get a much desired education. It is a tragic story of man's inhumanity to man in South Africa, and nature's harshness in Botswana, lightened by only a few faint rays of hope.

352 _____. Sunrise Tomorrow; A Story of Botswana. Farrar, Straus and Giroux. A fine novel of contemporary young people in a small, "backward" village in southern Africa, idealistic about progress but held back by tradition. The theme is universal, but the treatment of it by this author, an adopted member of a tribe in Botswana, is unique in its deep understanding of the young people in that emerging country. YA up

353 Paton, Alan. Cry, the Beloved Country. Scribner's, 1948. A widely read and influential novel, poetically written in Biblical prose style, of a Zulu country priest who goes to the big city of Johannesburg to search for an errant sister and long-lost son. The woman has become a prostitute, and the son has admittedly murdered a white man, a man dedicated to the reform of the colonial system. A tragic story deeply penetrating conditions in Colonial South Africa, conditions which have certainly not improved in the twenty-five years and more since the book came out. A

354 Rooke, Daphne. Twins in South Africa. Ill. by W. Lorraine. Houghton Mifflin, 1955. This book should have had a more intriguing title, for it is a good exciting mystery story about some hidden gold and a fabulous diamond and the terrifying adventures

of the 12-year-old Boer twins during their Christmas holidays in Zululand. I, YA

355 Ropner, Pamela. The Golden Impala. Ill. by Ralph Thompson. Criterion, 1958. A story, with an element of fantasy, of a 12-year-old South African boy, son of the warden of a game preserve, as he seeks to protect herds of impala from an unknown enemy. I, YA

356 Seed, Jenny. Tombi's Song. Ill. by Dugald MacDougal. Rand McNally, 1966. Tombi is a six-year-old Zulu girl who feels very important when she is sent alone to the store to buy sugar. On the way she is teased by some older people who tell her of a horrendous monster living in the forest, and when she hears a fearful noise on the way home she drops her bag of sugar which all spills out in the sand. How her song saves the day is the point of the story. E

357 _____. Vengeance of the Zulu King. Ill. (uncredited). Pantheon, 1970. A novel based on the diary and other writings of a white trader, Henry Fynn, called by the Bantu of Natal, "Mbuyazi, Prince of the Bay." He was the leader of an advance party of a trading company and stood up bravely against the fierce King Shaka of the Zulus. Shaka, admiring his nerve, defended him against all enemies. The principal character in the story, however, is a boy named Bongiseni who had escaped when Shaka destroyed his village, and again was forced to flee the vengeance of Shaka's brother after the King's death. The name of Fynn who died in Natal in 1861 is still held in honor by the Zulus. YA

358 Waldeck, Theodore. Lions on the Hunt. Ill. by Kurt Wiese. Viking, 1956. A story of a very young male lion of Zululand as he grows up and survives the perils of drought, fire, men (oh, especially men) and, finally the struggle for leadership of a pride. Good sound animal lore imaginatively presented. I, YA

359 Westwood, Gwen. Narni of the Desert. Ill. by Peter Warner. Rand McNally, 1968. A story of a child of the Kalahari Desert, the games the children play there, the foods they eat (whey they can find food) and their way of life--generally much different from anything westerners and even many other Africans know. And yet, as the story of Narni shows, these small people have the same ambition as children everywhere to prove themselves to their peers. E

360 Whitney, Phyllis A. Secret of the Tiger's Eye. Ill. by Richard Horwitz. Westminster, 1961. What more intriguing way to learn about another country and way of life than through a well plotted, entertaining mystery story? In this book, some children are taken to Capetown, South Africa, by their journalist father, to spend six months in learning to understand an entirely alien culture and people. In spite of the system of apartheid, Benita not only learns to know and love someone of a different color, but also learns to be more tolerant of one of her own whose approach to life differs from hers, and, best of all, to better understand herself as she probes for the secret of the tiger's eye. I, YA

Part Three

ASIA

ASIA IN GENERAL

Asia, as defined by one dictionary, is a continent "bounded by Europe and the Arctic, Pacific, and Indian Oceans." Rather a staggering concept, isn't it? Particularly so when you try to think of it in terms of its teeming and varied population. Somehow, it doesn't seem to work out very well to divide it up according to the points of the compass, as was done with the African continent. For one thing, the terms Near East and Mideast (or Middle East) are often used interchangeably, and "North" is never used at all (South Asia, and the very familiar Southeast Asia are). Accordingly the following arrangement will have to do: (1) The Soviet Union in Asia; (2) China and neighboring countries; (3) Japan and Korea; (4) Turkey; (5) The Mideast; (6) India and neighboring countries; (7) Southeast Asia.

Obviously there can be no generalizations about the continent as a whole, even though this short section is titled "Asia in General." What it contains simply are books that won't fit into the frames of any of the above divisions.

NON-FICTION

361 deKay, Ormonde. The East in the Middle Ages. Ill. with paintings. Golden Press, 1966. A handsomely illustrated history of China, Japan, and the Mongol and Moslem Empires, from 214 B.C. when the Ch'in emperors built the Great Wall of China, to 1644, the beginning of the Manchu dynasty in China, with charts of important events in the east between those dates. The text is so well organized that it makes the ancient history of the East easy to comprehend. YA

362 Fairservice, Walter A. Jr. Before the Buddha Came;

The Story of the Earliest Civilizations of the Far East. Ill. with photographs, maps and drawings by Jan Fairservice. Scribner's, 1972. A splendid book with a brief, clear chronology (from 2000 B.C. to A.D. 800) at the end. The content of the book can be summed up by quoting the last paragraph of the introduction: "It is the ancient world of the Far East before Buddhism that concerns us. It was the time when out of the simple life of prehistoric man emerged the splendid civilizations about which men still think and wonder." YA up

363 Joy, Charles R. Young People of South Asia. Ill. with photographs of the young people whose first-hand reports are collected in this book and with endpaper maps by Don Pitcher. Duell Sloan and Pearce, 1964. The countries represented by these accounts are: Thailand, Malaya, Burma, Pakistan, Nepal, India, Kashmir, Ceylon, Afghanistan, Iran, Iraq, and Syria and the young writers are of various racial, religious, and social classes. I

364 Lum, Peter. The Growth of Civilization in East Asia, China, Japan and Korea to the 14th Century. Ill. with maps, drawings and half tone reproductions. S. G. Philips, 1969. A concise, beautifully illustrated history of ancient China, Japan and Korea, with a chronology, bibliography and index, and enjoyable reading to boot. YA up

365 Sawyer, Martha and Reusswig, William. The Illustrated Book About the Far East: China, Tibet, Mongolia, Korea, Japan, Formosa, Manchuria, Siberia, the Philippine Islands. Grosset and Dunlap, 1961. A rich background book for readers of Asian novels and biographies, made by a husband and wife team, Martha the painter and William the writer. I up

366 Seeger, Elizabeth. Eastern Religions. Ill. with photographs and reproductions. Crowell, 1973. The rise and development of the far eastern religions and philosophies as revealed by the Buddha, Confucius, and Lao-tse, in geographical and historical arrangement, with illustrative stories and anecdotes. A timely book because of the current youth cults based, though not always correctly, on the religions of the East. YA up

Asia in General 77

BIOGRAPHIES

367 Barr, Pat. A Curious Life for a Lady; The Story of Isabella Bird, A Remarkable Woman Traveler. Ill. with 16 pages of photographs and 6 maps. Doubleday, 1970. Indeed she was a remarkable lady, this frail little Victorian woman who, at the age of forty, started traveling "for her health." Pretty rugged treatment, for she avoided all conventional tours, preferring to explore by herself the wildernesses of Australia and the Canadian Rockies and the least known parts Asia in the 1870s: Japan, opened only shortly before to westerners, Korea, Tibet, China, Malaya, Persia, and Kurdistan. At the age of seventy she visited the fierce warrior tribes of the Atlas mountains in Morocco. And about all these adventurous travels she wrote prolifically and entertainingly. A
368 Roland, Albert. Profiles from the New Asia; A Spectrum of Outstanding Men and Women of Indonesia, Singapore, Thailand, the Philippines, Japan and Other Asian Countries. Ill. with photographs. Macmillan, 1970. Most biographical books about the new Asia stress political leaders, but this one covers journalists, authors, artists, movie producers and such from all over Asia, but especially from the southeastern part. To list the names of all would bewilder the reader. YA up

FOLKLORE AND FICTION

369 Carpenter, Frances. The Elephant's Bathtub; Wonder Tales from Burma, Cambodia, Persia, Malaya, Arabia, Thailand, Iraq, India, Afghanistan, the Philippines, Ceylon, Vietnam, Indonesia, Annam, Laos, and the Pacific Islands. Ill. by Hans Guggenheim. Doubleday, 1962. I
370 Courlander, Harold. The Tiger's Whisker and Other Tales and Legends from Asia and the Pacific. Ill. by Enrico Arno. Harcourt Brace, 1959. Humorous tales from Arabia, Burma, Ceylon, China, India, Indonesia, Japan, Kashmir, Korea, Laos, Malaya, Persia, Polynesia and Yap Island, with notes on the stories appended. I
371 Nahmad, H. M. The Peasant and the Donkey, Tales of the Near and Middle East, with stories by Charles

Downing, Nadia Abu-Zahra, Feyyaz Kayacan and Mary Fergar. Ill. by William Pappas. Henry Z. Walck, 1968. A collection of Persian, Turkish, Arabic, Hebrew and Georgian stories of magic, mystery and common sense. I up

372 Stephan, Hanna. The Quest. Ill. by Antony Maitland, Tr. by Daphne Machin Goodall. Little Brown, 1967. A story of the wanderings of a young German boy, during his years from five to 14, in search of his mother from whom he became separated during World War II. Taken by a Russian soldier to the Caucasus, he then traveled through the Kirchis Republic, China, Tibet, India and, finally, Egypt. The story is based on original documents about a child lost in East Prussia and traced by the Red Cross nine years later. YA

373 Tooze, Ruth. Three Tales of Monkey; Ancient Folk Tales from the Far East. Ill. by Rosalie Petrash. John Day, 1967. Three monkey stories, each introduced by a paragraph about its origin: the first, from Cambodia, tells how the monkeys first invented music; the second from Ceylon (or Sri Lanka as it was named long ago and is now again named) illustrates the proverb that pride goeth before a fall; and the third is an Oriental version of "Puss in Boots" as told in Ceylon, Cambodia and Bali. E

TURKEY

Turkey is often considered part of the "Middle East," but its geographical and historical connection with Europe seems to demand a section by itself. Historically Asia and Europe clashed with each other there during the three centuries of the Crusades, and in the 17th century the Ottoman Empire extended to the very gates of Vienna. What is now left of that Empire is a republic, established in 1923 by Mustafa Kemal Ataturk.

NON-FICTION

374 Coolidge, Olivia E. The Trojan War. Ill. by Eduard Sandoz. Houghton Mifflin, 1952. The Homeric leg-

end, supported by archaeological discoveries, woven into a continuous narrative, with a table of characters. YA
375 Duggan, Alfred. The Story of the Crusades. Ill. by C. Walter Hodges' drawings, and with photographs of the major battle sites. Pantheon, 1964. A lively story of all the crusades from 1095 to 1291, with an epilogue and note on sources. YA
376 Graves, Robert. The Siege and Fall of Troy. Ill. by C. Walter Hodges. Doubleday, 1962. The stories from Homer's Iliad and Odyssey, supplemented with accounts of Latin and Greek writers. YA
377 Jacobs, David. Constantinople, City on the Golden Horn. Ill. with reproductions of paintings, mosaics, statuary architecture and maps. American Heritage, 1969. A biography of the 2700-year-old city, now Turkish Istanbul. YA
378 Pernoud, Regine. The Crusades. Tr. by Enid McCleod. G. P. Putnam's, 1963. For the serious reader, this history, recorded in the words of some who were there, is a long, but thoroughly rewarding book. Included are clear maps of the Near East and the routes of the first and second crusades. YA up
379 Schloat, G. Warren. Naim, A Boy of Turkey. Ill. with photographs. Alfred A. Knopf, 1963. The text and pictures show village life in Turkey to be still behind the times. E, I
380 Spencer, William. The Land and People of Turkey, rev. ed. Ill. with a map and photographs. J. B. Lippincott, 1972 (Portraits of the Nations Series). This book about the former Ottoman Empire and modern Turkey, after Ataturk's revolution, is entertaining as well as informative. YA up
381 Stewart, Desmond and the Editors of Life. Turkey. Time, Inc., 1965. Lavishly illustrated and with large endcover maps. A comprehensive book of Turkish history (long and intricate) and of modern Turkey, its achievements and problems. Appended are lists of historical dates, recommendations for further reading and the names of famous Turkish cultural figures and their principal works. YA up
382 Williams, Jay. Knights of the Crusades. American Heritage, 1962. Richly illustrated in color and black and white, with stories of the crusades and crusaders. I, YA

BIOGRAPHIES

383 Braymer, Marjorie. The Walls of Windy Troy: A Biography of Heinrich Schliemann. Ill. with photographs. Harcourt Brace, 1960. The story of Schliemann's life and his discovery of the actual site of ancient Troy, with an outline map and a time chart adapted from Wallbank and Taylor's Civilization, Past and Present, Vol. I. YA

384 Downey, Granville. Belisarius, Young General of Byzantium. Jacket design and map by Reynold Pollak. Dutton, 1960. The story of Justinian's general's first thirty years (505-535), his leading the Roman army to victory over the Persian invaders of Syria, his suppression of the Nika rebellion, and his African triumph. A map of the Roman world at this time, a long list of characters, and an afterword about sources is included. YA

385 Elkin, Sam. Search for a Lost City: The Quest of Heinrich Schliemann. G. P. Putnam's Sons, 1967. A well written biography of the German (1822-90) who always believed that the Trojan War as told by Homer was a true story and who set out determinedly to prove it by finding the actual site of Troy. The story of the Trojan War and that of the Wooden Horse are told in the first chapter: "Fact or Fiction." I

386 Heller, Deane Fons. Ataturk, Hero of Modern Turkey. Julian Messner, 1972. A biography of Mustapha Kemal (1881-1938) and the story of how, in the aftermath of World War I, he created the Turkish Republic out of the ruins of the Ottoman Empire, became its first president, and instituted revolutionary reforms. YA

387 Lengyel, Emil. They Called Him Ataturk. Ill. with photographs and maps. John Day, 1962. A dramatic biography of Mustapha Kemal, later called Ataturk (Father of Turkey) and his rise from peasant boy to general of the Sultan's army, to revolutionist and finally to president of the Republic of Turkey (1923-1938). He was the inspiration of many reforms and independent movements in such Arab countries as Syria, Iran and Egypt. In Turkey he established a constitution, and freedom of religion, abolished the fez, unveiled women, and replaced the Arabic script with the western alphabet. Not all these reforms took hold, but his accomplishments were, on the whole, phenomenal. YA up

Turkey

FOLKLORE

388 Ekrem, Selma. Turkish Fairy Tales. Ill. by Liba Bayrak. D. Van Nostrand, 1964. Twelve tales retold by the Turkish-born Selma Ekrem, from her memory of her old nurse telling them to her. There is a short introduction about the nurse and other story-tellers, and a glossary of Turkish words and expressions. I

389 Kelsey, Alice Geer (pseud.) Once the Hodja. Ill. by Frank Dobias. Longmans Green, 1958. The historical Hodja and Turkish folk hero lived about 600 years ago in the time of Tamerlane, but the legends about him, like American tales of Paul Bunyan, have grown taller and funnier with the centuries of telling in Turkey. The Hodja had a talent for getting into and out of trouble. E, I

390 Walker, Barbara K. The Courage of Kazan. Ill. by James and Ruth McCrea. Thomas Y. Crowell, 1970. "Long ago" so starts this humorous, brightly illustrated folk tale, "when the flea was a porter and the camel a barber, a timid fellow named Kazan set forth to find his courage." E

391. ————. The Ifrit and the Magic Gifts. Ill. by Ati Forberg. Follett, 1972. A most amusing folktale about three wandering soldiers, an ifrit and a princess. It wouldn't be fair to tell more except to explain than an "ifrit" in Turkish folklore is rather like a leprechaun in Irish. E

392 ————. Korolu, the Singing Bandit. Ill. by Nickzad Nodjaumi. Thomas Y. Crowell, 1970. A hero story, probably as well known to Turkish children as Robin Hood is to western ones. Korolu was a character of some 300 years ago whose name meant terror to the rich and protection to the poor. I

393 ————. Once There Was and Twice There Wasn't. Ill. by Gordon Kibbee. Follett, 1968. The folk hero of these seven stories (often nonsensical and often remarkably wise), is a boy named Keloglan. There is a brief author's note at the beginning, and after each story, credit is given to the person who helped in the translation. E, I

394 ————. Watermelons, Walnuts and the Wisdom of Allah and Other Tales of the Hoca. Ill. by Harold Berson. Parents' Magazine Press, 1967. There are hundreds of stories about Hoca (or Hodja), a story about him for every occasion. E, I

FICTION

395 Blatter, Dorothy. Cap and Candle. Westminster, 1961.
At the beginning of this novel of modern Turkey, Feliz Demir seems to have pretty much the same problems and pleasures as teenagers anywhere in the world, but as she grows up and after she has been capped as a nurse, she becomes involved in the larger problems of her country: the lack of doctors and nurses for the rural communities, the backwardness of the villagers and their resistance to change. She is torn between dedication to the nursing profession and domesticity, but to satisfy her parents she marries the young man they have chosen for her, with elaborate ceremonies. In the end her problem is resolved in a way that almost makes her believe in Kismet--what will be, will be. YA

396 Cervon, Jacqueline. Castaway from Rhodes. Tr. from French by Thelma Niklaus. Franklin Watts, 1973.
A novel, especially timely at present, of Turkish-Greek enmity. Washed ashore on a small island near the Turkish coast, Stavros, a young Greek of Rhodes, is saved from drowning by a tough crew of Turkish sponge-divers and his resemblance to a young Turk (not so tough) on the caique, is the beginning of an on again off again friendship between the two young men. After Turhan, the Turk, is badly beaten up risking his life for Stavros, the latter takes Turhan's place as a sponge diver and nearly loses his life. Centuries of hatred and prejudice between Turk and Greek is finally wiped out, at least between Stavros and Turhan. YA

397 Coolidge, Olivia. Tales of the Crusades. Houghton Mifflin, 1970. A collection of short stories about the most dramatic events and characters of the period, 1095-1291. YA

398 Dickinson, Peter. The Dancing Bear. Ill. by John Smee. Little Brown, 1972. A witty historical novel about a boy slave, a bear, and a holy man, set in 6th century Byzantium. At least it starts there, but Silvester travels a long way from Constantinople in his search for Ariadne who has been stolen away by the Huns. He is accompanied by Bubba, his charismatic bear, and Holy John, who had lived on top of a 12-foot pillar until the Huns came to ravage the city and the pillar fell from under him. YA up

399 Johnson, James Ralph. Camels West. Ill. by the

author. David McKay, 1964. A story about the importation of camels from Turkey to the southwest United States. YA

400 Kent, Louise Andrews. Two Children of Troy. Ill. by Elizabeth Tyler Wolcott. Houghton Mifflin, 1932. A well plotted historical novel of ancient Phoenicia at the time of King Solomon (10th century B.C.), about a brave boy of 14 and his equally brave sister of 13 and how they foiled some pirates. Interesting details of Tyrian trade in dyes, and of the Cedars of Lebanon, and of King Solomon's Temple in Jerusalem. I, YA

401 Krumgold, Joseph. The Most Terrible Turk; A Story of Turkey. Ill. by Michael Hampshire. Thomas Crowell, 1969. Young Ali of Istanbul discovers that his uncle is shooting at the tires of trucks because the truck traffic is spoiling his rabbit hunting. To get him to stop, Ali pretends to read him scare headlines about "truck murderers." A humorous story of a warm relationship between uncle and nephew. E, I

402 Rasp-Nuri, Grace. Yusuf, Boy of Cyprus. Tr. from German by J. Maxwell Brown, Jr. Criterion, 1958. Yusuf was only nine when he was kidnapped by a couple of potential murderers and trained for robbery, but he finally got away by his quick wits. Nevertheless he could never forget that the thugs were free and vengeful, not till near the very end of the book when, on his way to England by ship, suddenly they appear again. I, YA

403 Reeves, James. The Trojan Horse. Ill. by Krystyna Turska. Franklin Watts, 1969. The story told by a young Trojan boy escaping from Troy after the Greeks had taken it by trickery. E, I

404 Scott, Sir Walter. The Talisman (1825). Many editions, including paperback. A novel of the Crusades in which the principal characters are Richard Coeur de Lion and his noble enemy Saladin who cures Richard's sickness by the use of a talisman. A

405 Werfel, Franz. The Forty Days of Musa Dagh. Viking, 1934. A long, powerful and tragic novel of the defense by a group of Armenian villagers against the Turkish program of extermination during World War I. Some of the characters are historical, and all are fully realized individuals, those enduring the nightmare on Musa Dagh, and those involved in attempts to exterminate, or rescue, the Armenians. A

406 Whitney, Phyllis A. <u>Mystery of the Golden Horn.</u> Ill.
by Georgeann Helms. Westminster, 1962. The setting is contemporary Istanbul, but as Vickie Stewart, the daughter of a teacher in the American college there, becomes embroiled in the misadventures of another American girl (and a very mixed-up one) we find ourselves in old, historic Constantinople with its mosques and minarets and castles. I, YA

THE MIDDLE EAST
(Afghanistan, Iran, Iraq, Israel, Jordan,
Kuwait, Lebanon, Muscat and Oman, Palestine,
Saudi Arabia, Syria, United Arab Emirates)

Turkey and Egypt are also generally considered as part of the Middle East, but the former has a section to itself and the latter is included in that of Northeastern Africa. The list would be ever longer and more confusing if added to it were earlier and ancient names of countries in this part of the world, ancient ones such as Sumeria, Phoenicia, Assyria and Mesopotamia. The country so long known as "Persia" has been, since 1935, "Iran."

The Bible Lands call to mind such place names as "the Land of Canaan" and Judea. In this section I have chosen to simply use the name "Israel" in relation to Old Testament history and legend, and Roman Palestine in relation to the New.

Palestine is also the name of the former British mandate now divided between the State of Israel and the State of Jordan (Arab Palestine), and for this reason it is included above among the Middle Eastern countries, though, strictly speaking, there is at present no country as such. However this area of the mideast is in such a state of conflict and ferment that future names and boundaries are unpredictable.

NON-FICTION

407 Alden, Carolla. <u>Royal Persia, Tales and Art of Iran.</u>
<u>Ill. with full-color and black and white reproductions</u>
of works of art. Parents' Magazine Press, 1972.

This short pictorial history of Persia (now Iran) is based upon "Art Entertainments," a series for young people presented at the Metropolitan Museum of Art. I up

408 Asimov, Isaac. The Land of Canaan. Houghton Mifflin, 1971. Judaism and its offspring, Christianity, came from this territory, now split up between Syria, Lebanon, Israel and Jordan. This book is clearly organized and divided into twelve sections, beginning with "Before Abraham" and ending with "Rome Triumphant." There are maps throughout, and appended a table of dates covering all the ancient history of Canaan and Egypt, tables of genealogies (first of the Kings, and second of the Davidic dynasty), and index. YA

409 _____. The Near East, 10,000 Years of History. Ill. with maps and drawings. Houghton Mifflin, 1968. A fine comprehensive history of the Tigris and Euphrates valleys where western civilization began. In clear narrative style the author communicates his enthusiasm for the subject with the reader. And what an extensive subject it is, covering the Sumerians, Akkadians, Amorites, Assyrians, Chaldeans, Persians, Macedonians, Parthians, Sasanids, Arabs, Turks, and finally the Europeans. Appended is a comprehensive list of dates and index. YA up

410 Bahar, Hushang. Getting to Know Iran and Iraq. Ill. by Hazel Hoecker. Coward McCann, 1963. The long, complex history of these countries (Iran was formerly Persia and Iraq, Assyria), can only be skimmed over in a brief book, but, as in others of this series, there are appended historical outlines for each country and short vocabulary and pronunciation lists. I

411 Baumann, Hans. In the Land of Ur; The Discovery of Ancient Mesopotamia. Tr. by Stella Humphries. Pantheon, 1969. This author of several novels of ancient history, has here written non-fiction equally dramatically. Appended are the following: "Words, Places and People," "Famous Mesopotamian Explorers," "Major Excavations in Chronological Order," and "Chronological Table, with names of kings." YA up

412 Breetveld, Jim. Getting to Know Lebanon. Ill. by Harris Petie and with a map. Coward McCann, 1959. The modern story of this tiny country, about the size of Delaware, is interspersed with traces of its past; of the Phoenicians, Persians, Assyrians, Greeks,

Romans and European crusaders. The historical outline at the end tells us that it achieved its full independence in 1943. I

413 Caldwell, John C. Let's Visit Afghanistan. Ill. with photographs. John Day, 1968. A short but highly informative book about this remote, isolated country of the Hindu Kush mountains, high plateaus and deserts; about the invasions of Alexander the Great, Genghis Khan, and Islamic hordes; and about its modern constitutional monarchy and the pressures from surrounding countries and aid from the Soviets and Americans. I, YA

414 ———. Let's Visit the Middle East. Ill. with photographs and a map. John Day, revised edition, 1966. Much too much has happened and is still happening in this troubled area of the world for a book even revised as late as 1966 to be up to date, but there is good historical background here for a better understanding of current developments. I

415 Clifford, Mary Louise. The Land and People of Afghanistan. Ill. with photographs and a map. J. B. Lippincott, 1962 (Portraits of the Nations Series). The story of a mountain country of indeterminate population (since no census had yet been taken when this book was written); of its tribes, religion, the position of women, its government, and, of course, geography and history. YA

416 Cooke, David C. Kuwait, Miracle on the Desert. Ill. with 67 photographs. Grosset and Dunlap, 1970. A truly fantastic story of the sudden transformation, because of its oil riches, of a poverty-stricken desert land into a rich modern state, one in which there is no such thing as poverty or want. YA up

417 Copeland, Paul W. The Land and People of Syria, rev. ed. Ill. with photographs and a map. J. B. Lippincott, 1972 (Portraits of the Nations Series). The turbulent history of this small country includes invasions by Hittites, Phoenicians, Alexander the Great, Romans, Turks, Crusaders and others. The French held it in mandate after World War I until it became independent in 1946. Recently its relations with Israel have become increasingly tense. YA up

418 Cottrell, Leonard. Land of the Two Rivers. Ill. by Richard M. Powers. World, 1962. The ancient civilizations of Sumer, Babylon and Assyria (present-day Iraq) come alive for us in this book, as we read about the great Hammurabi, the Law Giver, and

The Middle East

Nebuchadnezzar and his son Belshazzar, who saw the writing on the wall. An exciting story of archaeological discoveries and a comparison of Sumerian and Bible stories that apparently makes Noah's flood a real event. Appended are a chronological chart of Mesopotamia and World Events, Books for Further Reading, Glossary and Index. YA up

419 Ellis, Harry B. Israel: One Land, Two Peoples. Ill. with photographs and maps by Walter Hortens. Thomas Y. Crowell, 1972. The story of the Jews from the time of Abraham, through the periods of exile and return, up to the development and continual problems of modern Israel, written in smooth narrative style and placing the Arab-Jewish conflict in clear perspective. YA

420 Fairservice, Walter A., Jr. Mesopotamia, the Civilization that Rose out of Clay. Ill. with photographs and drawings by Jan Fairservice. Macmillan, 1964. The story of the land between the Tigris and Euphrates Rivers, now known as Iraq, beginning with the Sumerian culture of about 3000 B.C. and ending with the Chaldean fall under the Persian onslought in 539 B.C.; based on archaeological evidence with a listing of some dynasties, kings, and important dates relating to the Sumerian, Babylonian, Assyrian and Chaldean periods, and with a glossary of mythological figures. YA

421 Gillon, Diana and Meir. The Sand and the Stars, The Story of the Jewish People. Decorations by Anita Bernarde. Lothrop Lee and Shepard, 1971. According to the Talmud, say the authors, the Jewish people would at times ride as high as the stars and at other times sink as deep as the sand on the shore. This story of the survival of the Jews throughout centuries of persecution is simply, clearly and briefly told and must probably, therefore, be somewhat oversimplified. YA

422 Gillsäter, Sven and Pia. Pia's Journey to the Holy Land. Ill. with color photography. Tr. from Swedish by Annabelle MacMillan. Harcourt, Brace and World, 1961. Beautiful color photography takes the reader with Pia and her father on their trip at a time when the boundaries of Israel and Jordan were different from what they are at present (1974). E up

423 Glubok, Shirley. Digging in Assyria (ed. from Nineveh and Its Remains, by Austen Henry Layard). Designed

by Gerard Nook, Foreword by Prudence Oliver Harper. Macmillan, 1970. In 1845 Austen Henry Layard began his excavations in northern Iraq (ancient Assyria) and worked without benefit of a team of scientists such as modern archaeologists have, more often hindered than helped by Turkish officials. This is his own story, adapted and abridged by Shirley Glubok and beautifully illustrated with pictures from museum collections. YA up

424 _____. Discovering the Royal Tombs at Ur (ed. from Ur Excavations: The Royal Cemetery by C. Leonard Woolley). Designed by Gerard Nook, special photography by Alfred Tamarin, Foreword by Prudence Oliver Harper. Macmillan, 1969. From the foreword: "the objects illustrated in this book are proof of the richness and importance of the Sumerians almost 4500 years ago." The tombs in the Royal Cemetery at Ur (the supposed birthplace of Abraham) were discovered by Sir Leonard Woolley in 1926. YA up

425 Henderson, Larry. The Arab Middle East. Ill. with map and photographs. Thomas Nelson and Sons, 1970. An important, timely and absorbing presentation of the Arab states in their conflict with Israel and the West. A much needed perspective on Middle East tensions, the countries considered being: Lebanon, Syria, Jordan, Arab Palestine and Saudi Arabia. Appended are a list for further reading, historical highlights, and index. YA up

426 Hinckley, Helen (Jones). The Land and People of Iran, rev. ed. Ill. with photographs and a map by Donald Pitcher. J. B. Lippincott, 1973 (Portraits of the Nations Series). The history of Iran (Persia) goes back over 2500 years to the founding of an empire that, at its height, reached from the Mediterranean to India. This book emphasizes that history and Iran's cultural and artistic heritage, but is also concerned with its present political and economic status. YA up

427 Holisher, Desider. Growing Up in Israel. Ill. with 71 photographs. Viking, 1963. The author, a professional photographer, formed a warm friendship with a family living in Nathanya, a new Israeli city on the Mediterranean coast. After a first chapter of history, he shows us the reborn Israel through the lives of the two children of the family, at home and in school and on visits to a kibbutz, to Jerusalem

The Middle East   89

and Haifa, to the excavations at Caesarea and other sites, and, in general, makes us feel their involvement with the progress of their country. I, YA

428 Honour, Alan. Cave of Riches; The Story of the Dead Sea Scrolls. Ill. by P. A. Hutchinson. Whittlesey House, McGraw-Hill, 1956. Written in almost fictional style, this account reads like an adventure story, especially in the beginning, 1947, when a Bedouin boy, searching for a lost goat, came upon the cave where the scrolls were found. The problems of deciphering them, authenticating them, finding buyers, etc. were complicated by the warring between Israel and Jordan and that story too is full of intrigue and adventure. I

429 Hussein of Jordan. My War with Israel--as told to, and with additional material by, Vick Vance and Pierre Lauer. Tr. from French by June P. Wilson and Walter B. Michaels. Ill. with photographs and a map. William Morrow, 1969. Here the King of Jordan tells how and why, in his opinion, his nation and his Arab allies were so badly beaten in the Six Day War of 1967. There is also a chapter giving the radical viewpoint of the Palestinian commandos. YA up

430 Irving, Clifford. The Battle of Jerusalem; The Six-Day War of June, 1967. Ill. with photographs and maps by Rafael Palacios. Macmillan, 1970. Unhappily this is only part of the continuing conflict between Israelis and Arabs as the war of 1967 was followed by that of 1973. A chronology of the six-day war is appended. YA up

431 Joy, Charles R. Getting to Know Israel. Ill. by Kathleen Elgin. Coward McCann, 1960. A good introduction to Israel but only an introduction because of the many changes since it was written. Jewish customs and holidays, un-changed, are well described. I

432 Keller, Warner. The Bible as History; A Confirmation of the Book of Books. Ill. with photographs. Tr. by W. William Neil. William Morrow, 1956. A book, as the author describes it, for churchmen and agnostics alike, about the archaeological finds and studies that have brought to light and life stories once considered purely theological material and pious reading for laymen. Beginning with the historical basis for the story of the Flood (and the fascinating hint that relics of the Ark may still be found) and going on through the Bible until, and through, the brief,

almost momentary history of the time of Jesus, the Apostles, and Paul's journeys, the author shows how archaeological discoveries support the historical truth of the Book which has had such a powerful and widespread impact on civilization. A

433 Kotker, Norman and the Editors of Horizon Magazine. The Holy Land in the Time of Jesus. Profusely illustrated. American Heritage, 1967 (Horizon Caravel Books). The story of Palestine under Roman control and of the life of Jesus and his followers. A list of suggestions for further reading and index are appended. YA up

434 Lansing, Elizabeth. The Sumerians, Inventors and Builders. Ill. in black and white and full color. With an introduction by Lamberg-Karlovsku, historical adviser. McGraw-Hill, n. d. A book about the great civilization that existed about 3000 B.C. and a progress report on archaeology in the land now called Iraq. YA up

435 Levin, Meyer. The Story of Israel. Ill. with photographs by Archie Lieberman and sketches by Eli Levin. G. P. Putnam's Sons, 1966. A story of how and why this small state came into being, how it has survived its birth pangs and imperiled infancy and of its condition at the time of writing, told largely through the lives of its dedicated leaders and supporters such as Herzl, Ben Gurion, Chaim Weizman, Rothschild and many many others. YA up

436 Lovejoy, Bahija Fattuhi. The Land and People of Iraq. Ill. with photographs and a map. J. B. Lippincott, 1964 (Portraits of the Nations Series). A good solid book of facts about the peoples, geography, history, religions and customs of this very old part of the world, considered the cradle of civilization and the setting for most of the stories of the Bible. YA

437 _____. Other Bible Lands. Ill. by Robert A. Jones. Abingdon Press, 1961. Concise histories and contemporary accounts of the many lands which were scenes of familiar Bible stories: Arabia, Iraq, Egypt, Jordan, Syria, Lebanon, Turkey and Iran. Five full page colored maps and a time chart of Bible history. YA

438 _____. Two Boys of Baghdad. Ill. with photographs. Lothrop Lee and Shepard, 1972. The writer, born in Iraq and making frequent visits to relatives there, is uniquely qualified to make the old city of Baghdad and the present-day life there of two boys, one rich and

The Middle East   91

        one poor, very real to young Occidental readers.
        The book also contains a short summary of recent
        Iraqian history, easy to assimilate and remember.
        I
439   Neurath, Marie.   They Lived Like This in Ancient
        Palestine. Ill. by Evelyn Worboys of the Isotype
        Institute. Franklin Watts, 1965. Interesting details
        of daily life and a map of Palestine and other Bible
        lands. I
440   Noble, Iris.   Treasure of the Caves; The Story of the
        Dead Sea Scrolls.   Ill. with photographs and map.
        Macmillan, 1971. An exciting account of the dis-
        covery of the scrolls, the bidding and bargaining that
        followed, the restoration to make them legible, and
        the preservation of them during the Six-Day War.
        YA up
441   Palmer, Geoffrey.   Quest for the Dead Sea Scrolls.
        Ill. by Peter Forster. John Day, 1965. The dis-
        covery of the scrolls, and following events, make a
        good historical detective story, told here in nine
        short, attractively decorated chapters. I, YA
442   Payne, Robert.   The Splendor of Persia. Ill. with line
        drawings by Leonard Everett Fisher and photographs.
        Alfred A. Knopf, 1957. An extremely readable book
        about Iran: its geography and history, its great
        kings and poets, and, finally, its awakening to the
        modern world. YA up
443   Pearlman, Moshe.   The Zealots of Masada: Story of a
        Dig. Ill. with photographs. Scribner's, 1967. An
        exciting archaeological story about the discovery and
        restoration of the ruins of the great palace stronghold
        of Herod the Great, built in 30 B.C., where, about
        a hundred years later, 960 Jewish Zealots chose
        death rather than surrender to the Romans. YA up
444   Philips, Ted.   Getting to Know Saudi Arabia. Ill. by
        Haris Petie. Coward McCann, 1963. A book about
        a country (once called just "Arabia") which, since
        oil was discovered there in 1938, and especially
        since the world energy crisis has been recognized,
        occupies a prominent place in all the news media.
        Appended are lists of a few Arabic words and ex-
        pressions, and some important dates in Saudi Ara-
        bian history. I
445   Rappaport, Uriel.   The Story of the Dead Sea Scrolls.
        Ill. by Milka Cizik and with photographs and maps.
        Harvey House, 1967. A thorough and readable ac-
        count of the discovery of the scrolls in 1947 and

further discoveries prompted by the first, with some quotations from the scrolls and their significance for archaeological and Biblical research. Also a brief review of Jewish history. YA up

446 Saggs, H. W. Everyday Life in Babylonia and Assyria. Ill. with maps and photographs and with drawings by Helen Nixon Fairfield. G. P. Putnam's, 1965. Excellent and very readable background for those interested in ancient history, fact or fiction, and in the archaeological digs in present-day Iraq and neighboring countries. YA up

447 Taylor, Alice. Iran (Persia). Ill. by Rafaello Busoni. Holiday House, 1955. An amazing amount of information is contained in this slim, colorful book, beginning with a list of "Fascinating Facts" and ending with "Highlights of Iran's History," and containing a fine map. I up

448 Weingarten, Violet. Jordan, River of the Promised Land. Ill. with photographs and map. Garrard, 1967. Bible stories are woven into the story of the river itself, and the author suggests that many supposed miracles such as the tumbling down of Jericho's walls, may have been actually caused by natural phenomena. Here, as all over the world, archeologists are finding historical foundations for many myths. I, YA

449 Werner, Jane. Iran, Crossroads of Caravans. Ill. by Iranian artists: Parviz Kalantari, Narreddin Zarrin Kelk, and Zaman Zamani. And with photographs and map. Garrard, 1966. An entertaining background book. It begins with a tall story, "The Moustache of Mahmoud," continues with the Iranian calendar of the months, the geography and history of Persia, and Iran's economy and industry, with emphasis on oil and rugs. And finally it ends with a boy visiting Isfahan, which, as his father says, "is half the world." I

450 Weston, Christine. Afghanistan. Ill. with photographs by the author and others and maps. Scribner's, 1962. Here the reader travels with the author through the exotic, little known kingdom and may find special interest in her intimate visits with women and girls. YA up

The Middle East

BIOGRAPHIES

451 Baker, Rachel. Chaim Weizman, Builder of a Nation. Julian Messner, 1958. A penetrating biography of the scientist and, for almost half a century, promoter of the Zionist cause (1874-1952). He was President of the World Zionist Organization for twenty-five years and first President of the newly founded nation of Israel. It is also the story of Zionism and the different factions in the movement. YA up

452 Camay, Joan. Ben-Gurion and the Birth of Israel. Ill. with maps and photographs. Random, 1967. The life story of a remarkable man, born in 1886 in the Pale of Russian Poland, and also of the small but impressive state of Israel, with a list of important dates in that country's history, from the era 1800 to 1500 B.C. (the period of the Patriarchs to the celebration of Ben-Gurion's 80th birthday in 1966. YA

453 Dayan, Ruth and Dudman, Helga. And Perhaps ... The Story of Ruth Dayan. Ill. with 8 pages of photographs. Harcourt Brace Jovanovich, 1973. The result of successful collaboration in which Ruth's total recall is sifted and organized by Helga Dudman, this is the autobiography of a truly liberated woman, a love story, and a testament of dedication and sacrifice for Israel. A

454 Diqs, Isaac. A Bedouin Boyhood. With a map of Palestine just after the 1948 war. Frederick A. Praeger, 1969. A book of memoirs, of particular interest because we have so little literature by Bedouin and their way of life is so foreign not only to Westerners but also to many peoples in the more settled parts of the Middle East. The author, at time of writing, was serving as a civil servant in Saudi Arabia. YA up

455 Honour, Alan. Treasures Under the Sand: Woolley's Finds at Ur. Ill. with drawings and photographs. McGraw-Hill, 1967. A biography of, in the author's words, "the last of the rugged individualists in the mainstream of archaeology." Archaeology has now become the work of institutions and teams. Charles Leonard Woolley (1880-1960), worked first under Sir Arthur Evans and had as his own assistant for a time, T. E. Lawrence (of Arabia). Prior to World I, both he and Lawrence served as spies on the Turks and Germans, but Woolley's great work was his discovery of Ur of the Chaldees, and this is the story of

that work. YA up

456 Kamm, Josephine. Gertrude Bell: Daughter of the Desert. Vanguard, 1957. A biography of an amazing English woman (1868-1926) who spent many years of her life in Arab countries, especially Syria and Iraq, and whose knowledge of the Arabian tribes and language was of such aid to the British in World War I that she has been compared in importance to "Lawrence of Arabia." The book, based largely on her letters and other writings, starts out slowly with more details of her childhood and youth than are needed in proportion to those of her exciting, adventurous middle age. YA up

457 MacLean, Alistair. Lawrence of Arabia. Ill. by Gil Walker. Random, 1962. The story of a man who became a legend in his own lifetime (1888-1935). Born in Wales, his childhood was spent in various parts of the world, but his involvement in the Arabs' revolt against Turkey and struggle for independence began when he first took a walking trip, all alone, through Syria, during his college days. A story of amazing leadership and endurance, with maps clearly showing the scenes of Arab fighting and a list of some other outstanding books about Lawrence, including two of his own. YA

458 Mann, Peggy. Golda, The Life of Israel's Prime Minister. Ill. with photographs. Coward McCann and Geoghegan, 1971. An inspiring biography of an intrepid human being who happened to be a woman and a Jew at a very important time in Jewish history. It is also a biography of the modern state of Israel. YA up

459 Mehdevi, Anne Sinclair. Persian Adventure. Alfred A. Knopf, 1953. It was more than an adventure when in 1945 American Anne Sinclair married the son of Hajji Malek, a great Iranian landowner, and, in 1951, went with him to Persia only to find herself in a feudal household, completely foreign to everything she had ever known. Her picture of the real Iran of the 1950s is highly entertaining and illuminating. Much of the book appeared in The New Yorker in condensed form. A

460 Miller, Shane. Desert Fighter, The Story of General Yigael Yadin and the Dead Sea Scrolls. Ill. with drawings and maps by the author and photographs. Hawthorne, 1967. A biography of a high ranking officer and planning chief in the War of Independence,

The Middle East 95

later Chief of Staff of the Israeli Defense Force, and, at present, one of the world's outstanding archaeologists, possibly his most important work being concerned with the Dead Sea Scrolls. YA up

461 Noble, Iris. Israel's Golda Meir, Pioneer to Prime Minister. Julian Messner, 1972. The story of a great woman, born in Russia in 1898, from her Milwaukee, Wis., girlhood to her position as Prime Minister of the new State of Israel, to which she has dedicated her life. Bibliography. I up

462 Pike, E. Roylston. Mohammed, Prophet of the Religion of Islam. Ill. with photographs and maps. Praeger, 1965 (a Pathfinder Biography). A fine, readable book with a table of dates and suggestions for further reading. YA up

463 Silverberg, Robert. The Man Who Found Nineveh; The Story of Austen Henry Layard. Holt Rinehart and Winston, 1964. A biography of the Englishman (1816-94) who, as a young man, excavated the ancient city of Nineveh. It is a story of high adventure as he traveled through the Mesopotamian desert country, encountering marauding Bedouin and Turks. Archaeology was an infant science in the early 19th century, and Layard was quite an amateur, but he laid the groundwork for later more scientific digging. There is a Mesopotamian chronology at the beginning of the book and a map of the territory (now Iraq) and a chapter at the end, "Assyria After Layard," about 20th century excavations. YA up

464 _____. To the Rock of Darius: The Story of Henry Rawlinson. Ill. with photographs and map. Holt Rinehart and Winston, 1966. A biography of the Englishman primarily responsible for the decipherment of cuneiform writing found on the "Rock of Darius" in ancient Persia, which opened up 4000 years of vanished history. Bibliography and index. YA up

465 Taslitt, Israel I. Soldier of Israel, The Story of General Moshe Dayan. Ill. with photographs. Funk and Wagnalls, 1969 (a Sabra Book). An inspiring biography of a brilliant tactician and fearless soldier, born in Palestine in 1915. I, YA

466 Warren, Ruth. Muhammad the Prophet. Franklin Watts, 1965. An attractively designed, short biography of the founder of Islam (570-632), completely factual as far as possible and with any surmises so labeled. YA

FOLKLORE

467 Brown, Marcia. **The Flying Carpet.** Ill. by the author. Scribner's, 1956. A good readaloud and story-telling version of the story from "Arabian Nights," taken from Richard Burton's translation. E, I

468 Bryson, Bernarda. **Gilgamesh, Man's First Story.** Ill. by the author. Holt, 1967. A splendidly designed and illustrated book of the Sumerian legend of Gilgamesh and his companion, Enkidu, from which we may find possible sources of the great mythological heroes, Hercules, Jason and Theseus. YA

469 Davis, Russell and Ashabranner, Brent. **Ten Thousand Desert Swords; The Epic Story of a Great Bedouin Tribe.** Ill. by Leonard Everett Fisher. Little Brown, 1960. An Arabian epic of the "Bani Hilal," Sons of Hilah, a great tribe of desert warriors of ancient Arabia, Iraq and Syria. YA

470 Ensor, Dorothy. **The Adventures of Hatim Tai.** Ill. by Pauline Baynes. Henry Z. Walck, 1962. An adaptation of Duncan Forbes' translation of the original legends of Hatim Tai, the great Persian hero of the 6th century. The author's note will interest students of Persian legends and folklore. I

471 Hampden, John. **Endless Treasure, Unfamiliar Tales from Arabian Nights.** Ill. by Kurt Werth. World, 1968. Fifteen stories which Mr. Hampden considered the best of (what he calls) "Shahrazad's" tales, with an interesting introduction. I

472 Hauff, Wilhelm. **The Caravan.** Ill. by Burt Silverman. Tr. by Alma Overholt. Thomas Y. Crowell, 1964. Original fairy tales, strung along night after night by the various members of a caravan crossing the Arabian desert, with a new story at each camping place. I

473 Hodges, Elizabeth Jamison. **A Song for Gilgamesh.** Ill. by David Omar White. Atheneum, 1971. Fiction based on the Gilgamesh legend, about a potter who discovers the mysteries of writing and nearly loses his life because of his ability to communicate by means of written symbols. Appended is a basic glossary of "Historical, Mythological, Geographical and Literary Words." YA up

474 Ish-Kishor, Sulamith. **The Carpet of Solomon, A Hebrew Legend.** Ill. by Uri Shulevitz. Pantheon, 1966. When the great King Solomon of the Old Testament is flown high above the earth on a magic

carpet, he feels like God and cannot even remember the name of the true God. Suddenly he finds himself alone on the top of a mountain and many terrifying experiences follow until, near the end, the most anguishing one recalls to Solomon the Name of God. I

475 Lang, Andrew. Arabian Nights. Ill. by William Dempster. Classic Press, Inc./Children's Press, 1968. A fine large-type edition with marginal notes and explanations, of Andrew Lang's (1844-1912) collection of the tales told by Scheherazade to postpone her Execution. I

476 Larson, Jean Russell. The Glass Mountain and Other Arabian Tales. Ill. by Donald E. Cooke. Macrae Smith, 1971. Six Middle East tales, cleverly arranged in a sort of chain reaction of bartering for high stakes. I

477 ———. Palace in Bagdad, Seven Tales from Arabia. Ill. by Marianne Yamaguchi. Scribner's, 1966. Adventure, humor and mystery are the main ingredients of these exotic tales, the charcoal drawings blending well with the retelling. I

478 Mehdevi, Anne Sinclair. Persian Folk and Fairy Tales. Ill. by Paul Kennedy. Alfred A. Knopf, 1965. Eleven tales collected by the author's many nieces and nephews in Iran from their old nurse, Nana Roosie, delightfully retold again and illustrated: stories which, as Mrs. Mehdevi says, are "filled with irony, sauciness and visuality." I up

479 Mozley, Charles. The First Book of Ancient Araby. Ill. by the author. Franklin Watts, 1960. The first story in this book is that about the story-teller, Scheherazade, who saved her life by telling the Sultan a new story every night for a thousand and one nights, always ending each at an exciting point to be concluded the next night. The stories included here are: "Aladdin and the Wonderful Lamp," "Ali Baba and the Forty Thieves," "The Fisherman and the Genie," "Sinbad the Sailor," "The Twice Blessed Arab," and the funny story of "Little Mukra." E, I

480 Pickard, Barbara Leonie. Tales of Ancient Persia; Retold from the Shah-Nama of Firdausi. Henry Z. Walck, 1972. The epic poem from which these legends were taken and so excellently retold, was composed by one of the greatest Persian poets. This book covers roughly the first half of the epic, telling of legendary kings and heroes such as Sohrab and

Rustem. The epic as a whole is an important part of World mythology, comparable to the Arthurian and Roland cycles and deals with pre-Islamic legendry, starting with stories of the Creation, and giving the history of Persia down to its conquest by the Arabs in the 7th century A.D. YA up

481 [Sinbad and] Reed, Philip. The Seven Voyages of Sinbad the Sailor. Designed, printed and illustrated by Mr. Reed. Atheneum, 1962. The author is supposedly Sinbad himself, but it is the designing, printing, and wood engravings by Reed that revive the old tales. I up

482 White, Ann Terry. Two Arabian Tales: Sinbad the Seaman and the Arabian Horse. Ill. by Vincent Colabella. Garrard, 1969. Two stories from "Arabian Nights," one familiar and one not. I

483 Wiggin, Kate Douglas and Smith, Norah A. The Arabian Nights' Entertainments, or a Thousand and One Nights. Ill. by Maxfield Parrish. With an introduction by Kate Douglas Wiggin. Scribner, 1909. From the introduction we learn that these ancient Persian, Indian, and Arabian tales, originally in Arabic, were probably arranged in the present form about 1450. This is an especially attractive edition (of the very many) because of its introduction and its illustrator. I

484 Yolen, Jane. The Girl Who Loved the Wind. Ill. by Ed Young. Thomas Y. Crowell, printed in Belgium, 1972. A fairy story with illustrations reminiscent of Persian miniatures, which are fairy tales in themselves. I

FICTION--BIBLICAL

485 Armstrong, William H. Hadassah, Esther the Orphan Queen. Ill. by Barbara Byfield. Doubleday, 1972. An attractively made and decorated version of the Biblical story of Esther, the wife of Ahaseurus (known to the Greeks as Xerxes), who, risking her own life, saved the lives of her Jewish people, exiles in Persia. I, YA

486 Asimov, Isaac. The Story of Ruth (from Asimov's Guide to the Bible). Maps by Rafael Palacios. Doubleday, 1968. Part One is about how the Book of Ruth came to be written; Part Two, the Bible story with passages from the New English Bible and

The Middle East

interpretation of those passages that give meaning to the ideal of the brotherhood of man. An exceptionally illuminating book about the Moabite girl who followed her mother-in-law to Judah. YA

487 Beatty, John and Patricia. A Donkey for the King. Ill. by Anne Siberell and with a map of Palestine at the time of the birth of Jesus. Macmillan, 1966. A little mute shepherd boy and his donkey become involved with the Holy Family during their escape from Herod's massacre of infant boys. I, YA

488 Bishop, Claire Huchet. Yeshua, Called Jesus. Ill. by Don Bolognese. Farrar, Straus and Giroux, 1966. In this short comprehensive book, the emphasis is on the Jewishness of Jesus, his Jewish ancestry, education, and observance of Jewish customs, but we also see where he was unique, not belonging to any of the sects--the Zealots, Essenes, Philistines, or Sadducees. There is some Jewish history and details of the life led by the boy, Yeshua, in Nazareth. Written by a Christian, the book is dedicated, "To the memory of John XXIII, Pope of Jewish-Christian Reconciliation and to that of Jules Isaac, its prophet." I

489 Bolliger, Max. Daniel. Ill. by Edith Schnidler, tr. by Marion Loenig. Delacorte, 1968. The dramatic Old Testament stories about Daniel woven into a continuous narrative; about his captivity at the court of Babylon, the miracles of the fiery furnace and the lions' den; about the conquest of Babylon by the Persians and the freeing of the Jews--all interspersed with songs from the Bible. I

490 Coolidge, Olivia E. People in Palestine. Houghton Mifflin, 1952. Seven short stories, set between the time of the birth of Jesus and A.D. 66 (the time of the great Jewish revolt), showing the social, religious, and political aspects of the period. The introduction explains the confusion of cultures at the time, among Greeks, Syrians, Jews and Romans. Though Rome was in power, the Greek influence was still strong, and the Jews were not united in themselves. The stories are of troubled individuals in troubled times, expanding upon Biblical biographies and themes. YA up

491 Edmonds, I. G. Joel of the Hanging Gardens. Ill. by Bob Parker. J. B. Lippincott, 1966. A tremendously exciting novel, based on the Book of Daniel and the history of Cyrus' conquest of Babylon, which

resulted in the Jews' being allowed to return to Jerusalem. YA
492 Fitch, Florence Mary. The Child Jesus. Ill. by Leonard Weisgard. Lothrop Lee and Shepard, 1955. So little is known of Jesus' boyhood, that here, as in all such stories, the writer has depended upon her own imagination and careful research into the period. E
493 Hanser, Richard. Jesus--"What Manner of Man Is This?" Simon and Schuster, 1972. A biography of the man, Jesus, showing what is known of his life and times and pointing out that "in the lives of the great religious innovators, the line between reality and allegory, and between biography and myth is not always sharply drawn." The italic passages in the book are all quotations from the King James version of the Bible. YA up
494 Haughton, Rosemary. The Carpenter's Son. Ill. with a map of the Holy Land. Macmillan, 1965. An historical novel about the "hidden years" of Yeshua's life, from babyhood to age 13 or 15 when he became a "man of the law." A glossary of Hebrew and Aramaic names is appended. YA
495 Hyman, Frieda Clark. Builders of Jerusalem in the Time of Nehemiah. Ill. by Don Bolognese. Farrar, Straus and Cudahy, 1960. It sounds like a background book doesn't it? But don't let the title throw you off. This is an exciting, well-plotted novel, based on the Book of Nehemiah in the Bible. Bani, Nehemiah's nephew, is reluctant to leave Persia when the Jews are allowed to return to Israel and his ideas frequently conflict with those of his Uncle, who, though a native of Persia, is also loyal to his ancestral and religious homeland of Israel. A story of divided loyalties back in the 5th century B.C. YA
496 Jenkins, Sara. Song of Deborah. John Day, 1963. Daughters of Valor Series. A novel based on chapters four and five of the Book of Judges in the Old Testament and careful research into the period, about Israel's only woman judge and prophet. A subplot concerns the savage revenge taken by Jael upon Sisera. Readers will probably turn (or return) to the Bible for the authentic "Song of Deborah," one of the Bible's great poems. YA
497 Malvern, Gladys. Behold Your Queen. Ill. by Corinne Malvern. David McKay, 1951. A novel about Esther, the wife of Ahasuerus (Xerxes) and her deliverance of

her own Hebrew people from the vengeance of Haman, the Amalekite. YA

498 _____. The Foreigner. Ill. by Corinne Malvern. Longmans Green, 1954. A novel, based on the lovely story of Ruth's devotion to her mother-in-law, Naomi, and an especially sensitive recreation of Ruth's character; her sacrifice in leaving her own land of Moab, her sister Orphah and her favorite idol; her suffering and exhaustion on the long walk to Judea, and, once there, her fortitude in the face of being rejected as a "foreigner." YA

499 _____. Saul's Daughter. Ill. by Vera Bock. Longmans Green, 1956. A novel about Michal (from the first Book of Samuel) who became the first wife of King David. YA

500 Meyer, Edith Patterson. The Three Guardsmen and Other Stories from the Apocrypha. Ill. by Howard Simon. Abingdon, 1960. Stories about Judith and Holofernes, Daniel in the Lions' Den, Esther the Queen, and Shadrach, Meshach and Abednego, to mention only some. Also a chapter of wise sayings and good advice from Ecclesiasticus and one about the Apocrypha and the Bible as a whole. I, YA

501 O'Neill, Mary. The Boy; A Novel of Christ's Boyhood. Doubleday, 1970. The most interesting feature of this book is the story of Jesus' boyhood pilgrimage to Jerusalem, with Mary and Joseph, an adventure-filled six days. I

502 Petersham, Maud and Miska. David. Ill. by the authors. Macmillan, 1938 and 1967. A retelling, with the Petershams' large colorful pictures, of the famous stories of David and Goliath, David and Jonathan, and, finally, of David as King. E, I

503 _____. Moses. Ill. by the authors. Macmillan, 1938 and 1958. The complete story of Moses from the discovery of him in the bullrushes by Pharaoh's daughter, to his death. E, I

504 _____. Ruth. Ill. by the adapters. Macmillan, 1938 and 1958. Simply told, in Biblical style, the story of the loving daughter-in-law who followed her husband's mother into a strange land. E, I

505 Speare, Elizabeth George. The Bronze Bow. Houghton Mifflin, 1961. A novel set in Roman Palestine, about some Zealots who were expecting a military Messiah but finally accepted the Christian message of the Messiah of Peace. YA

506 Stoutenburg, Adrien. Haran's Journey. Ill. by Laszlo

Kubinyi. Dial, 1971. An allegorical story of the desert journey of a young slave, following the Star and the Magi to Bethlehem. I

507 Turner, Philip. <u>Brian Wildsmith's Illustrated Bible Stories.</u> Ill. by Brian Wildsmith. Franklin Watts, 1969. Fortunate are the children who receive this book as their introduction to the Bible. The stories are told with simplicity and dignity, and the striking illustrations will make them a memorable part of the readers' literary experience. I up

508 Waddell, Helen. <u>The Story of Saul the King</u> (abridged by Elaine Moss from the author's <u>Stories from Holy Writ</u>). Ill. by Doreen Roberts. Constable Young, 1966. A picture book, to be sure, but one for children older than the usual "picture book set," as it is the Biblical story of the king who, as he grew strong in battle, grew weak in character, and, in his lust for power, disobeyed God. Helen Waddell is an eminent writer of historical fiction, and the paintings by Doreen Roberts fully complement the text. I up

509 Wahl, Jan. <u>Runaway Jonah and Other Tales.</u> Ill. by Uri Shulevitz. Macmillan, 1968. Five familiar Bible stories, simply told with refreshing humor, about Daniel, Noah, Jonah, David and Joseph. E

510 Wibberley, Leonard. <u>The Centurion.</u> William Morrow, 1966. An adult novel about Longinus, the Roman soldier delegated to crucify Jesus; a book faithful to the Gospels and enriched by the author's insight and imagination. A

511 Williamson, Joanne S. <u>Hittite Warrior.</u> Knopf, 1960. A first-rate historical novel, based on the story of Deborah and Barak in the Book of Judges, about an episode which took place about 200 years before the days of Saul and David and about 1200 years before the beginning of the Christian era. The principal character is a young Hittite, named Uriah, who tells of his travels after his country was conquered and the broadening of his horizons and understanding, and his finally coming to believe in the Hebrew God. YA up

FICTION--HISTORICAL

512 Fyson, J. G. <u>The Three Brothers of Ur.</u> Ill. by Victor Ambrus. Coward McCann, 1966. Set in Meso-

potamia (present-day Iraq) about 4000 years ago, this is an engrossing story about the family of Teresh the Stern. Haran, the youngest of the three brothers is the principal character because of his impulsiveness which gets him into all kinds of fixes. Two sisters also play parts in the novel. It is through one of Haran's misadventures that his oldest brother, Shanashazir, acquires the idea of one God more powerful than the clay idol broken by Haran. Various parallels are drawn with stories of the Bible. I, YA

513 _____. The Journey of the Eldest Son. Ill. by Victor Ambrus. Coward McCann, 1967. A sequel to The Three Brothers of Ur in which Shanashazir is the principal figure as he accompanies one of his father's trading caravans into the White Mountains, falls from a high precipice, and is given up for dead. YA

514 Haugaard, Erik Christian. The Rider and His Horse. Ill. by Leo and Diane Dillon. Houghton Mifflin, 1968. It might be well to turn to the last pages of this tragic novel before beginning the story, for the map there and short list of dates sets the time and place in which young David Ben Joseph leaves his rich merchant father and makes his way, first through the ruins of Jerusalem, and finally to the Masada, the last defence of the Zealots against the Romans, ending dramatically in April of A.D. 73. YA up

515 King, Clive. The Twenty-two Letters. Ill. by Richard Kennedy. Coward McCann, 1966. A scholarly, humorous and imaginative story of the beginning of celestial navigation, the introduction of cavalry, and, most important, the invention of the alphabet. A comparison of Egyptian hieroglyphics, Phoenician letters and modern letters is included. YA up

516 Kubie, Nora Benjamin. King Solomon's Horses. Harper, 1956. A skillfully plotted story about a boy's devotion to a filly he found abandoned soon after its birth and his travels with his horse on a trading expedition with King Solomon's famous horsemen to Egypt where he is confronted with the desperate choice between losing his beloved Bala or turning traitor to his King. I, YA

517 _____. King Solomon's Navy. Harper, 1954. Ill. by the author. An exciting novel of King Solomon's time (10th century B.C.) in which young Jared is captured and sent to work in one of the King's mines. He escapes and offers to sail in the King's navy on a

mission to the court of the Queen of Sheba. The slim Biblical basis for the story may be found in the First Book of Kings, but anyway it's a good rousing adventure novel. YA

518 Morgan, Barbara E. Hand of the King. Ill. by Howard Simon. Random House, 1963. A story of adventure and suspense in a town on the middle Euphrates around 1750 B.C., in which a 12-year-old boy plays a courageous part in a revolt against the hated king of Assyria and restores the Prince of Mari to his throne. The author's note explains that the town of Mari was completely destroyed, 20 or 30 years after this story, by the great King Hammurabi and that all the royal characters mentioned in the book really existed. YA

519 _____. Journey for Tobiyah; The Dramatic Adventures of a Slave Boy from Ancient Israel. Ill. by W. T. Mars and with a map. Random House, 1966. A novel based on historical events of about 700 B.C. during King Sennacherib's fourth campaign to subdue the people of Babylonia. An author's note tells of the archaeological discoveries providing this history, but one does not need to be an archaeologist to enjoy this exciting story. YA

520 Osborne, Chester G. The First Wheel. Ill. by Richard N. Osborne. Follett, 1959. A good fictional account of how the first wheel might have evolved, when Ashua, a boy of ancient Sumeria, thinks up a way of improving the log rollers that moved sledges, an invention which makes possible a victory for his people against attacking tribesmen. I

FICTION--CONTEMPORARY

521 Banai, Margolit. Yael and the Queen of Goats. Ill. by Friedel. Tr. from Hebrew by Ruth Reznik. Funk and Wagnalls, 1968 (a Sabra Book). An adventure story with a good plot about a very quick-witted little girl taking her goat to a faraway town in Israel to be entered in a goat contest. On her way, she, and we, learn a great deal about the land and people of Israel. I

522 Banks, Lynne Reid. One More River. Simon and Schuster, 1973. A novel about a rich, spoiled Canadian girl in her 15th year whose idealistic Jewish father takes her and her mother to live in a kibbutz

in Israel. Even a less affluent and spoiled girl would have felt the shock caused by this radical change in her life style, but gradually Lesley (and her parents) become adjusted to communal living, and just as they "have it made" the Six Days' War breaks out. Lesley's meeting with an Arab boy across the Jordan River brings out the Israeli-Arab tragedy. YA up

523 Biber, Yehoash. The Treasure of the Turkish Pasha. Ill. by Uri Shulevitz, tr. from Hebrew by Baruch Hochman. Scribner's, 1968. A novel of the early 20th century, in which Yumi, a one-time member of the guild of guardsmen protecting outlying villages in the Negev, is assigned to the dangerous task of recovering a treasure suspected to be hidden near the ancient monastery of St. Catherine at the very foot of the Sinai Peninsula. YA

524 Boyle, Kay. The Youngest Camel. Ill. by Ronni Solbert. Harper, 1939, 1959. A lovely and meaningful fantasy, "reconsidered and rewritten" (i.e., for the 1959 publication) by Kay Boyle, about the youngest camel's adventures in the desert, his ordeal of loneliness, his many temptations, and his finally coming to understand the invisibility of music, history, and love. E up

525 Byers, Betsy. The Dancing Camel. Ill. by Harold Berson. Viking, 1965. Camilla, the camel, was the last in a caravan, so hardly anyone noticed that she liked to dance all by herself. Finally, however, Abdul the Tricky caught on to it and traded his own camel for her. But when he tried to show her off for a fee, she refused to perform. Perhaps you can guess why. E, I

526 Catherall, Arthur. Red Sea Rescue. Ill. by Victor Ambrus. Lothrop Lee and Shepard, 1969. Two children of an Arab lighthouse keeper in the Red Sea, knowing their father is stranded on a desolate island in a wild storm, struggle to keep the light burning in the lighthouse, to send a message by radio, and to rescue their father, all these attempts being equally difficult and important. I

527 Cone, Molly. The House in the Tree: A Story of Israel. Ill. by Symeon Shimin. Thomas Y. Crowell, 1968. A simple little tale of a new boy in Israel wanting to build a tree house like the one he had had at home, but unable to find wood for it. But, as his aunt tells him, "Miracles happen in Israel." Much

information about Israel comes through as Yaakov seeks his miracle. E

528 Drewery, Mary. Hamid and the Palm Sunday Donkey. Ill. by Reginald Gray. Hastings, 1968. A very good story and a pleasant tour of such Biblical places as the Garden of Gethsemane, parts of old Jerusalem, Jericho and Amman, as a young Arab boy, accused of theft, travels about trying to find a witness to his innocence. An important figure in the story is his donkey, Haryat, named after an English tourist lady. I

529 Edwardson, Cordelia. Miriam Lives in a Kibbutz. Ill. with photographs by Anna Riwkin-Brick. Lothrop Lee and Shepard, 1971. A five-year-old Moroccan girl, a newcomer to Israel, resents very much having to live in a kibbutz, until she meets a playmate, Daniel, who shares with her a secret. E

530 Feder-Tal, Karah. The Stone of Peace. Ill. by Alie Evers, tr. from Dutch by H. R. Kousbroek. Abelard Schuman, n.d. A well-constructed plot built around the friendship of a Jewish boy, David, living in a kibbutz in the Negev, and an Arab Bedouin boy, Ahmed. They decide to work toward peace between Arabs and Jews through a campfire party for Ahmed and another Arab. They go a little too far when they let Ahmed drive one of the kibbutz tractors, but their intentions are good and in the end pay off, at least in a small way. I, YA

531 Forman, James. My Enemy, My Brother. Meredith Press, 1969. A serious novel of the friendship of a Polish Jew and the Arab son of a Muktar during the time of the partitioning of Palestine and the 1948 War. It goes back too to the desperate escape of Dan from Poland and the attitudes of his companions as they make their way to the mystical Promised Land. A novel of kibbutz pioneering, the Haganah and the Irgun and the ongoing conflict between Arabs and Jews. YA up

532 Gidal, Sonia and Tim. Sons of the Desert. Ill. with photographs. Pantheon, 1960. A background book about the Bedouin in the Upper Sinai near Beersheba, and also a story of a lost camel and how the boy who discovered it is suspected of stealing it. The authors were honored guests in a Sheik's "house of hair" and have written this book from within his family circle. I

533 Goldberg, Leah. Little Queen of Sheba; A Story of the New Immigrant Children in Israel. Ill. with 39 full-

page photographs by Anna Riwkin-Brick, tr. from
Hebrew by Shulamit Nardi. Union of American Hebrew Congregations, 1959. The story of an orphan
girl from Morocco who simply couldn't seem to adjust to kibbutz life but finally came to find inner
peace there. I

534 Groseclose, Elgin. The Scimiter of Saladin. Ill. by
Alan Moyler. Macmillan, 1956. A missionary's
son, who has been helping some archaeologists in
their "digs" in Iran, is intrusted with a jeweled
sword which, it is thought, might have belonged to
Saladin. The sword is stolen from him, however,
by a chief of the Mehdi tribe, and the lad, with his
Mohammedan friend, determines to recover it. A
thriller. YA

535 Hámori, László. Flight to the Promised Land. Ill. by
Mel Silverman, tr. by Annabelle Macmillan. Harcourt Brace and World, 1963. A novel based on the
actual experiences of a Yemenite Jewish boy when he
is flown to Israel from his very backward country
and encounters the revolutionary changes being brought
about there. His slow acceptance of the new technology, and life in a kibbutz, is shown with humor
and compassion. The first part of the book is about
life in Yemen, at least 300 years behind the times,
and the difficulties of flying the persecuted Jews out
of that country. YA up

536 Lampel, Rusia. That Summer with Ora. Tr. by Stella
Humphries. Franklin Watts, 1967. A novel of an
American Jewish girl of 13, rich and spoiled (Why
are American and Canadian girls always shown as
rich and spoiled? ... for the sake of the story, I
guess) spending her summer holidays with a family
in Jerusalem. We are shown her changing attitude
through the diary of her host's daughter, 15-year-old Ora, and also Ora's changing attitude toward the
American. I, YA

537 Lange, Suzanne. The Year; Life on an Israel Kibbutz.
S. G. Phillips, 1970. A realistic novel of the day-to-day experiences of an American college girl who
has left her senior year in America for a year of
dedication and hardship in an Israeli kibbutz. YA

538 Mehdevi, Anne Sinclair. Parveen. Alfred A. Knopf,
1969. A romantic novel, set in Persia in 1921,
about a daughter of divorced parents (American mother and Persian father), who, having been brought up
by her mother in Oak Park, Illinois, is sent at 16 to

Persia to visit her father and his young second wife, and suddenly finds herself transported into the sequestered world of Persian women of that period, living in an andarum guarded by a eunuch. Gradually she comes to find beauty and excitement in her father's country, especially after she meets a young English-educated Persian landlord. A delightful book about a changing Persia and a changing young lady. YA

539 Michener, James. The Source. Maps and diagrams by Jean-Paul Tremblay. Random, 1965. A massive historical novel of Bible lore, set in the framework of "digs" in Israel, and the lives of the young archaeologists and their discoveries. A history of the Jewish people in fictional form. A

540 Nurenberg, Thelma. My Cousin the Arab. Abelard Schuman, 1965. The foreword to this engrossing novel of the early settlers in Israel, gives briefly and clearly the history of the partition of Palestine and formation of the state of Israel. The novel is set in the period (1947) just before and up to the establishment of the new state by the United Nations. Glossary of foreign words. YA up

541 Ofek, Uriel. The Dog That Flew and Other Favorite Stories from Israel (tr. from the Hebrew). Funk and Wagnalls, 1969 (a Sabra Book). Eleven lively contemporary short stories about Israel from 1948 through the Six Day War. I, YA

542 Omer, Devorah. The Gideonites, The Story of the Nili Spies in the Middle East. Tr. from Hebrew by Ruth Reznik. Funk and Wagnalls, 1968 (a Sabra Book). A true and harrowing story, in fictional form, about the little known spy system, during World War I, in Palestine, when it was a Turkish province, and about some of the spies, particularly Sarah Aaronson and Absolem Feinberg, both of whom gave up their lives in their efforts to free Palestine from Turkish control by sending military information to the British. YA up

543 _____. Path Beneath the Sea. Tr. from Hebrew by Israel I. Taslitt. Funk and Wagnalls, 1969 (a Sabra Book). A novel about the frogmen in the 1967 Arab-Israel War, and about a 16-year-old Moroccan, determined to get to Israel to become a frogman. His determination pays off but not until he has learned to understand and control himself. Details of this frogmen activity in the 1967 war are still secret, but the

training and discipline of these young men is told in this book. YA

544 Potter, Bronson. Isfendiar and the Wild Donkeys. Ill. by Juan Carlos Barberis. Atheneum, 1967. Isfendiar is a Persian charcoal burner's son, imbued with the poetry and legends he has heard from the men around the kiln. I, YA

545 _____. Isfendiar and the Bears of Mazandaran. Ill. by David Omar White. Atheneum, 1969. A book filled with the mood and wisdom of Perisa, a sequel to Isfendiar and the Wild Donkeys. I, YA

546 Richard, Adrienne. The Accomplice. Ill. with a chart of the setting and cross section of the tell. Little Brown, 1973. A novel of conflicts between father and son and between Jews and Arabs in Israel. Benjy whose father is an archaeologist, forms a strong friendship with Fawzi, one of the young Arabs working on the dig and through that friendship becomes the unwitting accomplice of a young Arab terrorist who has been hiding in Fawzi's Village where he has been fed by Fawzi's Mother. For Benjy to reveal to his father what he knows of the Arab's plans (and deeds) would be to endanger Fawzi's home and village; for him not to do so is to endanger his father's work at the tell. YA

547 Rugh, Belle Dorman. The Crystal Mountain. Ill. by Ernest H. Shepard. Houghton Mifflin, 1955. An engaging story of three young American boys and an English girl, living in Lebanon, near sea and mountains, of their Arab friend, and an obnoxious new boy in the neighborhood, a mysterious Arabian visitor and an English governess, much like Mary Poppins. A thread of material about Lebanon's struggle for independence runs through the plot. A New York Herald Tribune Prize Book. I

548 _____. The Lost Waters. Ill. by Dorothy Bayley Morse. Houghton Mifflin, 1967. A novel set in the Lebanese mountains and interlaced with some Lebanese history and legend. The protagonist is an American girl who has several middle-class Arabian friends and there is a mystery involving some of their relations and their separate villages. I, YA

549 _____. The Path Above the Pines. Ill. by Dorothy Bayley Morse. Houghton Mifflin, 1967. Some of the children met in The Crystal Mountain appear again in this book set in Lebanon, the family of American boys, and Boadie, the patriotic British girl, but

there are new friends too, among them a distressingly scholarly boy from the international set. The boys form a club, and in trying to save their meeting place from stonecutters, they happen on a strange sound in the ravine, seeming to come from beneath the ground. Before this mystery is solved they visit a Crusaders' Castle where the scholarly boy proves himself worthy of membership in the club.

550 Shermaun, Li. The Golden Slippers. Ill. by Hildegard Roedelius, tr. by Anthea Bell. Abelard Schuman, 1961. The story line is not always clearly drawn, but the setting of modern Damascus is interesting and delightful as are the Syrian-Arab friends of 12-year-old Miranda, whose mother has recently died and whose father is not the amusing companion he once was. Miranda herself is a very real person, acting out historical and fabulous roles as she learns to accept the fact of her mother's death and the possibility of a stepmother. I

551 Shamir, Moshe. Great Day in Israel; Why Ziva Cried on the Feast of the First Fruits. Ill. by Cyril Satorsky, tr. by Tamara Kahana. Abelard Schuman, 1960. On the Day of the First Fruits, each class in Ziva's kibbutz was to give to the National Fund something the children had produced. Ziva planned that her class would give goat's milk cheese, but when the great day came, where was the cheese? E

552 Stinetorf, Louise A. The Shepard of Abu Kush. John Day, 1962. A novel set in Palestine at the time of the Division in 1947, when Arabs were forced to leave their homes and villages to the Jews and move into refugee camps. Most did not understand that they had sold their land and homes and even livestock, and even though there were some kind men among the British military who enforced the move, there was much bitterness. The story is about one Arab boy who is able to overcome his bitterness toward the British and the Jews. YA

553 Uris, Leon. Exodus. A long novel about the formation of the state of Israel, tracing the Jewish experience of persecution from long ago and in many countries to the final shocking treatment of the Jews in Germany under Hitler and the Nazis and leading up to the period of the British mandate when Jewish immigrants were denied admission to their Promised Land. A

554 Walden, Amelia Elizabeth. The Spy Who Talked Too

The Middle East 111

        Much. Westminster, 1968. A spy story, set in the rich oil sheikdom of Kuwait--novel, timely, intriguing. A
555 Watson, Sally. The Mukhtar's Children. Holt Rinehart and Winston, 1968. A novel of the early days of Israel as a state, about a new Israeli kibbutz near an Arab village and of how the young people from kibbutz and village show their elders new ways and attitudes, not without conflict and even violence, but, as the young people themselves learn, with tolerance too. Fine characterization of both old and young folks and humor in their dialogue, especially in the expletives. YA
556   . Other Sandals. Holt Rinehart and Winston, 1966. A story of two Jewish youngsters attempting to "live in each others' sandals" for a summer. A city boy with a hangup about his lameness goes to live in a kibbutz, and a kibbutz girl of 12 goes to the city for the summer, where some of her prejudices are upset by her meeting with a young Arab girl. A novel of serious thoughts treated with humor. I, YA
557   . To Build a Land. Ill. by Lili Cassel. Holt, 1957. A thrilling novel of the experiences and ordeals of a group of teenagers from widely different cultures and economic levels as they meet first in training camp in France, then sail on an illegal ship to Israel, learn to work very hard in a commune and finally get caught up in the war with the Arabs after Israel's declaration of independence. A glossary of Hebrew words and phrases and one of Arab words and phrases is appended. YA

THE SOVIET UNION IN ASIA

      Books listed in this section have mainly to do with Siberia though there are also a few stories of the Cossacks and of old Armenia. Most of the literary traditions of Russia, of course, are of European Russia (west of the Caucasus mountains).

NON-FICTION

558   Cohen, Daniel. <u>Conquerors on Horseback; The Nomad Empires of Attila, Genghis Khan and Timur.</u> Ill. with maps and drawings. Doubleday, 1970. A comprehensive, clear outline of the nomadic civilization of the Eurasian Steppes, beginning with the mid-12th century legend of Prester John, and ending in the 17th century with the end of the Mogul dynasty. YA up

559   Friend, Morton. <u>The Vanishing Tungus.</u> Frontispiece and map by Laszlo Kubinyi. Dial, 1973. A fascinating history and study of an exceptionally harmonious primitive culture, that of the Reindeer People of Siberia, from whom we of the 20th century might well take some lessons. YA up

560   Kennan, George. <u>Siberia and the Exile System,</u> abridged ed. With nine of the orig. illus. by George Frost. University of Chicago Press, 1958 (first pub. by the Century Co., 1891). Contains also an introduction by George Frost Kennan (1904-   ). The two large volumes of this original work became a sensation in 1891 when they were published and were said, by President Kalinin in the early days of the USSR, to have been "the Bible of the early revolutionists." They are still read by students of the Russian Revolution and the years just proceding it. However the abridged edition is simply a thrilling account of Kennan's journey in 1885 and '86 to the Tsarist prisons in Siberia. A

561   _____. <u>Tent Life in Siberia.</u> Ill. with reprod. of the orig. illus. by George Frost, and maps. New York Times Pub. Co., 1971 (reprint of 1910 ed.; first pub. in 1870). George Kennan, age 19 when he set out for Siberia, wrote humorously and vividly of his experiences and adventures during his two years, 1865-67, with the Western Union Russian-American Telegraph Expedition. He was one of a small force of young Americans, led by a Russian engineer, who surveyed and began building a telegraph line across Siberia, working often without maps, and with very few instruments, in sub-zero temperatures. A unique book about late 19th century Siberia. A

562   Portisch, Hugo. <u>Promise in the East: The New Siberia.</u> Ill. with photographs and a map. Little Brown, 1973. Tensions between the USSR and the People's Republic of China are made understandable

in this book about the far northeasterly territory of the Soviet Union. Of special interest to young readers, however, will be the chapters dealing with the way young people live, work and play in the new villages and cities of the taiga. YA up

BIOGRAPHIES

563 Hautzig, Esther. The Endless Steppe; Growing Up in Siberia. Crowell, 1968. Autobiography of a young Polish girl taken at the age of 11 from her gracious home in Poland to a slave labor camp in cold lonely Siberia, where, for five years, she endured incredible hardships with indomitable courage and ingenuity and even the ability to find beauty in the endless steppes. YA

564 Tchernavin, Tatiana. My Childhood in Siberia. Ill. with photographs. Oxford, 1972. Memoirs of the happy and exciting childhood of the author who was born in Moscow in 1887 and taken as a very little girl to Tomsk where her father was a professor of botany at the first Siberian university. I up

FOLKLORE

565 Ginsburg, Mirra. The Kaha Bird; Tales from the Steppes of Central Asia. Ill. by Richard Cuffari. Crown, 1971. The second collection of folk tales, tr. and ed. by Mirra Ginsburg, from various regions of old Russia, with a map showing the areas of their origin. E, I

566 ———. The Master of the Winds and Other Tales from Siberia. Ill. by Enrico Arno. Crown, 1970. The first volume of folklore, tr. and ed. by Mirra Ginsburg, many appearing in English for the first time, with an introduction about the diversity of people from whom these stories stem. I up

567 Guillot, René. Grishka and the Bear. Ill. by Joan Kiddell-Monroe, tr. by Gwen Marsh. Oxford Press, 1959. A "long ago" story about tribal customs among the Tushkins of northern Siberia. I

568 Tashjian, Virginia A. Once There Was and Was Not; Armenian Tales Based on Stories by Havannes Toumanian. Ill. by Nonny Hogrogian. Little Brown, 1966. The title is a traditional Armenian way of

starting a story. Seven rollicking tales, with delicate illustrations. I

569 ———. Three Apples Fell from Heaven; Armenian Tales Retold. Ill. by Nonny Hogrogian. Little Brown, 1971. Nine stories told originally by famous Armenian story tellers with the traditional Armenian ending: "Three Apples fell from heaven: one for the teller, one for the listener; and one for all the peoples of the world." I

FICTION

570 Aitmotov, Chinghis. The White Ship. Tr. by Mirra Ginsburg. Crown, 1972. A compelling story, half legendary, about the dream life of a lonely boy who believes that he will find his father on a white ship. The introduction explains the political implications of the story and the controversy caused by its publication in the Soviet Union. YA up

571 Arsenyev, Vladimir. With Dersu the Hunter. Adapted by Anne Terry White. Ill. with drawings and maps. George Braziller, 1965. The true story of a naturalist-detective who saved the life of a scientist in southeastern Siberia in the beginning of the century. YA

572 Bartos-Höppner, B. The Cossacks. Ill. by Victor G. Ambrus, tr. by Stella Humphries. Henry Z. Walck, 1963. A novel set in the period 1580-84, when the Russian hero, Yarmak captured the then capital of Siberia (later known as Tobolsk) and when the Stroganovs ruled over a large portion of Siberia. Map, chronological table of events and historical postscript. YA up

573 ———. Hunters of Siberia. Tr. by Anthea Bell. Walck, 1969. A stirring novel of the Siberian taiga (swampy forest) in the beginning of the 20th century; about the efforts of a dedicated forest commissioner to institute and enforce game laws with the (at first) unwilling help of a Caucasian exile and his son; and about the opposition of the Siberian natives to his interference with their way of life and the final conversion of the people to the realization of the need for conservation of wild life and the abolition of cruel methods of killing. YA

574 ———. Save the Khan. Ill. by Victor G. Ambrus, tr. by Stella Humphries. Walck, 1964. A strong

Soviet Union in Asia

novel for older readers about the conquest of Tatar Siberia by the Russians at the end of the 16th century, twenty years or so after the events in the novel The Cossacks. YA up

575 _____. Storm Over the Caucasus. Tr. by Anthea Bell. Walck, 1968. A novel about the Moslem leader, Iman Shamyl's defense of his country the Caucasus against Russian imperialism in the mid-19th century. YA up

576 Cretan, Gladys Yessayan. A Gift from the Bride. Ill. by Rita Fava Fegiz. Little Brown, 1964. Mari was a little Armenian girl who longed to learn to read and write, but in early 20th century Armenia it was not the custom for girls to go to school. It was a pleasant custom, though, for a bride to give presents to her wedding guests, and this bride had a very special one for Mari. E

577 Jones, Adrienne. Another Place, Another Spring. Ill. with maps. Houghton Mifflin, 1971. The maps clearly outline the almost year-long travels of Marya and her aristocratic mistress, from St. Petersburg across Siberia and then, Marya alone, across the Pacific to Fort Ross in California still in Russian hands. It is a touching love story and also a story of the exile system of the Czars in the 1840s and the exhausting hardships of travel through Siberia as the young women evade the Russian police on their trail. YA up

578 Kalashnikoff, Nicolas. The Defender. Ill. by Claire and George Louden. Scribner's, 1951. A Bambi-like story about a Siberian tribesman and his friendship with wild mountain rams. I

579 _____. My Friend Yakub. Ill. by Feodore Rojansky. Scribner's, 1951. The story of a Tatar and his life in a small Siberian town in the early part of the century. I

580 Lavolle, L. N. The Jade Gate. Ill. by P. Rousseau, tr. from French by Hugh Shelley. Abelard Schuman, 1963. A novel of high courage and adventure in central Asia where Russia, China, Tibet and Pakistan meet. A Chinese girl and an Afghan boy, detached from a caravan of Kazaks that is fleeing from invaders, cross the Takla Makan desert to the Himalayas, surviving near starvation and bitter weather (both cold and hot) and learning that "all nomads are brothers." YA

581 Linevski, A. An Old Tale Carved Out of Stone. Tr.

from the Russian by Maria Polushkin. Crown, 1973.
The setting of this fine novel is Neolithic Siberia and
the story is based on stone carvings still lining the
rocky coast of the White Sea. The theme is the universal one of youth defying tradition, seeking new and
better ways of life. The principal character is a
young shaman-in-spite-of-himself. YA up

582 Ritchie, Rita. Pirates of Samarkand. Ill. by Robin
Jaques. W. W. Norton, 1957. A mystery story,
set in the 13th century in central Asia, about two
brothers whose father is captain of a cargo ship on
the river between Bokhara and Samarkand, a stretch
badly beset by pirates. By raising hawks to sell to
a merchant in Samarkand, the boys seek to discover
the pirate chief, and it is one of their kestrels who
provides a clue. Interesting details of falconry in
that time and place. I, YA

583 Said, Kurban (pseud.). Ali and Nino; A Novel. Tr.
from German by Jenia Graman. Random House,
1970. Set in the Trans-Caucasus, the crossroads
of Moslem Persia and western Europe, this is the
love story of a Moslem "desert man" and a Christian Armenian girl symbolizing the clash between
East and West, Asia and Europe. Independently of
its social significance and deeper meanings, it is
an excellent novel, with characters as memorable as
some of Tolstoy's. It is a story of humor, idealism,
furious action and vivid pictures of the lives of aristocratic families in Baku and Teheran in the period
of World War I. A

584 Solzhenitsyn, Alexander. One Day in the Life of Ivan
Denisovich. Tr. from Russian by Ralph Parker,
with an Introd. by Marvin Kalb and Foreword by
Alexander Tvardsky, ed.-in-chief of Novy Mir. E. P.
Dutton, 1963 (Signet Modern Classic paperback).
This autobiographical novel about the plight of a
Russian citizen in one of Stalin's notorious slave
labor camps, first appeared in Russia's leading literary magazine, Novy Mir, during Khrushchev's more
liberal regime and was the first major literary work
to be published in the Soviet Union that concerned
the slave labor compounds. It is a powerful saga of
endurance, courage and cruelty. A

585 Verne, Jules. Michael Strogoff, Courier of the Czar.
Ill. by N. C. Wyeth. Scribner's, 1923. The pictures by the famous illustrator provide an added attraction to a wildly imaginative story set in Greater

India and Neighbors 117

Russia and Siberia in the years 1815 to 1840. YA
586 Würthle, Fritz. The Prince of Fergana. Ill. by Paul
Flora. Tr. from German by Patricia Crampton.
Abelard Schuman, 1962. The adventures of Zadir
El-din Mohammed Babur who became Khan of Fergana (in Turkistan) at the age of 11 and later began
the Mogul dynasty which ruled India for centuries;
taken from his own memoirs. YA

INDIA AND NEIGHBORING COUNTRIES
(Bangladesh, Bhutan, Burma, Nepal,
Pakistan, Sikkim, Sri Lanka)

When the Indian subcontinent became independent of
Britain in 1947, it was partitioned into the two countries of
India and Pakistan (East and West). The two parts of Pakistan were separated by almost 1000 miles of Indian territory,
and as a result of its rebellion and the Pakistan-India war
in 1971, East Pakistan became the separate independent nation of Bangladesh. Tiny Sikkim came into the news in 1974
when its government was taken over by India. Ceylon became the Republic of Sri Lanka in 1972.

NON-FICTION

587 Bothwell, Jean. The First Book of India. Ill. with
photographs. Franklin Watts, 1966-1971. A book
to make one long to go there, well organized as to
its wealth of information about geography, history,
politics, religion and culture, it is also eminently
readable and should particularly interest readers of
Jean Bothwell's many Indian novels. A list of the
18 states of India, with their capitals and language
are appended, with a glossary and some suggestions
for further reading. YA up
588 _____. First Book of Pakistan. Ill. with photographs and maps. Franklin Watts, 1962. The titles
of these two books on India and Pakistan sound as
though they were meant for elementary readers, but,
while they are written clearly and simply, they may
well interest all ages of children and adults. When
India received its independence from Great Britain

in 1947, parts of it split off into West and East Pakistan, the latter now Bangladesh. YA up

589 Bowles, Cynthia. At Home in India. Ill. with photographs. Harcourt Brace, 1956. A remarkable book in many ways; first of all in the acute perceptions of the author who was only 15 when, as the daughter of the American Ambassador, she went to spend two years in India. It is outstanding too, in its coverage of many sections of the vast country and the many types of towns and villages she visited from north to south and east to west. This was India in the early years of its independence, 1951 to 1953. YA up

590 Bryce, Winifred. India, Land of Rivers. Ill. with photographs and a map; with a Foreword by Rameshwari Nehru. Thomas Nelson Sons, 1966. A most comprehensive, well-organized, readable history and portrait of India, ancient and modern, with a reading list and chronology. YA up

591 Fairservice, Walter A., Jr. India. Ill. by Richard Powers. World, 1961. This beautifully decorated story of India's history, geography, religions and social customs, written in entertaining, narrative style, has, appended, a chronological chart of India and World Events, and a scholarly list of suggestions for further reading. YA up

592 Gidal, Sonia and Tim. My Village in India. Ill. with 50 photographs and a map drawn by Anne Marie Jauss. Pantheon, 1956. This was the first of the Gidal's "My Village" series, in each of which we visit a family and through that visit, learn a great deal about the country and its customs. In this book our host is Dhan, a Hindu boy. Glossary and map. I

593 Hillary, Louise. A Yak for Christmas; Sir Edmund Hillary's Wife and Children on a Himalayan Holiday. Ill. with photographs. Doubleday, 1969. In 1966, the wife and children (age 12, 10, and 7) of Sir Edmund Hillary, the conqueror, with Tensing, of Mt. Everest, set out, with another mother and her three daughters (14, 12, and 10), the Perl family, to join their husbands and fathers in Sherpaland for the Christmas holidays, camping and mountain climbing in the Himalayas. What valiant mothers! and what valiant children! Mrs. Hillary writes of the often hazardous, and seldom comfortable, experience with delightful humor and deep appreciation of the scenery

and people of Nepal and India. A
594 Kandell, Alice. Sikkim the Hidden Kingdom. Ill. with photographs in color and black and white by the author. Doubleday, 1971. An enchanting book, in both text and pictures, about a truly fantastic country, recently "absorbed" by India. The author, a friend of the American queen of Sikkim has given us a very complete account of the geography, peoples, history, religion and economy of the "hidden kingdom." I up
595 Kessel, Joseph. The Valley of Rubies. Tr. from French by Stella Rodway. David McKay, 1960. A thrilling, exotic true travel-adventure book, in fictional mystery story form, with fascinating details of a remote area of Burma, the precious jewels found there, and the business of ruby mining and trading. A
596 Landry, Lionel. The Land and People of Burma. Ill. with photographs and a map. J. B. Lippincott, 1968 (Portraits of the Nations Series). A serious study of the "Golden Land" intended for high school students. Past and present are intertwined, but the emphasis is on the present as of 1969. YA up
597 Lang, Robert. The Land and People of Pakistan. Ill. with a map by Donald T. Pitcher and photographs. J. B. Lippincott, 1968 (Portraits of the Nations Series). A solidly informational book of a new country, formed from part of India and divided into two parts (until the war which made East Pakistan into Bangladesh). Its past history is actually Indian history, its present is a troubled one, and its future problematical. YA up
598 Larsen, Peter and Elaine. Boy of Nepal. Ill. with photographs by Peter Larsen. Dodd Mead, 1970. The pictures tell about Nepal so well that even very young readers will surely enjoy this book about so different a life from theirs. E, I
599 Laschever, Barnett. Getting to Know India. Ill. by Kathleen Elgin. Coward McCann, 1960. Although not up to date, this is a well condensed account of the subcontinent that is India: its history, culture, and especially religions and the great leader of passive resistance, Mahatma Gandhi. Appended are lists of historical dates, Hindi words, and how to pronounce the foreign words in this book, and index. I
600 _____. Getting to Know Pakistan. Ill. by William deJ. Rutherfoord. Coward McCann, 1961. About the

strangely divided country which had been part of India until after Indian independence from Britain was accomplished in 1947. The two parts of Pakistan (before the formation of Bangladesh) were separated by 1000 miles of India and were dramatically different in geography, language, religion and customs. A glossary of Urdu words with their English parallels and an historical outline are appended, and it is to be hoped that the book will soon be updated. I

601 Modak, Manorama R. The Land and People of India, rev. ed. Ill. with photographs and a map. J. B. Lippincott, 1960 (Portraits of the Nations Series). A book needing another revision but nevertheless valuable because of its picture of old India and an interpretation of the Indian civilization from an Indian citizen's point of view. YA up

602 Rama Rau, Santha. Home to India. Harper, 1944-45. A young lady of a Brahmin family, who has been educated and mainly brought up in England, returns to her homeland in 1939, and records her impressions of it with warmth and humor, revealing, at the same time, her growing understanding of the land and people and of herself. Some intimate glimpses of Gandhi, Nehru and Tagore are added interests in this delightful book. A

603 _____. This Is India. Ill. with 16 pages of photographs and endpaper map. Harper, 1954. A personal guide, by a gracious Indian lady, educated in England and America, to some especially interesting parts of India and to a better understanding of the various Indian peoples. A

604 Redford, Lora Bryning. Getting to Know the Central Himalayas: Nepal, Sikkim, Bhutan. Ill. by Lewis Zacks. Coward McCann, 1964. A book about three countries, set among the greatest peaks in the world, between China and northern India. Except for stories about the Mt. Everest climbers and the Sherpa guides and Nepal's capital city, Katmandu, these countries are quite "out of this world" to westerners. I

605 Rice, Edward. Mother India's Children; Meeting Today's Generation. Ill. with photographs. Pantheon, 1971. An illuminating book made up of interviews with teenagers of traditional India, changing India, and Indian cities and with an immigrant to Israel and an emigrant from Tibet. It should be of great interest to the many young people of the Western world who are fascinated by gurus, yoga, books of medita-

India and Neighbors

tion, and Indian music. YA up

606 Schloat, G. Warren. Uttam, A Boy of India. Ill. with photographs. Alfred A. Knopf, 1963. About the life of a 13-year-old boy in a typical small Indian village, as he learns to be a farmer. I

607 Spencer, Cornelia (Yaukey). Made in India. Ill. by Allen Lewis. Alfred A. Knopf, 1946, 1957. The story of India's people and their gifts to the world, vividly described and illustrated. YA

608 Watson, Jane Werner. India, Old Land, New Nation. Ill. by Indian artists: Shanti Dave, A. A. Almelkar, G. R. Santosh, B. Prabha, and Bani Prassano. Garrard, 1966. A great deal of information is packed into this colorfully illustrated, good story-telling book. I

609 Wibberley, Leonard. The Epics of Everest. Ill. by Genevieve Vaughan-Jackson. Farrar Straus and Young, 1954 (Ariel Books). The thrilling story of the several attempts to climb to the top of Mt. Everest, with lists at the end of the book of the principal personnel of the expeditions, for, as the author says in his final chapter, the real victors were all those who made the attempt, and the final achievement was the result of teamwork. A bibliography, arranged chronologically is appended. YA up

610 Wilber, Donald N. The Land and People of Ceylon, rev. ed. Ill. with photographs and a map. J. B. Lippincott, 1972. A picturesque description of the island of Sri Lanka (as the country now calls itself) is that of a pearl pendant from India, and that is a good way of finding its geographical location. Though independence was achieved in 1948, Sri Lanka is still in the throes of social and political turbulence, clearly explained in this book. YA up

BIOGRAPHIES

611 Apsler, Alfred. Fighter for Independence, Jawaharlal Nehru. Julian Messner, 1963. An absorbing biography, written only a year before his death, of the man (1889-1964) who was influential in bringing India to independence. It is also a history of India during the lifetimes of his father and grandfather and his own 75 years. A disciple of Gandhi, he could not always follow the Mahatma's line of passive resistance, but he endured altogether 3,262 days in prison be-

cause of his efforts to bring about independence without violence. YA

612 Cohen, Joan Lebold. Buddha. Ill. by Mary Frank. Delacorte, 1969 (a Seymour Lawrence Book). A biography which must of necessity be a blend of myth and legend and history, of Prince Siddartha, born in what is now Nepal in 568 B.C. Though the religion he founded has been the prevailing one in Asia for over 2000 years, there are no contemporary written accounts of his life. In this legendary biography we learn about Buddha's "wheel of law," "eightfold path," and "four noble truths" leading to enlightenment. I, YA

613 Coolidge, Olivia. Gandhi. Ill. with photographs. Houghton Mifflin, 1971. A full length, penetrating biography of the saintly Indian (1869-1948) as a man and a politician, and of the history of his passive resistance movement and its impact upon India and the world. Glossary of Indian terms. YA up

614 Eaton, Jeanette. Gandhi, Fighter Without a Sword. Ill. by Ralph Ray. William Morrow, 1950. An excellent fictionalized biography of the leader of the powerful passive resistance movement that so greatly aided India's progress to independence (1869-1948). YA

615 Edwardes, Michael. Nehru: A Pictorial Biography. With 136 illustrations in photogravure. Viking, 1962 (a Studio Book). An easy way to study 20th century history of India, for Jawaharlal Nehru was born in 1889 and lived until 1964. YA up

616 Garnett, Emmeline. Madame Prime Minister, The Story of Indira Gandhi. Ill. with photographs. Farrar Straus and Giroux, 1967. A biography of Jawaharlal Nehru's daughter, who seems never to have known a normal carefree childhood and youth; nor a time when her father, aunts and uncles were not being carried off to jail in the cause of Indian independence; nor a time when her mother was completely well. Born in the same year and month as the Russian revolution, her whole life was dedicated, as were the lives of her Nehru relatives, to the cause of independence and, when that was achieved, to the development of her country. YA up

617 Godden, Jon and Rumer. Two Under the Indian Sun. Alfred A. Knopf, 1966. A unique book that defies classification. Memoirs of the childhoods of these two English sisters in Colonial East Bengal, now

Bangladesh, in the early 20th century. In their own words, "an evocation." A

618 Guthrie, Anne. Madame Ambassador, The Life of Vijaya Lakshmi Pandit. Ill. with photographs. Harcourt Brace and World, 1962. A biography of a younger sister of Jawaharlal Nehru (born in 1900) and, like her brother, a leader in the movement for Indian independence, who went to jail three times for the cause. It is a family story as well as the story of a great woman, Ambassador to several important countries and one-time president of the General Assembly of the United Nations. YA up

619 Kamm, Josephine. Malaria Ross; A Story Biography. Ill. by Anne Linton. Criterion, 1963. Ronald Ross was of English parentage, but was born in India in 1857 where his father was a British officer in the Indian army. Ronald was sent to school in England but spent most of his life in India where his study of mosquitoes (and imagine dissecting a mosquito), led to his discovering the cause and prevention of malaria. He was also a pianist, composer and writer. YA up

620 Lamb, Beatrice Putney. The Nehrus of India; Three Generations of Leadership. Ill. with photographs and a map. Macmillan, 1967. A remarkable family saga because of the continuity of leadership for over 100 years. Motilal was born in 1861, his son, Jawaharlal in 1889, and his daughter, Indira in 1917, becoming Prime Minister in 1966. And there were many other relatives and connections who led in the struggle for independence. YA up

621 Lengyel, Emil. Mahatma Gandhi, Great Soul. Ill. with photographs. Franklin Watts, 1966. An excellent biography of the "Mahatma," which means "Great Soul" (1869-1948). YA

622 Masani, Shakuntala. Nehru's Story. Ill. by the author. Oxford Press, 1949. A short simple story of Jawaharlal Nehru up to the time he was sixty. The book was first written for boys and girls of India. E, I

623 Mehta, Ved. Daddyiji; A Biography of Amolak Ram Mehta. Farrar, Straus and Giroux, 1972. This biography of the author's father (1895-   ) first appeared in the New Yorker magazine, and seems more of a family-saga novel than pure biography, almost an East Indian "Buddenbrooks," in which the reader becomes completely involved with the Mehta family as he reads. The family tree at the beginning is extremely helpful as is the extensive glossary

at the end. A
624 Nevins, Albert J. St. Francis of the Seven Seas. Farrar, Straus, 1955 (a Vision Book). A biography of St. Francis Xavier (1506-52), a founder, with St. Ignatius de Loyola, of the Society of Jesus, who spent 11 years in India and the Far East. YA
625 Peare, Catherine Owens. Mahatma Gandhi; A Biography for Young People. Ill. with photographs. Henry Holt, 1950. Introduction by Handas T. Muzumdar. This book should not be limited to any specific age group. Glossary and bibliography. YA up
626 Reynolds, Reginald. The True Story of Gandhi, Man of Peace. Ill. by Parviz Sadighian. Cover painting by Mary Gehr. Children's Press, 1964. A biography (1868-1948), simply told and attractively arranged, with an endpaper map of India and Pakistan and index of place names. I, YA
627 Russell, Jack. Clive of India. G. P. Putnam's Sons, 1965. An exciting life story of Robert Lord Clive, known as the founder of an empire. He was born in England in 1725 and died there in 1774. The introduction summarizes the history of the colonization of India and growth of the East India Company. YA up
628 Zinkin, Taya. The Story of Gandhi. Ill. by Robert Hales. Criterion, 1966. A thoughtful, candid study of the man and the politician, and the story of how independence finally came to India, along with partition. YA

FOLKLORE

629 Aung, Maung Htin. A Kingdom Lost for a Drop of Honey and Other Burmese Folk Tales. Ill. by Paw Oo Thet. Parents' Magazine Press, 1968. A collection of 15 Burmese folktales (taken from Dr. Htin Aung's scholarly books on Burmese folklore), with introduction, excellent notes and exceptionally interesting design and illustrations. I up
630 Cassedy, Sylvia and Thampi, Parvathi. Moon-Uncle, Moon-Uncle, Rhymes from India. Ill. by Susanne Suba. Doubleday, 1973. A sort of Indian Mother Goose book, of rhymes mostly a hundred years old or more. E
631 Gaer, Joseph. The Adventures of Rama. Ill. by Randy Monk. Little, Brown, 1954. One of the great love stories of the world, adapted from the great Hindu

epic, the "Ramayana," of the Hindu god, Vishnu, the Preserver, who came in the mortal form of Prince Rama, to save mankind from evil. YA

632 ———. The Fables of India. Ill. by Randy Monk. Little Brown, 1955. Of interest to adults is the introductory section on fables and fabulists, what a fable is, and an explanation of the sources of these Indian fables. Bibliography and index. I up

633 Gobhai, Mehlli. The Legend of the Orange Princess. Ill. by the author. Holiday House, 1971. An ancient legend of Chandpur and a mysterious princess. E up

634 Gray, J. E. B. India's Tales and Legends. Ill. by Joan Kiddell-Monroe. Henry Z. Walck, 1961. A rich book of short stories chosen from the ancient literature and folklore of India and centering on the two great stories of Nala and Damayanti, and on the "Ramayana." I, YA

635 Guillot, René. The Elephants of Sargabal. Ill. by Felix Hoffman, tr. by Gwen Marsh. Criterion, 1957. An exotic, legendary story of the Bengal jungle, in which the Princess Narayana is saved from her enemies by some elephants, led by an elephant boy and some outcast children finding freedom in Sargabal. YA

636 ———. The 397th White Elephant. Ill. by Moyra Leatham. Tr. by Gwen Marsh. Criterion, 1957. A charming fable about a child prince in old India and two white elephants, showing that "happiness is not a thing you can sell." E, I

637 Haviland, Virginia. Favorite Fairy Tales Told in India. Ill. by Blair Lent. Little, Brown, 1973. Nine easy-to-read stories, selected by the head of the Children's Book Section of the Library of Congress. E, I

638 Hitchcock, Patricia. The King Who Rides a Tiger and Other Folktales from Nepal. Ill. by Lillian Sader. Parnassus Press, 1966. A dozen varied and colorful stories from western Nepal in the Himalayas, with notes about them and a glossary of Nepali words. I

639 Hodges, Elizabeth Jamison. Serendipity Tales. Ill. by June Atkin Corwin. Atheneum, 1966. The word "serendipity" derives from the ancient name of Ceylon (now Sri Lanka) and has come to mean "the gift of finding valuable or agreeable things not sought for" which is the theme of these stories. I, YA

640 _____. The Three Princes of Serendip. Ill. by
Joan Berg. Atheneum, 1966. Taken from the same
sources as the 5th century Serendipity Tales this is
a continuous story of three princes who were sent by
their father to find the secret formula for "Death to
Dragons" and of the unexpected rewards they received
during their mission. I, YA

641 Merrill, Jean. Shan's Lucky Knife; A Burmese Folk
Tale. Ill. by Ronni Solbert. W. R. Scott, 1960.
The story of a clever country boy outwitting a sly
rascal on a boat trip to Rangoon. E, I

642 Seeger, Elizabeth. The Five Sons of King Pandu; The
Story of the Mahabharata, adapted from the English
translation of Kisari Mohan Ganguli. Ill. by Gordon
Laite. Scott, 1967. A handsomely illustrated lengthy
version of the great Indian epic, with a long preface
which may be of more interest to folklore scholars
than to the general reader. But one never knows.
YA up

643 _____. The Ramayana; adapted from the English
translation of Hari Prasad Shastri. Ill. by Gordon
Laite. Scott, 1969. The author's introduction to
this beautiful book explains that the "Ramayana" is
one of the two great epics of India (the other being
the tale of the Pandavas and Kursavas which are part
of the "Mahabharata") and that it contains a gospel
as important as any of the Hindu scriptures. It is
mainly the story of Rama and his wife Sita and continues a religious tradition from the earliest times to
the present day. There is a list of the characters
in the epic and a guide to pronunciation of proper
names. YA up

644 Serage, Nancy. The Prince Who Gave Up a Throne; A
Story of the Buddha. Ill. by Kazue Mizumura.
Thomas Y. Crowell, 1966. Prince Siddhartha was
born in the kingdom of Kapilavastu on the border of
India and Nepal, possibly about 556 B.C. and here
is the legend about him, delicately illustrated and
simply told; of how visions of old age, suffering and
death led him to give up all worldly riches and glory
and found the religion of Buddhism. The story is
based on extensive research and the drawings are in
the mood of the Ajanta Cave frescoes. I

645 Siddiqui, Ashraf, and Lerch, Marilyn. Toontoony Pie
and Other Tales from Pakistan. Ill. by Jan Fairservice. World, 1961. Twenty-two tales from both
East and West Pakistan, a few of which are already

known, though most have been collected from oral sources and are published here for the first time.
E, I

FICTION

646 Arora, Shirley L. <u>What Then Ramon?</u> Ill. by Hans Guggenheim. Follett, 1960. A story of the meeting of the old and new worlds. Ramon, an Indian boy living in the hill country where some Americans have bungalows to escape the heat of the plains, helps a teacher lady to find rare plants and thus earns enough money to buy a long coveted book. I, YA

647 Batchelor, Julie Forsyth. <u>A Cap for Mul Chaud.</u> Ill. by Corinne B. Dillon. Harcourt Brace and World, 1950. A little Indian boy is invited by his uncle to go to the big city of Bombay but is ashamed to go without a cap. He finally finds work and earns enough money to buy the cap he wants, only to lose all the money to a bully. And then--read and see.
E, I

648 Bonham, Frank. <u>Burma Rifles; A Story of Merrill's Marauders.</u> Thomas Y. Crowell, 1960. A story specifically written to commemorate the heroism of the 14 Nisei volunteers with the 5307th Composite Unit, popularly known as Merrill's Marauders, whose very presence behind the enemy lines involved courage beyond the line of duty. YA

649 Booz, Elizabeth Benson. <u>The Seal of Jai.</u> Ill. by Paul Kennedy. Macmillan, 1968. An adventure novel of east India based on events that actually took place somewhere in the early 1930s: the attempted murder of a Bengal Raja by his wife and the search for him by his 14-year-old nephew up into the Himalayas, through Sikkim, Bhutan and into Tibet. The court scene in Dacca that climaxes the story may be legendary but is believed by the Bengalese villagers. YA

650 Bothwell, Jean. <u>Dancing Princess.</u> Harcourt Brace and World, 1965. This is the second book of a trilogy set in the Mogul period of the late 16th century, during the reign of Emperor Akbar, and following <u>The Promise of the Rose</u> though not actually a sequel to it. The story is of a fictional princess and the treasure of the Black God in a monastery in Upper India, and is based on the "Ain-i-Akbari," an account of the court of Akbar, the greatest of all Mogul

emperors, compiled by a court writer. YA

651 _____. Defiant Bride. Harcourt Brace and World, 1969. The third of the Akbar trilogy, following Dancing Princess, centering on Akbar's minor campaign to annex Kashmir, which was ruled by the Sultan of Chak. The heroine is a young girl of a nomad tribe of the Himalayas, a tribe dwelling in Abkar's empire but in sympathy with the kingdom of Kashmir. Ruins of a fort begun by Akbar can still be seen in Lahore. YA

652 _____. The Emerald Clue. Harcourt Brace and World, 1961. The third in a series of mystery novels set in India at the time of transition from British control to independence (the 1940s) about the grandchildren of Sir Ranjit Singh who seek the new freedom promised at that time. It follows Search for a Golden Bird and gives, as do all of Bothwell's novels, a cast of characters and an author's note about the time setting. YA

653 _____. Little Boat Boy. Ill. by Margaret Ayer. Harcourt Brace and World, 1945. An eight-year-old boy, living on a "mat-boat" on a lake in Kashmir, longs to go to school where he might have friends of his own age, but his parents lack the money for school fees, and are already in debt to a greedy money-lender for the schooling given to his older brother. So Hafiz amuses himself as best he can, running into several misadventures in the process. E, I

654 _____. The Missing Violin. Ill. by Arthur Marokvia. Harcourt Brace and Co., 1959. An American professor and his family, consisting of wife, four children and housekeeper-friend, leave their New Jersey home, shortly after World War I, for a year in Rajapur, northern India. The principal characters in the story are 12-year-old twin boys whose adjustment to this completely alien culture is so gradual that they themselves are surprised to discover, at the end of the year, that they actually want to stay on in India. There is a slight mystery within the plot, but it has less importance than the story of the whole family's adaptation to the East Indian world. Only Barbara, aged 14, fails to fit in, and the story of her later years there is continued in a sequel to this book, The Silver Mango Tree. I

655 _____. Omen for a Princess; The Story of Jahanara, Royal Poet of the Seventeenth Century. Abelard

Schuman, 1963. A novel based on the true story of a princess, the daughter of Mumtaz-i-Mahal for whose tomb the Taj Mahal was built. Seeking to comfort her father, the Mogul emperor, Shah Jahan, and give him an outlet for his grief, she actually designed the Taj Mahal. YA

656 _____. The Promise of the Rose. Harcourt Brace and Co., 1958. The first of a trilogy (followed by Dancing Princess) set in late 16th century India in and near the court of the Mogul Emperor Akbar, about Aruna Rahmat Abulin, a ward of the emperor, and her refusal to be married to a stranger in far-off Lahore. The cast of characters in the beginning is helpful as always in these historical novels. YA

657 _____. The Red Scarf. Harcourt Brace and World, 1962. A mystery novel about a young man, the "English-returned" superintendent of police of the Daura District Headquarters at Daurapur, just after independence. YA up

658 _____. Ride, Zarina, Ride. Harcourt Brace and World, 1966. A novel of mystery and romance, set in the late 16th century court at Agra, of Akbar the Great. The author's note gives the historical background of the story of 18-year-old Zarina who is impatient with her single lot. YA

659 _____. Ring of Fate. Harcourt Brace, 1957. A romance and story of the conflict between the old and the new in the Punjab in the post World War I period. YA up

660 _____. River Boy of Kashmir. Ill. by Margaret Ayer. William Morrow, 1946. The story of a Kashmiri school boy in the years before India's independence, who finds a silver box in the mud near the post office, and is pursued by a greedy money lender because of it. Beautiful details of Kashmir and interesting characterizations of Haviz' schoolmates, teachers, the cook, and Haviz' family. I

661 _____. Search for a Golden Bird. Ill. by Reisie Lonette. Harcourt Brace, 1958. Set in the late 1940s when India was about to achieve independence from the British Empire, this is the second of a trilogy of mystery novels, following The Thirteenth Stone and preceding The Emerald Clue, about three grandchildren of the Prime Minister of Jaipur, Sir Ranjit Singh. The author's note is of special interest for its material about India's independence and the problems it posed. YA

662 _____. The Silver Mango Tree. Harcourt Brace, 1960. A sequel to The Missing Violin this is a novel about Barbara Tennant's return to India after four years of college at Berkeley, California. She had never been happy when she had lived there at the age of 14, largely because of her unwillingness at that time (and age) to try to adjust to strange customs, and now, eight years later, her feelings about India are confused because of her involvement with a fascinating Indian prince who presses her to marry him. YA up

663 _____. The Thirteenth Stone. Harcourt Brace, 1957. The first of three mystery novels about the grandchildren of Sir Ranjit Singh, Prime Minister of Jaipur, before India's independence, followed by Search for a Golden Bird and The Emerald Clue. YA

664 _____. White Fawn of Phalera. Harcourt Brace and World, 1963. A novel, set in the jet age, but dealing with age-old traditions and superstitions in a village in northeast India, about a young American nurse working in a mission compound. Aside from the nurse's story, there are interesting details about puppetry, an important dramatic and costume art in both old and new India. YA

665 Bryant, Chester. The Lost Kingdom. Ill. by Margaret Ayer. Julian Messner, 1961. The story of a 13-year-old boy, very knowing in the ways of wild animals, who seeks to find a roadway through the jungle, and during his search discovers the secret of the seven-headed cobra mark on his chest. I, YA

666 Buck, Pearl. The Big Fight. Ill. by Mamoru Funai. John Day, 1964. Based on an incident Pearl Buck once saw in India, this is an amusing little story about a tiger and a leopard who were supposed to fight each other for the benefit of an American movie company. E, I

667 Cadell, Elizabeth. Sun in the Morning. Ill. by Mildred Coughlin. Morrow, 1950. A charming, gently humorous novel about three girls living in Colonial India in the early 1920s: one French and two English. One of the English girls is the narrator, beginning her story when she is ten and the other two slightly older. At the end, the girls are grown-up and facing separation from each other as they fall in love and become engaged. YA

668 Catherall, Arthur. Thunder Dam. Ill. by Omar Davis. Criterion, 1964. A thrilling suspense story in which

a 17-year-old Burmese lad battles intrigue and superstition as he tries to get his father's teak logs out of the jungle before the monsoon hits. YA
669 Chandler, Charlotte. Kumar. Ill. by Robin Jaques. W. W. Norton, 1965. A novel of village and farm life in south India where the caste system still held in 1945, and of Kumar who has grown up with the separation from "untouchables" but gradually outgrows that concept, partly through his friendship with one of that caste, and partly through the efforts of an American pastor giving the villagers American aid in food. I, YA
670 Channel, A. R. Rogue Elephant. Ill. by D. Watkins Pitchford. Macrae Smith, 1963. Don't put this book down until you've finished it, or if you have to be interrupted, don't waste any time getting back to it. It is the story of a Burmese boy whose dearly-loved tame elephant has become branded as a "rogue" and of how Ma Thi O is ordered to bring him in to be shot. There are thrills aplenty of floods and ruthless bandits and the authentic sounds and atmosphere of the Burmese jungle. I, YA
671 Dobrin, Arnold. To Katmandu; A Story of Nepal. Ill. by the author. Thomas Y. Crowell, 1972. The story of a farm boy living near Katmandu, the capital city of Nepal, who longs to join the mountain climbers and Sherpas but who has to realize that he is not yet ready to climb the "Goddess of the Wind." E, I
672 DuBois, Theodora. Tiger Burning Bright. Farrar Straus, 1964. A novel about the Sepoy Rebellion, 1857-9, and an American girl, the daughter of missionaries, who escapes the massacre at Meerut and who, with the aid of an American telegraph engineer, rescues a group of 11 children, an Irish nurse, and a difficult English woman from the murderous Sepoys. (Sepoy--a native East Indian soldier equipped and disciplined in European style.)
673 Evarts, Hal G. The Secret of the Himalayas. Scribner's, 1962. An American college freshman is chosen as a member of a scientific expedition going to the Himalayas in Nepal in search of the yeti or "abominable snowman." He encounters many natural dangers and also the apparent enmity of a fellow member of the expedition. YA
674 Forsberg, Vera. Salima Lives in Kashmir. Ill. with photographs by Anna Riwkin-Brick. Macmillan, 1971. Kashmir must be one of the most beautiful places in

the world, but not a good place for a girl who wants desperately to go to school and has to wait for her grandfather's permission. E

675 Forster, E. M. Passage to India. Harcourt Brace, 1924, Harbrace Modern Classics, 1952. A compassionate and ironic novel about racial and social tensions in early 20th century, colonial India, also about the universal conflict between the ruler and the ruled. Adela Quested comes to India to visit her fiancé and try to decide whether she could be happy as the wife of an English city magistrate there. In her attempts to understand the Indians, she finds herself the center of a racial crisis and learns that she definitely cannot live in the Anglo-Indian world. An enduring novel for both its content and literary style. A

676 Godden, Rumer. Black Narcissus. Random House, 1939, 1st Modern Library edition, 1947. A small community of Anglican nuns acquire a former general's palace in northern India for a convent, hospital and school. They are warned that the project won't succeed, that a brotherhood of monks with the same intentions had left after only a five-month trial; but Superior Sister Clodagh insists that "nothing is impossible with God." The palace is haunted by the shades of the old general's "ladies" whom he once kept there and whose lingering laughter, as well as the awesome view of Kanchenjunga, the altitude of the site, and the difficulties with the villagers they came to serve but whom they could not understand-- and most of all the loneliness--changed all the sisters in one way or another--even Sister Clodagh. A

677 _____. Kingfishers Catch Fire. A love affair with Kashmir was both Sophie's doing and undoing. As a young widow she comes, with only her two young children and Kashmiri servants to stay in a lonely valley, where she tries to lead a life like that of the Indians there. Though the experiment ends in near-tragedy, she knows that she will always be homesick for Kashmir. A moving, sensitive and exciting novel with many memorable characters. A

678 Grant, Eva. A Cow for Jaya. Ill. by Michael Hampshire. A Break-of-Day Book, 1973. A simple adventure story with realistic drawings that give the young reader a picture of India's village life and customs. E

679 Hallard, Peter. Kalu and the Wild Boar. Ill. by W. T.

Mars. Franklin Watts, 1973. A story of a boy's promise to his injured father to kill the wild boar that is destroying crops, and of how, with the help of an old Sikh, he keeps his promise. I, YA

680 Herrmanns, Ralph. In Search of the Abominable Snowman; A Story from Nepal. Ill. with dramatic color photographs by the author. Doubleday, 1969. Bevod, a boy of Katmandu, was so timid that he considered himself cowardly and felt that he might overcome his cowardice if he could find his ideal of strength and courage, the "abominable snowman." So he set out to climb the highest mountain in the world, Chomolungma (which we know as Everest) but has to turn back only to discover that though he had not succeeded in finding the god of courage, he had, in his search, found strength and courage in himself. A handsome book to own. I

681 Jacob, Helen Pierce. A Garland for Gandhi. Ill. by Lillian Sader. Parnassus, 1968. The story of a little girl in an Indian fishing village who finds learning to spin very difficult, but whose earnest efforts are rewarded when Gandhi passes through her village on his "salt walk." I

682 Jhabvala, R. Prawer. Amrita. W. W. Norton, 1956. First published in Great Britain in 1955, under the title To Whom She Will, this is a delicious comedy of manners, set in contemporary Delhi, hilariously funny but moving too, and as full of life as an eastern bazaar. Amrita thinks she is desperately in love with Hari, and he thinks he adores her, but neither family approves of their marriage and plot together to prevent it. A

683 Kalish, Betty McKelvey. Eleven! Time to Think of Marriage, Farhut. Ill. by Alton Raible. Atheneum, 1970. A charming, poignant story, based on that of a real Farhut, living in Bengal during the time of British control, who was forced to marry and go into "purdah" at the age of 13. (Purdah means seclusion, along with other women, from the outside world.) The fictional Farhut is a little tomboy who has to grow up very quickly and become a lady in purdah, and who is aided in escaping that fate by an understanding father. I, YA

684 Kent, Louise Andrews. He Went with Vasco da Gama. Ill. by Paul Quinn. Houghton Mifflin, 1938. Fiction, based on sound research, about a pair of boys who accompany da Gama on his perilous voyage to

India near the end of the 15th century, a story filled with humor and adventure. I, YA

685 Kinist, Esther. Paji. Ill. by Harold Price. McGraw-Hill, 1946. The story of a little boy of Ceylon who rejects the idea of carving the same objects day in and day out and realizes the value of originality in art and the beauty of simple objects, like a carving of his own "dreamy dish-faced bullock." Delightful details of Ceylon--its jungles, old temples and mythical statues. E

686 Kipling, Rudyard. All the Mowgli Stories. Ill. by Kurt Wiese. Doubleday, 1936. Both Jungle Books in one volume. I

687 _____. The Jungle Book, Vol. I (1894). Ill. by Kurt Wiese. Doubleday, n.d. The central figure of both Jungle Books is the human Mowgli, brought up by Mother Wolf and taught the ways of the jungle. I

688 _____. The Jungle Book, Vol. II (1895). Ill. by J. Lockwood Kipling. Doubleday, n.d. A continuation of the story of Mowgli and his jungle animal friends. I

689 _____. Kim (1900). Doubleday, n.d. A novel of Indian life in the late 19th century, built around the travels of an Irish orphan and an old lama from Tibet, in quest of a mystic River of the Arrows. Eventually Kim's experiences make him an asset to the English Secret Service in which he distinguishes himself while still a boy. YA up

690 _____. Wee Willie Winkie and Other Stories (1889). Various ed. A book of short stories about English colonialism in the late 19th century. The title story is about the six-year-old son of an officer of the British-Indian army, living on the army post and coming to the rescue of the fiancée of his hero, Lieutenant Brandis. A

691 Lavolle, L. N. Nhoti, Son of India. Ill. by J. P. Legueret, tr. by Hugh Shelley. Abelard Schuman, 1960. A novel of unusual contemporary interest because of its setting, first Calcutta, and later the border of India and East Pakistan (now Bangladesh). It tells of the arbitrary division between agricultural and industrial areas and the religious conflicts between Moslem and Hindu. Vivid descriptions of drought, starvation, beggarly existence and, on the brighter side, the circus world of wrestlers, dancers, fakirs and trained animals, are woven through the plot con-

cerning Nhoti's secret, divulged only at the end. For added measure are two Indian fables, told by Nhoti to earn money or rice for some of the starving people across the Pakistani border. I, YA

692 Lindquist, Willis. Burma Boy. Ill. by Nicolas Mordvinoff. Whittlesey House, 1953. A short adventure novel of a boy and a great bull elephant who has grown wild and dangerous, with a brief vocabulary of Burmese words. I

693 Louden, Claire and George. Rain in the Winds; A Story of India. Ill. by the authors. Scribner's, 1952. The Loudens know well how to weave a story through informational material; and do so in this book, of a boy and his elephant friend and their combined share in new developments in India. E

694 Masters, John. Nightrunners of Bengal. Viking, 1951. A novel of the horrendous mutiny in the Indian Presidency of Bengal in 1857, in which Indian soldiers, the Sepoys, turned on British officers and murdered them and their women and children. Most of the incidents are drawn from official reports, contemporary letters and Anglo-Indian tradition, but the places actually visited and the people actually met in the story are fictitious. A glossary of off-stage people and places is appended, and the meanings of Hindustani words are usually made clear in their context. A

695 Mehta, Rama. The Life of Keshav; A Family Story from India. McGraw-Hill, 1969. A novel which involves the reader in the family life of an Indian schoolboy and the world of his village, with its gossip and festivals and very early marriages. When Keshav acquires a scholarship for a rich man's school, he finds himself caught up in a dilemma, being neither completely accepted by his new schoolmates nor understood by his old playmates. An outstanding story of old and new India, with a glossary of Indian words. YA up

696 _____. Ramu; A Story of India. Ill. by W. T. Mars. McGraw-Hill, 1966. Foreword by Santha Rama Rau. Through the story of the ambitions and experiences of a mischievous young boy, one catches a non-tourist look at a small Indian town where the living may be poor but where life is rich. At the beginning of the book is quite an extensive list of Indian words, their meanings and pronunciation. I

697 Mukerji, Dhan Gopal. Gayneck; The Story of a Pigeon.

Ill. by Boris Artzybasheff. E. P. Dutton, 1927.
The life and training of a carrier pigeon and his service in World War I, told partly about him and partly by him. I, YA

698 _____. Kari the Elephant. Ill. by J. E. Allen.
E. P. Dutton, 1922. The principal character of this book happens to be an elephant, and the relationship between him and the boy narrator, Hari, provides the continuity of the plot. But this is not just another exciting book of jungle tales. The word "ecology" was certainly not a household word in 1922, but this story concerns itself with the ecology of the Indian jungle. A thread of the Hindu religion also runs through it. I, YA

699 _____. Hari the Jungle Lad (1924). Ill. by Morgan Stinemetz. E. P. Dutton, 1946. A thrilling story of jungle lore--of tiger hunting, elephant tracking, monkeys, panthers, cobras and other creatures, great and small. Though it is a sequel to Kari the Elephant and might be more enjoyable read after that, it stands alone very well. I, YA

700 Murphey, Eleanor A. Nihal. Ill. by Ezra Jack Keats. Thomas Y. Crowell, 1960. Art work and text blend to make this an atmospheric story of the island of Ceylon (now Sri Lanka), and the gentle people there, and of 12-year-old Nihal who grew to love and understand the sea, though he could never be a fisherman. I up

701 Nirodi, Hira. Chikka. Ill. by Constance McMillan. Reilly and Lee, 1962. Eleven-year-old Chikka runs away from his small village to the city of Bangalore where he has all sorts of new and exciting experiences and where he learns that the quality of honesty is the same in the big city as in his home village. I

702 Potter, Jeffrey. Elephant Bridge. Ill. by Roberta Moynihan. Viking Press, 1957. A grand jungle story of World War II. Maung Po, living in central Burma was considered too young to join his brothers when they marched off to war, but, determined to join the fighting somehow, he slipped away from home in the night to try to catch up with the soldiers. Before long, however, he felt so weary that he simply had to sleep for a while, and suddenly he was awakened by an elephant who lifted him up in his trunk and carried him off with the wild herd which took him as one of their own. A beautiful

story of the boy's identification with the elephants and his part in their fight against the enemy. I

703 Rama Rau, Santha. Remember the House. Harper, 1956. A splendid novel in which humor and compassion are joined, of a young Indian woman on the threshold between two worlds. The time setting is 1947, the last year of British rule and the last year of the India of Baba's childhood and youth. But she does not feel sad about it as does her father. Rather she hopes and believes that independence will make her life more exciting and romantic as it seems to be with a young American couple to whom she has become warmly attached. And yet--various events and a visit to her very wise old grandmother give her a new maturity and an understanding of herself and of the fact that there are many kinds of love.

704 Singh, R. Lal and Lownsbery, Eloise. Gift of the Forest. Ill. by Anne Vaughan. Longmans Green, 1942. A lovely story of a 10-year-old boy and his adopted tiger cub and of a superstitious serving man who feared and hated the tiger as a cub and even more when it grew big. The boy's grandfather had no fear of, nor hatred for, any of the Lord's creatures and was able to overcome the evil of those who did possess those qualities. The Hindu religion pervades the story. I

705 Sommerfelt, Aimee. The Road to Agra. Ill. by Ulf Aas. Criterion, 1961. An endearing and engrossing story of two small children and a dog, making a long and dangerous journey on foot from their small village in northern India to Agra where little Maya, who has trachoma, may receive treatment and hopefully a cure. Theirs is indeed "an incredible journey." A glossary of unusual words in the story is appended. I, YA

706 _____. The White Bungalow. Ill. by Ulf Aas, tr. by Evelyn Ramsden. Criterion, 1964. A sequel to the prize-winning Road to Agra in which the brother, now 16, faces the hard decision between supporting his family in their poverty-stricken village in northern India or accepting a scholarship that would lead to a medical career in the new India. Glossary of unusual words in the book. I, YA

707 Spittel, Richard. Savage Island. Criterion, 1959. A Robinson Crusoe type of plot, set in 17th century Ceylon in which young Hans, the sole survivor of a shipwreck, narrowly escapes death from wild animals

and reptiles and a tribe of aboriginal Veddas. I, YA

708 Styles, Showell. Sherpa Adventure. Ill. by Matvyn Wright from the author's Sketches. Vanguard, 1960. No mountain climbing enthusiast of whatever age should miss this novel of a listless, 16-year-old Scot whose doctor prescribes the Himalayan climate for his lung trouble. His uncle, who is an intrepid mountain climber takes him along on an expedition, but not wanting him to go too high, leaves him for four weeks in a Sherpa village, only 12,000 feet up. There he is befriended by the son of a Sherpa guide who does as much for the Scottish boy as does the climate. YA

709 Sucksdorf, Astrid Bergman. Chendru--The Boy and the Tiger. Ill. with full color photography by the author. Harcourt Brace and World, 1960. English version by William Sansom. Chendru, a member of the Munas, a primitive tribe in central India, is given a tiger cub by his father, and he and the tiger grow up together, but it is a question as to how long their friendship can last. The Munas are beautiful people and the author photographs them as they go about their daily tasks. The tiger is also beautiful, and readers of all ages may enjoy the book. I up

710 Thampi, Parvathi. Geeta and the Village School. Ill. by Ronni Solbert. Doubleday, 1960. Here again is a story of the old and new India and how hard it is to face the unknown. Geeta, a little village girl, is terribly afraid of the new school which has just been built in her village, but well--a promise is a promise. E

CHINA AND NEIGHBORING COUNTRIES
(Hong Kong, Manchuria, Mongolia, Taiwan, and Tibet)

The ancient land of China whose history reaches back to 2205 B.C., is now split into two hostile parts: the People's Republic of China (mainland China) and the Republic of China, on the island of Taiwan (Nationalist China). As Formosa, Taiwan was a possession of Japan from 1895 to 1945, restored to China in 1945, and, since 1949 has been the seat of the Republic of China.

China and Neighbors

Manchuria, a region of northeastern mainland China, was the home of the Manchu dynasty, who ruled China from 1644 to 1911. The area was under Japanese control from 1931 to 1945, when it was called Manchukuo. The Mongolian People's Republic was proclaimed in 1921 but did not achieve independence from China until 1945.

Hong Kong, comprising the island of Hong Kong and adjacent mainland bordering southeast China, is a British Crown Colony which was acquired from China in 1841. The large mountainous country of Tibet has long had a history mingled with that of China, to whom they surrendered their government, after a Chinese Communist invasion, in 1951.

NON-FICTION

711 Appel, Benjamin. Why the Chinese Are The Way They Are. Maps and jacket by Samuel H. Bryant. Little Brown, 1968. A unique approach to the history and the current (as of the 1960s) condition of China. In the prefatory note to the reader, Mr. Appel explains that he researched the questions asked about China by boys and girls and the conceptions and misconceptions they had formed about that country. Each chapter lists some of their questions and the author's answers in which he tries to explain why, the Chinese being as they are, we should not expect them to adopt to our political system or our ideals of democracy, yet still hope that they will try to understand us. YA

712 Caldwell, John C. Let's Visit Formosa. Ill. with photographs. John Day Co., 1956. Because this book was published 17 years ago, the political situation described on page 9 is out of date. However the geography, history and the varied peoples and their legends are still valid. Appended are a chronological history, a summary of facts, and a short list of source and reference books. E, I

713 Eberte, Irmengarde. Pandas Live Here. Ill. with photographs. Doubleday, 1973. The giant pandas are especially intriguing because they are so hard to find and so short-lived in captivity. This is a history of panda-hunting in China, Tibet and Nepal, and a study of their lives in zoos. All ages

714 Edmonds, I. G. Taiwan, the Other China. Ill. with photographs by the author and maps by Jack H. Ful-

ler. Bobbs-Merrill, 1971. An excellent history and contemporary story of the island formerly called "Formosa." YA up

715 Glubok, Shirley. The Art of China. Ill. with photographs. Macmillan, 1973. Illustrates art forms from the pottery of the Neolithic period to the elegant porcelains of the Ming dynasty. I up

716 Goldston, Robert. The Long March, 1934-1935: A Red Army Survives to Bring Communism to China. Ill. with photographs. Franklin Watts, 1971 (a World Focus Book). A relatively small book, but containing, besides the detailed story of the incredible march, a chronology of China's history and a list of the principals in the events of that period, among whom were the Dowager Empress, Sun Yat-sen, Lenin, Chiang Kai-shek and Mao Tse-tung. YA up

717 ――――. The Rise of Red China. Ill. by Donald Carrick and with photographs. Map by Irving Werstein. Bobbs-Merrill, 1967. "Truly," says the author, "if one reads the history of China as a record of who slew whom and who begat which emperor, then Chinese history can overmatch that of any other nation for profusion of detail, confusion of names and sheer mass." Yet out of this profusion, Mr. Goldston has constructed a clear and pleasantly readable history of China from the 13th century to 1966, introducing brief biographies of contemporary Chinese leaders. YA up

718 Harrer, Heinrich. Seven Years in Tibet. Ill. with 40 pages of photographs. E. P. Dutton, 1954. With an introduction by Peter Fleming, tr. by Richard Graves. The German author was in Asia on a Himalayan expedition when World War II began and he was taken prisoner by the British. After two failures he finally succeeded in escaping from the POW camp in India into Tibet where, under the most difficult circumstances, he finally reached the Forbidden City of Lhasa, where he eventually became tutor to the Dalai Lama. A

719 Harrington, Lynn. China and the Chinese. Ill. with photographs by Richard Harrington. Thomas Nelson, 1966. A comprehensive book about the People's Republic of China, with an excellent map and a chronology of Chinese history and related world events; also a list of "Other Books to Enjoy" and index. A minimum of political comment. YA

720 ――――. The Grand Canal of China. Ill. with photo-

graphs and maps. Rand McNally, 1967. The author
and her photographer spent 11 weeks in the People's
Republic of China in 1965 so there is much in the
book of current interest besides the history of this
great canal, which connects five of China's greatest
rivers and which reached its "grand" stage in the
time of Kublai Khan. Included is a glossary of one-
syllable Chinese words frequently used in place-names.
YA

721 Hay, John. Ancient China. Ill. with maps and photographs and drawings by Rosemonde Nairac and Pippa
Brand. Henry Z. Walck, 1974 (Walck Archaeologies).
A beautifully illustrated and well organized account of
the major archaeological finds in China from the first
decades of this century until the present. It is good
to know that the earlier investigations done by foreign
archaeologists with the Chinese, have been continued
under the present regime, even with the blessing of
Chairman Mao. The finds include the discovery of
the Peking Man and evidence of the Neolithic Age.
A chronology covers the time from 6000 B.C. to the
establishment of the People's Republic in 1949. YA
up

722 Hirschfeld, Burt. Fifty-five Days of Terror; The Story
of the Boxer Rebellion. Ill. with maps. Julian
Messner, 1964. An absorbing account of the rise
of the Boxers, the causes of the rebellion and the
lack of understanding of those causes by the corrupt
rulers of China as well as the foreigners from many
countries, who were attacked. Excitingly told, with
profiles of many of the individuals, foreign and Chinese, involved in the days of terror, the book reads
like a novel. YA up

723 Joy, Charles R. Getting to Know Hong Kong. Ill. by
Claudine Nankivel. Coward McCann, 1964. An introduction to the crowded island near the mainland
of China, a British Crown Colony since 1843. Appended is an historical outline, a page of Mandarin
words and phrases with their English equivalents,
and a pronounciation guide. I

724 Kublin, Hyman. China. Ill. with maps and photographs.
Houghton Mifflin, 1972. An up-to-date introduction
to Chinese history and thought, with two pages of informative "time tables" and an extensive bibliography.
YA up

725 Lewis, Richard. The Moment of Wonder. Ill. with
paintings by Chinese and Japanese Masters. Dial,

1964. A poetry anthology with an editorial preface about Oriental poetry, explaining the haiku form in particular. An author index is appended. YA

726 Lum, Peter. Great Day in China; The Holiday Moon. Ill. by Peter Thompson. Abelard Schuman, 1963. New Year's Day in China resembles American Christmas, New Year's and the 4th of July all rolled into one. The Chinese "Kitchen God" is a sort of Santa Claus, and the fireworks are glorious and noisy. What a day! E

727 Munro, Eleanor C. Through the Vermillion Gate; A Journey into China's Past. Illustrations from many collections. Pantheon, 1971. A double-purpose book well arranged: a modern story of archaeological discovery and an ancient one of the T'ang era, established in A.D. 618, and memorable for its rich flowering of art, commerce and government. Appended is a comparative history chart. YA up

728 Neurath, Marie and Ellis, John. They Lived Like This in Ancient China. Ill. by John Ellis. Franklin Watts, 1966. A fine visual story of ancient China with clear simple text and pictures. E, I

729 Pine, Tillie S. and Levine, Joseph. The Chinese Knew. Ill. by Ezra Jack Keats. McGraw-Hill, 1958. A book about many Chinese inventions of long long ago and how we depend on the same scientific ideas today, with suggestions of experiments to be made, using these principles, making an abacus, for instance. E, I

730 Schloat, G. Warren. Fay Gow, A Boy of Hong Kong. Ill. with photographs. Alfred A. Knopf, 1964. The picture story of the daily life of a 12-year-old boy who lives aboard a boat anchored in the Hong Kong Bay of Aberdeen, amidst a forest of boat masts. E, I

731 Scott, John. China, the Hungry Dragon. Ill. with maps by Ernest Adelberg. Parents' Magazine Press, 1967. A book concerned predominantly with recent history: the introduction of Marxist ideology, the rise of Mao Tse-Tung, the development of Chinese industry, transportation and technology, and China's relations with the Soviet Union and the United States. Because it is this kind of a book, it should be read with an open mind, remaining ever aware of often sudden changes in international affairs and the controversial aspect of political systems. Appended are tables of China's economic development, and biographical sketches of

China and Neighbors 143

important political figures in China. YA up
732 Seeger, Elizabeth. The Pageant of Chinese History, 4th ed. Ill. by Bernard Watkins. David McKay, 1962. This long, well-organized panoramic view of Chinese history was first published in 1934. Obviously, events have outrun it even since the 1962 updating but for the past history of China it provides an excellent and readable resource. YA up
733 Sharp, Jean Bowie. After You, Marco Polo. Ill. with photographs. McGraw-Hill, 1955. An adventure travelogue, written with warmth and humor by an intrepid woman who, with her photographer husband, set out to retrace the travels of 13th century Polo, from Venice to Peking. As they were turned back at the Chinese border, this title may seem misplaced here. However I felt that the author's determination to walk in the steps of that adventurous explorer entitled it to be considered in this section. A
734 Silverberg, Robert. The Long Rampart; The Story of the Great Wall of China. Chilton, 1966. The history of China is traced through the fantastic history of this wall, from 214 B.C. to the present. YA up
735 _____. Wonders of Ancient Chinese Science. Ill. by Marvin Besunder. Hawthorne, 1969. The history of China is interwoven with the history of her inventions and a discussion at the end of what set China apart from other ancient nations in her inventiveness. A table of Chinese dynasties is given at the beginning. I, YA
736 Snow, Edgar. Red Star Over China, 1st. rev. & enl. ed. Ill. with photographs from the original edition and newly selected pictures and endpaper maps; Introd. by Dr. John K. Fairbank. Grove Press, 1968 (first pub. in 1938). Snow was 22 when he first went to the Far East as a journalist, and had made his home in China for seven years when, in 1936, he ran Chiang Kai-shek's blockade, entered the Communist-held portions of China, and was the first westerner to interview the Communist leaders. The new edition includes further interviews with Mao Tse-tung (hitherto unpublished outside of China); a chronology of 125 years of Chinese revolution; a chart of the present leadership of the Chinese Communist party, conversations with Chou En-lai and others and a great deal else of interest and value. A
737 Spencer, Cornelia (Yaukey). The Land and People of China, rev. ed. Ill. with photographs. J. B. Lip-

pincott, 1972 (Portraits of the Nations Series). This revision contains chapters on the changes in the traditional way of life brought about by the Communist regime under Mao Tse-tung and China's position in international politics. YA

738 _____. Made in China; The Story of China's Expression. Ill. by Kurt Wiese, Foreword by Lin Yutang. Alfred A. Knopf, 1965. From the Foreword: "Perhaps it will serve to whet the reader's appetite to go farther in his research; perhaps it will do no more than make him see with keener, more appreciative eyes, the value of the things the Chinese value-- beauty, wisdom and democracy" (Lin Yutang's words). Bibliography appended. YA up

739 _____. Yangtze, China's River Highway. Ill. by Kurt Wiese and with photographs; maps by Fred Klein. Garrard, 1963. In the early 1960's in the Yangtze River basin lived 200 million people, at that time one tenth of the human race (the figure is much higher now in 1975). It is China's Main Street which is all one needs to say about the importance of this well organized, finely illustrated and very readable background book. I

740 Toland, John. The Flying Tigers. Ill. with photographs. Random Landmark, 1963. About the daring exploits of Chennault's A.V.G.--American Volunteer Group, who began fighting the Japanese in China even before Pearl Harbor; a flamboyant, reckless bunch, using unconventional methods of air warfare and downing an incredible number of Japanese planes in China and Burma. I, YA

741 Werstein, Irving. The Boxer Rebellion; Anti-Foreign Terror Seizes China, 1900. Ill. with photographs. Franklin Watts, 1971 (a World Focus Book). The exciting story is introduced by a brief summary of the rebellion and a list of principals and at the end, a brief chronology of the events of the first Opium War, 1839-42, and of the fall of the Manchu dynasty in 1912 and formation of the Chinese Republic. YA up

742 Yutang, Lin. The Chinese Way of Life. World, 1959. Life as it was in northern China in the 1930s, and as being shown to an American-born Chinese boy. The last chapter, "China Today," takes up very briefly the history after 1937 and here, Lin Yutang understandably expresses his own strongly anti-Communist bias. A fine chronol-

ogy chart of the Chinese World and other world events is appended. YA

BIOGRAPHIES

743 Archer, Jules. Chou En-lai. Hawthorne Books, 1973. A biography of the strong diplomatic No. 2 man in the People's Republic of China who came from an aristocratic background but grew to be a confirmed communist. An exceptionally charming personality emerges from this book, a portrait of a man who could communicate with all sorts and conditions of people--peasants, soldiers, foreign statesmen, almost anyone, it seems, except Chiang Kai-shek. YA up

744 _____. Mao Tse-tung. Hawthorne Books, 1972. This biography of the Chinese leader (1893-) is also a history of China from the mid-twenties to 1972. Mao appears at first as a rather kindly, simple man devoted to the Chinese peasantry, but the story of the Long March reveals his staunch courage and indomitable will. His later ruthlessness which caused the torture and murder of thousands whose politics did not tally with his is no different from that of Chiang Kai-shek, but however he is judged his final place in history will be one of heroic size. One wishes that a map had been included in the book. YA up

745 Baker, Nina Brown. Sun Yat-sen. Ill. by Jeanyee Wong. Vanguard, 1946. An exceptionally readable biography of the founder of the Chinese Republic (1867-1925), written in fictional style. A list of authorities consulted is appended. YA

746 Block, Irvin. The Lives of Pearl Buck; A Tale of China and America. Ill. with photographs. Thomas Y. Crowell, 1973. More about China than America because China became part of Pearl Buck in her childhood. A fine sensitive portrait of a great writer and a great woman (1892-1973). YA up

747 Buck, Pearl. The Man Who Changed China; The Story of Sun Yat-sen. Ill. by Fred Castellon. Random House, 1953 (a Landmark Book). A biography of Sun Yat-sen (1867-1925), and the story of his crusade to establish the Republic of China, a story of repeated failures and frustrations but undying perseverance and hope. I

748 Buehr, Walter. The World of Marco Polo. Ill. by the author. G. P. Putnam's Sons. A short vividly illustrated story of the life and travels of the 13th century Venetian explorer. I

749 Chapman, Walker (Silverburg). Kublai Khan, Lord of Xanadu. Designed by Mina Baylis. Bobbs-Merrill, 1966. As fourth successor to his grandfather, Genghis Khan, Kublai Khan reigned on the Mongol throne first and then on the Dragon throne of the Middle Kingdom as first Yuen Emperor of China, from 1260 to 1294. For a clearer understanding of his background and relationships, see Sons of the Steppe by Hans Baumann (Walck, 1958), with its chronology. This biography is built upon the writings of Marco Polo, Kublai's ambassador for 17 years, who took back to Venice many of the details contained in this book. A colorful exotic story, with a chapter on "The Aftermath," a bibliography and map. YA up

750 Dupuey, Trevor Nevitt. The Military Life of Genghis: Khan of Khans. Maps by Dyno Lowenstein. Franklin Watts, 1969. A biography (1162-1227), with emphasis on military strategy. Appended are a chapter on "Principles of Military Leadership and Military Theory," a chronology and an index. YA

751 Eunson, Roby. Mao Tse-tung, The Man Who Conquered China. Ill. with photographs. Franklin Watts, 1973 (an Associated Press Book). A biography, giving an unbiased account of Mao's successes and failures and, above all, his well-nigh incredible strength. Bibliography and index. YA up

752 Grousset, René. Conqueror of the World: The Life of Ghingis Khan. Tr. from French by Marian McKeller and Denis Sinor, with preface notes and bibliography by Denis Sinor. Orion Press, 1966. A definitive, scholarly biography of the mighty Khan, with detailed end-cover maps. A

753 Haldane, Charlotte. The Last Great Empress of China. Bobbs-Merrill, 1965. An absorbing biography of the Empress Yehonala (or Tzu Hsi), the powerful and enigmatic ruler of China from 1861 to 1908. She was born in 1835 and died in 1908, and the book includes a history of China during that period and up to 1960. It is full of fascinating detail and characterizations and particularly exciting in its chapters on the Boxer Rebellion. Appended are chapter notes, a general index, and a helpful index of Chinese names, so confusing to Occidental readers. A

China and Neighbors

754 Han Suyin. A Mortal Flower. Putnam, 1966. Bantom paperback, 1972. A combination of autobiography and history by a Eurasian author. The former concerns her very troubled youth in the '20s and '30s, with glimpses of her later life interspersed. The history reveals personal impressions and opinions of such people as Chiang Kai-shek, Mao Tse-tung, Chou En-lai and many other prominent contemporary figures. A

755 Kelen, Betty. Confucius in Life and Legend. Thomas Nelson, 1971. A biography of the great teacher whose real name was K'ung Ch'in and who lived circa 551 to 472 B.C., about the time of Buddha in India and the Golden Age of Greece. It includes many of his precepts which seem to apply as well today as they did 2500 years ago. For instance, "the aim of politics is to uphold the right. Lead people by doing right. Then no one else will do otherwise." YA up

756 Komroff, Manuel. Marco Polo. Ill. by Edgard Cirlin. Messner, 1952. A short biography of the Venetian traveler to China (1254?-1324). YA

757 Lamb, Harold. Genghis Khan and the Mongol Horde. Ill. by Elton Fax. Random House, 1954. A good short, lively biography (1162-1227) of the Mongolian who made himself master of half the world. I

758 _____. Genghis Khan, The Emperor of All Men. Ill. with photographs. Robert M. McBride, 1927. The story of the great Khan's life from his birth in 1162 to his death in 1227, how he united all the Mongol tribes and then proceeded to conquer the Chinese, Persians, Turks and others until he had expanded his empire to the very gates (and through some of them) of eastern Europe. The afterword carries on the history, after Genghis' death to the rule of his grandson, Kublai Khan, with chapters on "The Massacres," "The Laws of Genghis Khan," "Prester John" and other aspects of the Mongol Empire. YA up

759 Li Shu-fan. Hong Kong Surgeon. Ill. with photographs; Preface by Morris Fishbein, M.D.; and Foreword by Felix Martí Ibáñez. E.P. Dutton, 1964. An autobiography of a Chinese doctor whose fifty years of medical practice were studded with amazing adventures and miraculous escapes during periods of revolution in China and, in Hong Kong, harrowing ordeals during the Japanese occupation. The book may be read with special interest by doctors and medical students, but there are also stories about big game

hunting, and older adults will be interested in his theories about staying young. He never gives his own age. YA up

760 Preston, Edna Mitchell. Marco Polo, A Story of the Middle Ages. Ill. by Edward Leight. Macmillan, 1968. Although the story of Marco Polo's 13th century travels to the court of Kublai Khan has been told over and over again, it never seems to lose its attraction, and this is a fresh vivid presentation of the famous travelogue. I, YA

761 Price, Olive. The Story of Marco Polo. A fictionalized account of the fabulous adventures of the Polos, Marco, his father and uncle, as they traveled to far Cathay in the 13th century and took back to Italy the first reports of the East, reports which led many explorers, including Columbus, to seek a western route to the Orient. I

762 Rugoff, Milton, and the Editors of Horizon magazine. Marco Polo's Adventures in China. Consultant, L. Carrington Goodrich. Ill. with paintings, maps and illuminations, many of the period. American Heritage, 1964. A book, like all American Heritage books, which brings the story glowingly alive. I up

763 Spencer, Cornelia (Yaukey). Chiang Kai-shek, Generalissimo of Nationalist China. Ill. with photographs. John Day, 1968. A biography of an extraordinary and controversial figure, from his birth in 1887 to the present, as he lives in virtual exile on the island of Taiwan. A map and helpful glossary of names. YA up

764 _____. Sun-Yat-sen, Founder of the Chinese Republic. John Day, 1967. A well written and organized biography of the man who turned away from his early career in medicine to become a revolutionary leader and the founder of the People's Republic of China. A bibliography, chronology, divided list of references and index are appended. YA

765 _____. Three Sisters; The Story of the Soong Family. John Day, 1939 (Junior Literary Guild). A biographical novel about all the Soongs, though especially the three sisters who became Mesdames Kung, Sun, and Chiang Kai-shek. It is also about their father, Charlie Soong, their mother, "Miss Ni," and their three brothers, T. V., T. L. and T. A. The outstanding character is Ching-ling who eloped with Dr. Sun Yat-sen. YA up

766 Thomas, Lowell, Jr. The Dalai Lama. Duell, Sloan

and Pearce, 1961. A biography of the Dalai Lama, now an exile in India since the takeover of Tibet by the Chinese Communists, and the story of his escape to India. Born in 1935, he was only five years old when he was "discovered" as the reincarnation of the God, Chenrezi. The author of this book, with his father, Lowell Thomas, Sr., was presented to the Dalai Lama in Lhasa in 1949. YA up

FOLKLORE

767 Alexander, Frances. Pebbles from a Broken Jar; Fables and Hero Stories from Old China. Ill. with scissor-cuts. Bobbs-Merrill, 1967. Eighteen fable-like stories, "brief, wise and pleasing," with indications of the period of their origins, the oldest being from the 6th century B.C. E, I

768 Beaton-Jones, Cynon. The Adventures of So-Hi. Ill. by John Ward. Vanguard, n.d. A charming fairy story of a little Chinese boy who flies away with his kite and meets a sad but loveable dragon. Together they have a series of adventures and narrow escapes all over the world. I

769 Birch, Cyril. Chinese Myths and Fantasies. Ill. by Joan Kiddell-Monroe. Walck, 1961. A collection of folklore including myths of creation, fairy and ghost stories, and fantasies about "the revolt of the demons." I

770 Carpenter, Frances. Tales of a Chinese Grandmother. Ill. by Malthe Hasselriis. Doubleday, 1937. A lovely book, not only for the stories themselves, collected from many sources, nor for the full-page color illustrations in Chinese tradition, but for the details of family life in Old China that frame the tales. I, YA

771 Chang, Isabelle. Tales from Old China. Ill. by Tony Chen. Random, 1969. These fables and stories are too amusing and full of wisdom to be suggested for any one age group. Take, for instance the fable called "The Trap," the moral of which is, "In the face of mutual destruction it is fatal to waste time in debate." All ages

772 Chrisman, Arthur Bowie. Shen of the Sea; Chinese Stories for Children. Ill. by Else Hasselriis. E. P. Dutton, 1925 and 1953. Winner of the 1926 Newbery Medal, this book contains 16 stories, fascinating,

amusing, and, beneath the surface, revealing wise and practical Chinese philosophy. I

773 Holland, Janice. You Never Can Tell. Ill. by the author. Scribner's, 1963. Adapted from the translation by Arthur W. Hummel from the Book of Huai Nan Tzu (before 122 B.C.). Indeed, you never can tell, as you shall see. E

774 Hume, Lotta Carswell. Favorite Children's Stories from China and Tibet. Ill. by Lo Koon-Chiu. Charles E. Tuttle, 1962. Nineteen traditional tales collected by Mrs. Hume during the 22 years she lived in western China--animal tales, creation stories, even a Chinese version of the Cinderella story--with many illustrations (12 in full page color), done in the classic Chinese brush style. I

775 Knight, Mary. The Fox That Wanted Nine Golden Tails. Ill. by Brigitte Bryan. Macmillan, 1969. Another of the many "three wishes" fables but with an unusual ending. E, I

776 Larson, Jean Russell. The Silk Spinners. Ill. by Uri Shulevitz. Scribner's, 1967. Both text and line drawings have beauty and humor and an Oriental "feel" in this fabulous fairy tale about Lin Po's search for the lost silk spinners. E, I

777 Lin, Adet. The Milky Way and Other Chinese Folk Tales. Ill. by Enrico Arno. Harcourt, Brace and World, 1961. A collection of her own childhood favorites by a daughter of Lin Yutang, their written sources mentioned in her acknowledgments. I

778 Mandel, Oscar. Chi Po and the Sorcerer: A Chinese Tale for Children and Philosophers. Ill. by a Chinese scroll in ink by Lo-Koon Chiu. Charles E. Tuttle, 1964. A biographical fantasy of a real Chinese artist, Ch'i Po-Shih, who died in 1957. "From a chance encounter with this man's story," writes Mr. Mandel, "the present tale was born." The 20-odd sections of ink drawings actually compose one continuous painting in which the adventures of Chi Po are unfolded. The story is filled with kindly but satirical humor and should be required reading for all bureaucrats, especially those in Moscow, Washington and Peking. All ages

779 Merrill, Jean. The Superlative Horse; A Tale of Ancient China. Ill. by Ronnie Solbert. W. R. Scott, 1961. A truly meaningful story based on an old Taoist tale, in which an unknown country boy is delegated to choose a superlative horse for the Khan.

The qualities he must seek are such as might be sought in men and women as well as horses. I
780 Ritchie, Alice. Treasure of Li-Po. Ill. by T. Ritchie. Harcourt Brace, 1949. Six original folktales.
781 Thomas, Leslie. The Story on the Willow Plate. Ill. by the adapter. William Morrow, 1940. You will have to lick your own plate clean to find all the details of this story--if you have a willow plate. E, I
782 Treffinger, Carolyn. Li Lun, Lad of Courage. Ill. by Kurt Wiese. Abingdon, 1947. This story of a boy, who is called a coward because he feared the sea, is based on a legend about a mountainous island off the China coast where Li Lun is sent alone to plant seven grains of rice and told not to return from the top of the mountain until he has grown seven times as many grains. I
783 Wahl, Jan. The Wonderful Kite. Ill. by Uri Shulevitz. Delacorte Press, 1970 (a Seymour Lawrence Book). Ping Ling buys a magic kite, and hanging on to its tail he is carried off into fantastic adventures with strange companions: a dragon, an emperor, eagles, and the man in the moon. The graceful and colorful pictures are rooted in Chinese art and tradition. E, I
784 Wyndham, Robert (Hyndman). Tales the People Tell in China. Ill. by Jan Yang. Julian Messner, 1971. A collection of folklore, with notes on sources, which merits the attention of serious students of Chinese culture. One, in particular, has been adapted for propaganda purposes by the Peking government. I up

FICTION

785 Anderson, Joy. The Pai-Pai Pig. Ill. by Jay Yang. Harcourt Brace and World, 1967. A most amusing story of two Taiwan boys, Su-ling and Yang-yang, competing for the prize money for the fattest pig to be presented at the annual pai-pai festival. Su-ling would not let anyone see his pig during the fattening process, so there was great suspense when the big day arrived. The story is also told by the detailed pen and ink drawings of the young Chinese artist, Jay Yang, who lives on Taiwan. E, I
786 Andrews, Roy Chapman. Quest in the Desert. Ill. by Kurt Wiese. Viking Press, 1950 (Junior Literary

Guild). A thrilling novel of the Gobi desert in Mongolia, based on the author's actual experiences when he spent ten years exploring central Asia for the American Museum of History. One of the major characters in the story is Wolf, a dearly loved dog who accompanied him and to whose memory the book is dedicated. YA

787 _____. Quest of the Snow Leopard. Ill. by Kurt Wiese. Viking, 1955. An exciting fictional story of a real zoological expedition, made by Dr. Andrews in 1916-17, to the province of Yunnan in southwest China and to the Tibetan frontier. The natural history, the names of villages, and everything about the native tribesmen is true. Andrews killed a yellow tiger as his fictional character, Ken Lewis, does in the story, and all the adventures here narrated were experienced by him or friends of his, except for the actual trapping of the snow leopard. YA

788 Baumann, Hans. Sons of the Steppe. Oxford Press, 1958. A long novel, rich in details of Mongol life under Genghis Khan in the 13th century, about two "inseparable" brothers, Kublai and Arik Buka, gradually growing apart as Kublai turns away from savagery and battles and Arik considers him a traitor because of his pacifism. The chronological table at the end is helpful for all books about the great days of the Mongols. YA up

789 Bro, Margueritte. The Animal Friends of Peng-U. Ill. by Seong May. Doubleday, 1965. A fantasy about how a fox, a rooster and two hens helped poor kindly, unselfish Peng-U acquire a son. E, I

790 _____. Su-Mei's Golden Year. Ill. by Kurt Wiese. Doubleday, 1950. Twelve-year-old Su-Mei, living in a Chinese village devastated by the Japanese in 1940, tries to prove that her father's modern ideas for saving their wheat from blight is better than the old superstitious ones about "black devils." I

791 Buck, Pearl S. The Good Earth. John Day, 1931 (Pocket Book, 1974). A Pulitzer Prize novel and modern classic, telling in prose with a Biblical rhythm, the life story of a simple Chinese farmer who rises to become a wealthy landowner but is never truly at ease far from the soil. A

792 _____. The Three Daughters of Madame Liang; A Novel of China Today. John Day, 1969 (Pocket Book, 1974). It is interesting to read this much later novel by Pearl Buck (who died in 1973) soon after reading,

or rereading, The Good Earth, published nearly 40 years earlier, for in the character of Madame Liang, and her attitude toward the new China, one senses something of the character and attitudes of Mrs. Buck herself. Madame L., a revolutionist in her youth, in later years regrets the changes brought about by the revolution and sends her three daughters to America to be educated in a free atmosphere. Fearful about their futures if they return to Mao's China, she nevertheless longs to see them. Two do return, though for different reasons, and with different reactions to Communist control and suppression of individualism. A

793 _____. The Water Buffalo Children and the Dragon Fish. Ill. by William A. Smith. John Day, 1943-44 (Dell Yearling Book, 1966). Two short stories about the relationship of Chinese and American children in missionary circles before World War II. E, I

794 Byrne, Donn. Messer Marco Polo. Ill. by C. B. Falls. Century, 1921. A poetic, imaginative little novel about Marco Polo's romance, at the court of Kublai Khan, with little Golden Bells. Pure fiction. A

795 Carlson, Dale. The Beggar King of China. Ill. by John Gretzer. Atheneum, 1971. A biographical novel about Chu Yan-chang, the son of a poor farmer who became leader of some rebel bandits called the Red Turbans and finally, in 1368, Emperor of all China. Written with humor and excellent characterizations, it may also increase our understanding of modern China, and particularly Mao's "Long March" and his belief in the importance of the peasants. YA up

796 _____. The Mountain of Truth. Ill. by Charles Robinson. Atheneum, 1972. A mystical, futuristic novel of the "Order of the Children of the Mountain of Truth," a book which will either turn a reader on or off immediately, according to his taste for fantasy and mysticism. The story takes place in Tibet in a future time when the Chinese have given up and gone home and the Dalai Lama has been restored. YA

797 Cavanna, Betty. Lo Chau of Hong Kong. Ill. with photographs by George Russell Harrison. Franklin Watts, 1963. Through the experience of a little boat-dweller who finds a treasure in the aftermath of a typhoon, we learn much about the British Crown Colony of Hong Kong. I

798 Cheney, Cora. The Treasures of Lin Li-Ti. Ill. by Marvin Besunder. Hawthorne, 1969. A young Chinese boy, separated from his family during the evacuation of Chinese from Communist China to Formosa (Taiwan), and lost in the hordes of Chinese seeking refuge on the island, is taken in by some kindly priests and almost commits himself to the priesthood, but hopes of finding his family and the wish to be a scholar send him back out into the streets to beg. Fiction but based on real events. I, YA

799 Cordell, Alexander. The Traitor Within. Ill. by Victor Ambrus. Thomas Nelson, 1973. A novel of Red China in the 1940s in which 15-year-old Chau Wai Ling confides in Bigba, a water buffalo whom he counts as his best friend, that he really is a coward although he has received a medal for bravery in the Red Guard Boys' Battalion. Suffering from a wound received from a Nationalist Chinese air attack on the commune where he lives, he suffers even more deeply from the taunts of his school and battalion mates who insist that his father, reported missing and probably dead, has actually defected to Chiang Kai-shek. With a blend of humor and sadness tension builds up as the commune awaits another attack from the Nationalist air force. Is Ling's father truly a traitor? Or is the real traitor Ling's own fear? Only Bigba the water buffalo knows the answers. YA

800 Costain, Thomas B. The Black Rose. Doubleday, 1945. First Avon paperback printing, 1973. An historical novel in the grand tradition, long, picaresque and romantic, beginning and ending in England but most of the action taking place in central Asia and China in the time of Kublai Khan. A

801 David, Kurt. Black Wolf of the Steppes. Ill. by Hans Baltzer. Tr. from German by Anthea Bell. Houghton Mifflin, 1972. A novel of warfare on the steppes of Mongolia in the early 13th century and about the development of Temujin into the famous Genghis Khan as observed by his boyhood friend, Black Wolf. YA up

802 Dejong, Meindert. The House of Sixty Fathers. Ill. by Maurice Sendak. Harper, 1956. This suspenseful story of a small Chinese boy and his beloved pig, carried away from his family while asleep in their sampan, into Japanese occupied territory and trying to find his way back without detection by Japanese soldiers, is based on a true event. The author was

one of the "sixty fathers." I up
803 Evarts, Hal G. Mission to Tibet. Scribner's, 1970.
The historical background of this thrilling novel is
factual, but the characters and incidents are fictional. The time setting is 1948 when the Communists
were driving the Nationalists out of mainland China.
A U.S. Air Force plane is lost in far-western China
and one of its passengers was a V.I.P. scientist
possessed of atomic information that would be of
great value to the Chinese. The fate of these flyers
never comes to light, and four Americans set out to
learn it and to try to rescue any survivors, especially the atomic scientist. YA up
804 Flack, Marjorie. The Story About Ping. Ill. by Kurt
Wiese. Viking Press, 1965. An ever popular story
about a little duckling's adventures on the Yangtze
River. A good one for first-graders to read aloud
to kindergarten brothers and sisters. E
805 Fukei, Arlene. East to Freedom. Westminster, 1964.
A tense novel of the Communist takeover of China,
about a young girl trying to adjust to the resulting
changes. Even her fiancé accepts the Marxist faith
of Mao and the necessity for brutality in support of
that faith. Mei-lin strives to "go along" with him,
but finally, revolted by the lack of freedom, makes
her escape to Formosa. YA up
806 Hersey, John. A Single Pebble. Alfred A. Knopf,
1956. A deceptively simple short novel about a
young American engineer's trip by junk, up the
Yangtze River in the early 1920s, a slow hazardous
journey during which the once self-confident young
man becomes more and more bewildered by the contrast between the age-old patience and superstitions
of the Chinese "trackmen" and his own native reliance
on progress and technology. A
807 Hobart, Alice Tisdale. Oil for the Lamps of China.
Bobbs-Merrill, 1933; Pyramid Books edition, 1963.
A long novel, in three parts, of early 20th century
China (and Mongolia) after the downfall of the Manchu
dynasty. Stephen Chase, a young American employee,
and a cog in the machinery of a giant oil company,
struggles to maintain his individuality and dignity in
the dehumanizing organization that also threatens his
marriage. The cover of the Pyramid paperback is
misleadingly lurid for this is not the story of a Don
Juan but of a sensitive, idealistic young Puritan imbued with the American work ethic while recognizing

the values of a changing China. A

808 _____. Yang and Yin. Bobbs-Merrill, 1936. This follows Oil for the Lamps of China and, like it, is the story of opposing cultural values, here affecting a young American doctor in China, his medical career, and his marriage. Yin, in Chinese philosophy, the negative, dark and feminine principal, and Yang, the positive, bright and masculine one, symbolize the problems of understanding between husband and wife and between old and new cultures. A

809 Holland, Cecelia. Ghost on the Steppe. Ill. by Richard Cuffari. Atheneum, 1969. As a punishment for lying to his father, young Djela, a Mongolian prince, is sent off to a far north station for a month of herding the family flocks of horses and cattle. The camp is on the fringes of a deep forest, thought by the natives to be haunted by a great white beast which kills stray cattle, screaming wildly as it does so. Djela thinks it is a real creature but is not too sure, as he sets out with great trepidation, but also with the courage of his ancestor, Genghis Khan, to seek and destroy whatever the "thing" may turn out to be. I, YA

810 Hsiao, Ellen. A Chinese Year. Ill. by the author. M. Evans, 1970 (dist. J. B. Lippincott) (a Two Worlds Book). An autobiographic story about a year in the author's childhood which she and her little brother spent visiting their grandfather in Cheng-Chiang after their grandmother's death. Their experiences include going through the funeral rites, celebrating New Year, worshipping their ancestors and learning to know a new school and different children before returning to Nanking. I

811 Huggins, Alice Margaret. The Red Chair Waits. Ill. by Jeanyee Wong. Westminster, 1948. A realistic novel of 1948 China, and the beginning of the youth movement, with an appealing love story. Shu-lan, a young school teacher rebels against the marriage arranged by her parents and a go-between, and refuses to marry the young man whose "red chair waits." YA

812 Kent, Louise Andrews. He Went with Marco Polo. Ill. by Leroy Baldridge and Paul Quinn. Houghton Mifflin, 1935. As in her other "He Went With" books, Mrs. Kent has constructed a good story about the adventures of a young fictional companion of Marco Polo in his 13th century travels. I, YA

China and Neighbors

813 Lattimore, Eleanor Frances. The Chinese Daughter.
Ill. by the author (as are all the books listed below).
William Morrow, 1960. The story of a little Chinese
girl, adopted by missionaries in North China in the
first quarter or so of the 20th century, and the choice
she finally had to make between her real parents and
those by adoption. E, I

814 ———. The Fisherman's Son. Morrow Junior Books,
1948 and '59. The story of small Liang, the only
son of a Chinese fisherman who lived with his parents and three sisters on a river houseboat; about
how he learned to cast a net and how he rescued one
of his little sisters from the river. E, I

815 ———. The Journey of Ching Lai. Morrow Jr.
Books, 1957. Ching Lai didn't think he was stealing the black donkey he found standing loose at the
foot of the long steps up to the White Cloud Temple.
And truly he didn't; he merely climbed on its back
and the donkey stole him and carried him off on an
exciting journey. E

816 ———. Little Pear. Harcourt Brace and World,
1931. The story of a farmer's little son in the early
20th century. Little Pear tried very hard to be good
but not quite hard enough because he was so curious
and independent. E, I

817 ———. Little Pear and His Friends. Harcourt
Brace, 1934. The further adventures and misadventures of Little Pear, the small boy with the shaven
head except for a spot of hair tied up in a little pigtail. He lived in the village of Shegu, in the China
of 50 years ago. E, I

818 ———. Little Pear and the Rabbits. William Morrow, 1956. How Little Pear finds a way to buy a
very small donkey. E

819 ———. The Little Tumbler. William Morrow, 1963.
This story has a mystery plot in addition to the usual
delightful description of Chinese life in the early days
of the century. What was the mystery concerning
"Ba"? And what did the paper say--the paper he
carried in his shoe? E, I

820 ———. More About Little Pear. William Morrow,
1971. Another book about the little Chinese boy of
50 years ago, now grown to the age of seven and so
able to get into more mischief than ever. E, I

821 ———. Peachblossom. Harcourt Brace and World,
1943. The story of a little girl who has to move
from place to place because of the Japanese bombers,

and who carries with her everywhere she goes a precious doll that plays an important part in her life. E, I

822 ―――. The Questions of Lifu. Harcourt Brace, 1942. A story of World War II and a little boy who runs away to find his soldier father, but finds a little sister instead. E

823 ―――. Three Little Chinese Girls. William Morrow, 1948, 7th printing, 1963. Jasmine was the youngest of the three sisters and the most troublesome, but Young Tiger, visiting his aunt next door, chose to give her the best New Year's present. A pleasant picture of middle-class town life in the early 20th century. E

824 ―――. Willow Tree Village. Morrow Junior Books, 1955. When little Mimosa changed clothes with her nurse's little girl and ran away to the city she didn't realize how much anxiety she was going to cause her parents and her nurse who was responsible for losing her. And lost she was for quite a while until she came to Willow Tree Village. E

825 Lewis, Elizabeth Foreman. To Beat a Tiger. Holt Rinehart and Winston, 1962. A novel of 16 boys banding together in their struggle for survival in the International Settlement of Shanghai in the late 1930s, sharing hunger, cold, and constant danger from Japanese invasion. The title comes from an old proverb: "To beat a tiger one needs a Brother's help." Forced to steal and plunder, they nevertheless keep hoping for a day when they can find honest work. YA

826 ―――. Young Fu of the Upper Yangtze (John C. Winston, 1932). Ill. by Kurt Wiese. Special 40th anniv. ed., Holt Rinehart and Winston, 1972, with new drawings by Ed Young and revised background notes and introduction by Pearl Buck. Newbery Prize novel for 1932. A young country boy is apprenticed to a coppersmith in Chungking. As he learns the craft he also grows in wisdom through dangerous and exciting experiences and through his contacts with various people, such as his tart but kindly employer who teaches him to read and write, and a "barbarian" foreigner and especially his fellow workers. A glossary and background notes are appended. I, YA

827 Lewis, Thomas P. The Dragon Kite. Ill. by Errol Le-Cain. Holt Rinehart and Winston, 1974. A little Tibetan boy visits the city on his eighth birthday, to

China and Neighbors

see the huge dragon kite flown by the monks in the monastery, and decides to stay and become a monk. E

828 Liu, Beatrice. Little Wu and the Watermelons. Ill. by Graham Peck. Follett, 1954. The story, set in southwest China around 1942, is about a 10-year-old boy of an ancient tribe who wants very much to buy some sort of jewelry for his mother and finally earns enough money to do so, but comes to realize that there is something his mother wants more than jewelry. E, I

829 Mühleweg, Fritz. Big Tiger and Christian. Ill. by Rafaello Busoni, tr. by Isabel and Florence McHugh. Pantheon, 1961. A long humorous adventure story about a Chinese boy and his western friend accidentally caught up in the "generals' wars" of 1922 and sent on a mission across the Gobi desert. Included is a map of their travels and a glossary of foreign expressions and Mongolian words, also explained in footnotes as they occur in the text. YA

830 Polland, Madeleine. Mission to Cathay. Ill. by Peter Landa. Doubleday, 1965. A novel about an actual Jesuit missionary of the late 16th century, Father Matteo Ricci, who built the first Christian mission in China. The plot involves a small boy whom the priest befriends and the daughter of a wealthy mandarin who, in trying to escape a revolting marriage, endangers the boy's life and Father Ricci's mission. I, YA

831 Rankin, Louise. Daughter of the Mountains. Ill. by Kurt Wiese. Viking, 1948. When 10-year-old Momo acquires a valuable red-gold terrier puppy from Lhasa, an astrologer tells her that it will bring her adventure and good fortune. His predictions come true when, in another year, the dog is stolen from her by a wool trader passing through her village on the Jelep La Pass of Tibet, on his way to Calcutta. As soon as Momo learns of the theft she sets off in pursuit of the wool merchant, and the reader follows her breathlessly over the mountain route, down through Sikkim to Calcutta. Vivid descriptions of the mountain passes and the view of "turquoise India" from above, and a well-made plot make this book a memorable reading adventure. I

832 Reiss, Malcolm. China Boat Boy. Ill. by Jeanyee Wong. J. B. Lippincott, 1954. Set in China near the Burmese and Tibetan borders, this is a mystery

story centering on a silver cormorant called "Precious Grief" in the possession of the Tien family. Why does Teng of the Buzzards desire that particular cormorant so intensely? And what is Scarface the smuggler planning to do? A dull title for an exciting book. I, YA

833 Ritchie, Rita. The Golden Hawks of Genghis Khan. Ill. by Lorence Bjorklund. E. P. Dutton, 1958. A mystery novel of high adventure and falconry in Karakorum and the surrounding lands of the Khan of Khans in 1218. The story begins with young Jalair running away from his grandfather in Samarkand to recover the golden hawks which he believes were stolen from his father, Darian. Why are the Mongols so anxious to capture Jalair? What is the meaning of the hawk and thunderbolt design? Who is Torgul? And where, in the end, does Jalair's primary loyalty lie? YA up

834 ———. Secret Beyond the Mountains. E. P. Dutton, 1960. A novel set in Mongolia and Tibet in the early 13th century. The mystery in this book centers on a strange black and white beast which is considered by many of the Khan's hunters to be an evil spirit. To prove its material reality, Genghis Khan allows a young warrior to travel to Tibet. Especially interesting are details of life in the Khan's court and the great Mogul hunt, lasting two months, and the entertainments provided the hunters during their rest periods. The bibliography shows extensive research. YA up

835 ———. The Year of the Horse. Ill. by Lorence F. Bjorklund. E. P. Dutton, 1957. The story of perilously exciting adventures of a Mongol boy in Mongolia in 1211, as he tries to clear his dead father's name of the unjust accusation of treachery. YA up

836 Sherer, Mary Huston. Ho Fills the Rice Barrel. Ill. by Marion Greenwood. Follett, 1957. Young Ho, age 12, lives with his family on the camphor plateau of Formosa and goes, with his father, to Taipei with loads of camphor for shipment to the United States. Even in the mid 20th century, after the Japanese had left the island, there were still some headhunters in the deep wild forest near the Han's little hut, so the journey to Taipei provides dangers aplenty. I

837 Slobodkin, Louis. Moon Blossom and the Golden Penny. Ill. by the author. Vanguard, 1963. A happy story

China and Neighbors

about a little girl and a miraculous penny. Or <u>was</u> it miraculous? Was it even really golden? E

838 Todd, Ruthven. <u>Tan's Fish.</u> Ill. by Theresa Sherman. Little Brown, 1958. Tan, a little boy living in Canton, collects tropical fish and one day is thrilled to find an entirely new one, but when his discovery becomes known, people flock to the site of his discovery and take out so many of "Tan's fish" that he fears they will be exterminated. E

839 Weiss-Sonnenburg, Hedwig. <u>Plum Blossom and Kai Lin.</u> Ill. by the author. Franklin Watts, 1960. A love story, set in China shortly after the fall of the Manchu dynasty in 1911, a turbulent time of conflict between the government and guerrilla bands. Plum Blossom is the daughter of a farmer so poor (and constantly being robbed of what little he has by wandering soldiers) that he and her mother sell her to the head wife of the house of Wang where she meets the spoiled son of the family, Kai Lin. Spoiled at first to be sure but after he has been to an American school, he changes his ways and tries to change Plum Blossom's too. YA

840 Wood, Esther. <u>Silk and Satin Lane.</u> Ill. by Kurt Wiese. David McKay, 1963. First published in 1939, this lovely story of a little Chinese tomboy whose misadventures frequently turn out for the best has understandably had many printings. It is set in the ancient city of Shaoling in the early 20th century when little girls were not considered of much value. E

841 Wu, K. C. <u>The Lane of Eternal Stability.</u> A long historical novel about three generations of the House of Ho in the turbulent years from the Boxer Rebellion in 1900 to the Communist takeover in 1950, written by a Chinese author, once secretary to Chiang Kai-shek and governor of Formosa, who broke with Chiang and emigrated to the United States in 1953. An inside view of the transition of "the Lane of Eternal Stability" to its new name of Lenin Lane. Endpaper map. A

JAPAN AND KOREA

The books listed here are about two Japans and two

Koreas. Japan is divided in a time sense: the country before its emergence from isolation in the mid-19th century and as part of the world community. Korea is divided geographically and politically into North Korea and South Korea.

NON-FICTION

842 Appel, Benjamin. Why the Japanese Are the Way They Are. Maps by Samuel H. Bryant. Little Brown, 1973. A revealing account of Japan's history and way of life and the mystique of the Japanese--their conflict between two spirits: the way of the Warrior, the "giri," and the way of human sensitivity, the "ninjo." YA

843 Behn, Harry. Cricket Songs: Japanese Haiku. Ill. with pictures selected from Sesshu and Other Japanese masters. Harcourt Brace and World, 1964. It would be a beautiful little book to own. All ages

844 Bellerophon Press. A Coloring Book of Japan. 1971. A unique way to study the history of Japanese art, going back to the 7th century. The coloring would not be easy, but the pictures of the famous actors of Japan and drawings of scrolls and scenes are exciting and informative. Any age

845 Bird, Isabella L. Unbeaten Tracks in Japan; An Account of Travels in the Interior, Including Visits to the Aborigines of Yezo and the Shrine of Nikko. (1st pub., G. P. Putnam, 1880). Ill. with only three exceptions, by engravings of the author's sketches and Japanese photographs. Charles E. Tuttle, 1973. With an introduction by Terrence Barrow, Ph.D. A travel book in the form of letters to her sister in England by a courageous lady of 47, written in 1878, not very long after Japan had been opened to westerners. Imagine a frail middle-aged Victorian lady traveling alone through many places where no white person had ever been seen, enduring a variety of hardships which would have daunted a strong young man. And Miss Bird claimed she was traveling for her health! A

846 Buell, Hal. Festivals of Japan. Ill. with photographs. Dodd Mead, 1965. Japan is a land of festivals combining religion, history and legend. It would be great to be able to visit Japan at some of these festival times, but the next best thing is a book like this. I up

Japan and Korea

847 Carr, Rachel. The Picture Story of Japan. Ill. by Kazue Mizumura. David McKay, 1962. From the title you might think this just a picture book, but in addition to the rich illustrations, the text is updated and informative, and there is a list of the rulers of Japan in an appendix. I up

848 Dilts, Marion May. The Pageant of Japanese History, 3d ed. Ill. by photogravures from Japanese art, and drawings by Toyojiro Onishi. David McKay, 1961. First published in 1938, this updated history provides an absorbing and rewarding reading experience. Appended are outline charts of cultural history and governmental periods, copious chapter notes, a glossary and dictionary of Japanese proper names and index. YA up

849 ———. Two Japans. Ill. with photographs. David McKay, 1963. Half of this book is about Japan's emergence from isolation and the latter half is about Japan in the world community. A unique feature is a chapter called "A Challenge to Christianity," which discusses the many religious traditions and forms in Japan, and the growing ecumenicalism. YA up

850 Edelman, Lily. Japan in Story and Pictures. Ill. with photographs. Harcourt, Brace, 1953. A good, brief introduction to both rural and city life in Japan (as of 20 odd years ago). E, I

851 Evans, M. Fulmer. The Land and People of Korea. Ill. with 25 photographs by the author and a map. Macmillan, 1962 (repr. with correct., 1968). "Chosen, The Land of Morning Calm" is the beautiful name the Koreans give their country. An outstanding feature of this book is the appendix; How to Reach Korea--the Currency--Music--Religion--Education--Travel--National Day--Geography--Agricultural Products. YA up

852 Gidal, Sonia and Tim. My Village in Korea. Photographs by Tim Gidal. Pantheon, 1968. At the beginning of each of the "My Village" books is a two-page map drawing of the village visited and its immediate environs. Here we visit young Hong Sung-je who shared with us his daily life in his small village, thirty miles south of Seoul. Appended are a map of all Korea, and a postscript giving a short history, and a glossary. I

853 Glubok, Shirley. The Art of Japan. Designed by Gerard Nook. Special photography by Alfred Tamarin.

Macmillan, 1970. The well-chosen reproductions exemplify the spirit of Japanese art, and the simple, instructive text occupies the same page or opposing one as the illustration. I up

854 Icenhower, Joseph B. Perry and the Open Door to Japan, July, 1853; An American Commander Ends Centuries of Japanese Occupation. Ill. with reproductions of paintings and a map of Perry's route. Franklin Watts, 1973 (a World Focus Book). A short concise story of the great "opening" giving at the end of the text of the Treaty of Kanagawa. Bibliography and index. I up

855 Kirk, Ruth. Japan, Crossroads of East and West. Ill. with photographs by Bob and Ira Spring. Thomas Nelson, 1966. An excellent coverage of Japanese history and way of life, with a bibliography, list of United States-Japan sister cities, a chronology, and basic facts on geography, government, economy and the Japanese language. YA up

856 Kuhn, Ferdinand. Commodore Perry and the Opening of Japan. Ill. by J. Graham Kaye. Random House Landmark, 1953. The story of the events of 1853 vividly and entertainingly told and illustrated. I, YA

857 Lewis, Richard. The Moment of Wonder; A Collection of Chinese and Japanese Poetry. Ill. by Chinese and Japanese Masters. A fine anthology with an editorial preface about Oriental poetry in general and the Haiku form in particular. An author index appended. (Also noted under China.) YA up

858 _____. The Way of Silence, The Prose and Poetry of Basho. Ill. with photography by Helen Buttfield. Dial, 1970. An exquisite book, combining biography, poetry and photography in such a way as to give the reader a sensing, as he reads, of "the way of silence." I up

859 Lifton, Betty Jean. Return to Hiroshima. Photographs by Eikoh Hosoe. Atheneum, 1970. Each page of this tragic book has on it one or more photographs, some showing the horrors of the bomb, some showing the city today, and many showing survivors of August 6th, 1945, while the text points up, page after page, the lesson of Hiroshima:
"Of the old, have they forgotten?
Of the Young do they remember?
Of the wounded, have they healed?" I up

860 Mears, Helen. The First Book of Japan. Ill. by Kathleen Elgin. Franklin Watts, 1953. Since the publi-

cation of this charmingly illustrated book, Japan has progressed so fast and far industrially that the last chapter, "Today in Japan," had best be ignored. Otherwise it is an enjoyable picture of what still remains of traditional Japan. E, I

861 Merrill, Jean and Solbert Ronni. A Few Flies and I, Haiku by Issa (Kobayashi). Ill. by Ronni Solbert, tr. by R. H. Blyth and Nobuyuki Yuasa. Pantheon, 1969. A selection of these very short poems about very small things and creatures, by the Japanese poet, Issa, born in 1763. All ages

862 Morton, W. Scott. The Japanese; How They Live and Work. Ill. with photographs and a map. Praeger, 1973. An excellent summary of Japanese history, religions, art and the present-day government, industry and foreign relations. A practical reference book on Japan, splendidly organized and readable. Invaluable for prospective visitors to Japan. YA up

863 Neurath, Marie. They Lived Like This in Old Japan. Ill. by Evelyn Worboys of the Isotype Institute. Franklin Watts, 1966. All about the olden days in Japan, beautifully depicted. I

864 Prechtl, Louise Boylston. Come Along to Japan. Ill. with photographs by James Rovert Prechta. T. S. Denison, Minneapolis, 1962. A trip to Japan without leaving your favorite reading corner. I

865 Reynolds, Robert L. and the Editors of American Heritage. Commodore Perry in Japan. Ill. with paintings, prints, photographs and maps of the period. American Heritage, 1963. Consultant, Douglas MacArthur II. A colorful number in the American Heritage series with the story of Commodore Matthew Galbraith Perry's arrival in Japan in 1853, how he was received, and the consequences of his "opening the door." YA

866 Roberts, John G. Black Ships and Rising Sun: The Opening of Japan to the West. Ill. with photographs. Julian Messner, 1971. The American naval squadron steamed into the waters of Japan in 1853, but it was many years before Japan's acceptance of foreigners and her transformation into one of the world's great powers. Not an easy book to read because of the difficult (for Occidentals) Japanese names and the various conflicting factions there, but a careful reader will be well repaid by a clearer understanding of our one-time enemy and present competitor and friend. YA up

867 Schloat, G. Warren. Junichi, A Boy of Japan. Ill. with photographs. Alfred A. Knopf, 1964. This book with its diagrammatic drawing of Junichi's area will almost make you feel that you have visited Junichi in the city of Kamakura. I

868 Solberg, S. E. The Land and People of Korea, rev. ed. Ill. with photographs and a map. J. B. Lippincott, 1973. There are now, it seems, two Koreas: the Democratic People's Republic of Korea in the North, and the Republic of Korea in the South, with a demilitarized zone in between. The author explains very clearly and objectively the origins of the Korean War which ended in 1953, leaving the present division, but the book ends on a note of hope for a united country sometime in the future if only the big powers will keep out. YA up

869 Spencer, Cornelia (Yaukey). Made in Japan; The Story of a Country's Arts. Ill. by Richard Powers and with photographs. Alfred A. Knopf, 1963. With a backdrop of history as a first chapter the book is an introduction to the art of the Japanese and the unique quality of its beauty. I, YA

870 Taylor, Theodore. Air Raid--Pearl Harbor; The Story of December 7, 1941. Ill. by W. T. Mars. Thomas Y. Crowell, 1971. An exciting readable book, important because it is based on interviews with participants as well as written accounts, the scene shifting back and forth between Washington and Tokyo. I up

871 Vaughan, Josephine Budd. The Land and People of Japan, rev. ed. Ill. with photographs. J. B. Lippincott, 1962 (Portraits of the Nations Series). Included with chapters on the geography, daily life, arts and religion, are five chapters of history: the early history, the days of the shoguns, the period of isolation, the period of expansion, and the occupation by the allied forces. YA

872 Vining, Elizabeth Gray. Windows for the Crown Prince. Ill. with 16 pages of photographs. J. B. Lippincott, 1952. The personal story of an American Quaker's four years as private tutor to the Crown Prince of Japan, from 1946 to 1950, showing the great changes in the country after its defeat in World War II and at the same time showing the continuing emphasis of the Japanese on beauty and courtesy. Mrs. Vining opens windows for the Crown Prince but also for westerners from which to view Japan and its imperial

family. A
873 Watson, Jane Werner. Japan, Islands of the Rising Sun. Ill. with color art work and photographs and endsheet maps by James Bier. Garrard, 1968. A comprehensive and colorful book of historical and contemporary Japan, introducing some legendary material. The flower calendar is delightful. I

BIOGRAPHIES

874 D'Amelio, Dan. Taller Than Bandai Mountain; The Story of Hideyo Noguchi. Ill. by Fred Banbery. Viking, 1968. A fictionalized biography of a Japanese doctor (1876-1928) who overcame physical and financial handicaps to become an honored member of the Rockefeller Institute for Medical research in the United States. I, YA
875 Fukuda, Hanako. Wind in My Hand; The Story of Issa, Japanese Haiku Poet. Ill. by Lydia Cooley. Golden Gate Junior Books, 1970. The poet was born Yataro Kobayashi, in 1762, but for his haiku writing he used the name of Issa, meaning a cup of tea, for, as he said, his poems were simple things, as simple as a cup of tea. I up
876 Levine, I. E. Behind the Silken Curtain; The Story of Townsend Harris. Julian Messner, 1961. A biography (1804-1878) of the man who became the first U.S. consul general to Japan after the island country had been opened to trade with the outside world. The first part of the book deals with his youth when, being denied higher education, he managed to educate himself so thoroughly that he became a successful merchant and founded the College of the City of New York. However, the years spent in the Orient provided his greater claim to fame, and though his diplomatic achievements have not received the attention rightly due in the United States, there are still memorial shrines to him in Japan. YA up
877 Nakamoto, Hiroko. My Japan, as told to Mildred Mastin Pace. McGraw-Hill, 1970. The autobiography of a Japanese woman who was a young girl in Hiroshima at the time the atom bomb was dropped. She tells of her life working in a factory during World War II when she was often cold and hungry. Though she herself was badly burned and lost many friends and relatives in the holocaust, she tells her story

without bitterness. YA

878 Ripley, Elizabeth. Hokusai, A Biography. With 71 pages of illustrations. Lippincott, 1968. An art book and lively biography (1760-1849) of the Japanese painter and illustrator--which is as it should be, for he was a particularly lively and often amusing nonconformist, on whose gravestone (after the fifty names he had used at different times during his career) is engraved, "Old Man Mad About Painting." YA

879 Sugimoto, Etsu Inagaki. Daughter of the Samurai. Ill. by Tekesin Ishii, with an Introd. by Christopher Morley. Doubleday, Doran, 1925. The memoirs of a woman who was raised in the Samurai tradition in the late 19th century and who, after her early marriage, came to America and eventually became an instructor in Japanese language and history at Columbia University. A

880 Yoshida, Jim, with Hosokawa, Bill. The Two Worlds of Jim Yoshida. With a Foreword by Senator Daniel K. Inouye. William Morrow, 1972. An autobiography of a Nisei, forced to serve in the Japanese army in World War II and voluntarily serving in the American army in the Korean war. It is Jim's own account of his two war experiences, his difficulty in recovering American citizenship, and most significantly, his success in overcoming hatred for the Japanese who treated him brutally while he was in their army, and resentment against America, the land of his birth, for its treatment of the Nisei. YA, A

FOLKLORE

881 Bang, Garrett. Men from the Village Deep in the Mountains and Other Japanese Folk Tales. Tr. and ill. by Garrett Bang. Macmillan, 1973. Twelve varied stories, mainly humorous and some ecological in theme. E, I

882 Carpenter, Frances. People from the Sky; Ainu Tales from Northern Japan. Ill. by Betty Fraser. Doubleday, 1972. Frances Carpenter has an interesting individual way of presenting folklore (see her Tales of a Korean Grandmother, next), one which makes the reader feel that he or she is one of the children

listening to the original story-teller. Here it is the grandfather who tells the tales, never admitting that he doesn't believe them all. I

883 _____. Tales of a Korean Grandmother. Ill. with reproductions of old Korean paintings. Doubleday, 1947. As in her "Tales of a Chinese Grandmother" the old woman's folk stories are combined with a continuous series of events in the lives of the grandchildren. The colorful reproductions of old paintings are enchanting. I

884 Coatsworth, Elizabeth. The Cat Who Went to Heaven. Ill. by Lynd Ward. Macmillan, 1930 and 1958. A poor artist is commissioned to paint a picture of Buddha and relives the life of Buddha during his meditations. Into the picture go many incarnations of the Buddha in animal forms but never in the form of a cat, and the artist's cat, Good Fortune, feels very badly about this and so---. I

885 _____. Cricket and the Emperor's Son. Ill. by Juliette Palmer. W. W. Norton, 1962. Cricket, a silk merchant's poor apprentice so treasures the written word that he saves every scrap of paper he can find that has written characters on it. On one he discovers continually changing stories with which he entertains the sick son of the Emperor, to the benefit not only of the Prince but also of himself and his mother. I

886 Cocagnac, A. M. The Three Trees of the Samurai. Ill. by Alain deFoll. Harlin Quist, 1969 (a Here-and-There Book). Adapted from a Japanese "No" play about an aged and destitute Samurai who destroys his last three trees (symbols of his class) in order to build a fire to warm a pilgrim seeking refuge from the snowstorm. The make-up of the book, with its two page spread illustrations in strong colors and of large figures, gives an effect of stage sets, and the text is almost marginal. E up

887 Edmonds, I. G. The Case of the Marble Monster (orig. title, Ooka the Wise). Ill. by Sanae Yamazaki. Bobbs-Merrill, 1961 (Scholastic Books paperback, 1972). Ooka, the judge, is a combination of Sherlock Holmes and the Biblical King Solomon and this is his case book. I

888 _____ The Possible Impossibles of Ikkyu the Wise; Tales of a Japanese Hero. Ill. by Robert Byrd. Macrae Smith, 1971. Highly amusing stories retold, of a man who lived over 600 years ago and who felt

that the impossible is always possible if one has his
wits about him. I
889 Hodges, Margaret. The Wave. Ill. by Blair Lent.
Houghton Mifflin, 1964. Adapted from Lafcadio
Hearn's Gleanings in Buddha-Fields. A retelling of
a retelling of a folktale about an old man's sacrifice
to protect his fellow villagers from a coming tidal
wave. I
890 Jewett, Eleanore M. Which Was Witch; Tales of Ghosts
and Magic from Korea. Ill. by Taro Yashima. Viking, 1953. A delightful collection of 14 fairy tales,
ghost stories and folktales from Korea with notes on
sources. I, YA
891 Johnson, W. Ryerson. Gozo's Wonderful Kite. Ill. by
Lois Lignell. Thomas Y. Crowell, 1951. An original fantasy about a painting by a famous painter of
300 years ago. The picture was of five wild geese
flying, and when Gozo pasted it on his kite and flew
the kite, the leading goose flew right out of the picture. And that was not all that happened. E
892 Kirkup, James. The Magic Drum. Ill. by Vo-Dinh.
Knopf, 1973. A fantasy based on a classical Noh
drama, in which a little boy becomes part of his
drum. I
893 Lifton, Betty Jean. The Dwarf Pine Tree. Ill. by
Fuku Akino. Atheneum, 1963. A legend of how a
little pine tree, trained in the Japanese way, suffers
gladly to restore health to an ill princess. E, I
894 McAlpine, Helen and William. Japanese Tales and Legends. Ill. by Joan Kiddell-Monroe. Henry Z. Walck,
1959. Twenty-eight stories, epics, legends, folk and
fairy tales of Japan, with a glossary and a note on
"The Tales of the Heike," a famous Japanese epic
narrative of the 12th century. I, YA
895 Sakade, Florence. Japanese Childrens' Stories. Ill.
by Yoshio Hayashi. Charles E. Tuttle, 1959. In
this collection are 15 Japanese traditional stories and
also two original stories by a contemporary Japanese
writer of childrens' stories, Hirosuke Hamada. E,
I
896 Stamm, Claus. Three Strong Women; A Tall Tale from
Japan. Ill. by Kazue Mizumura. Viking, 1962. A
funny story, delightfully retold and illustrated, of a
young man who, on his way to wrestle before the emperor, comes up against a girl who is stronger than
he is. Attention, women liberationists. E, I
897 Uchida, Yoshiko. The Dancing Kettle and Other Japanese

Folk Tales. Ill. by Richard C. Jones. Harcourt Brace, 1949. Fourteen fairy and folk tales, some long unavailable and some hitherto unknown, with the Japanese sources given for each story. Glossary appended. I

898 _____. The Magic Listening Cap; More Folk Tales from Japan. Ill. by Kazue Mizumura. Harcourt Brace, 1955. Fourteen folk tales related with humor and charm and exhibiting elements of folklore from other lands. E, I

899 _____. Rakubei and the Thousand Rice Bowls. Ill. by Kazue Mitzumura. Scribner's, 1962. A humorously, delightfully illustrated (as is always the case with this illustrator) tale of what happened when a farmer and his family were taken from their home to live in luxury in the household of a great lord. E

900 _____. The Sea of Gold and Other Tales from Japan. Ill. by Marianne Yamaguchi. Scribner's, 1965. Twelve Japanese folk tales, covering a wide range of subjects, charmingly illustrated in charcoal drawings, usually divided into three panels, each showing separate parts of the story. I

901 Yamaguchi, Tohr. The Golden Crane; A Japanese Folktale. Ill. by Marianne Yamaguchi. Holt Rinehart and Winston, 1963. The author's note about the setting and circumstances in which he heard this story is a tale in itself. I

FICTION

902 Anderson, Paul. Yong Kee of Korea. Ill. by Yong Hwan Kim. Young Scott, 1959. How Yong Kee, who was only eight years old when he first begged to go with his father to gather grass on the mountain, had to wait until he was nine to understand that it is the way we act that makes wishes come true. E

903 Breck, Vivian. The Two Worlds of Noriko. Doubleday, 1966. Noriko, a Nisei, adopted daughter of an elderly Japanese couple, is in love with a young dental student Ken she met at the University of Californis in Berkeley. As a commencement present she is given an unwelcome gift from her foster parents: a two-week tour of Japan and then a three-month visit to their old home in the country. Not

too sure of Ken's love for her, she is reluctant to leave home but equally reluctant to disappoint the old people who have been so kind to her, and so she leaves for Japan. The novel is a love story and a "generation gap" story, but principally the story of Noriko's inner conflict, caused by her Japanese inheritance and her American ideal of personal freedom. YA up

904 Bruckner, Karl. The Day of the Bomb. Tr. from German by Frances Lobb. Van Nostrand, 1961. This book won the Austrian National Prize for 1961. A mistitled semi-fictional story of the after effects of the bomb on Sadako Sasaki and her brother who, as little children, survived the blast, only to succumb to its effect ten years later. YA

905 Buck, Pearl. The Big Wave. Ill. with prints by Hiroshige and Hokusai. John Day, 1948. This small classic is about life and death and the dangers two Japanese boys face: one, that of the sea, and the other, that of a threatening volcano, and how it is only with courage that one is truly alive. This book will appeal to older children and young adults because of the depth of meaning in the story itself and also because of the pictures by the two famous artists: Hokusai who lived between 1760 and 1849, and Hiroshige, 1797 to 1858. I up

906 _____. Matthew, Mark, Luke and John. Ill. by Mamoru Funai. John Day, 1966. A touching story of four Korean orphans, deserted by their American soldier fathers and their Korean mothers who were ashamed of them. I

907 Cavanna, Betty. Noko of Japan. Ill. with photographs by George Russell. Franklin Watts, 1964. Noko, at 12, wishes she were a boy, but finally comes to the conclusion that she can be feminine and skilled in the arts of flower arranging and tea service, and at the same time, develop her mind. Some may disagree with the thesis, but anyone can enjoy the pictures and stories of Noko's sightseeing trips. I

908 Clark, Roger W. Ride the White Tiger. Ill. by Kim. Little Brown, 1959. In the main, a true story of a young Korean whose father was captured early in the war by the North Korean Communists, who then rescued his mother, her new baby and his small brother from the bombing of Seoul, and then went back to join the army in regaining Seoul. The Korean lad is fictional, but what happens to him in the story hap-

pened, in many cases, to Kim, the illustrator of this exciting novel. I, YA

909 Crockett, Lucy Herndon. Pong Choolie, You Rascal. Ill. by the author. Holt, 1951. A different sort of war story, depicting the dire confusion of nationalities fighting in North Korea in the early 1950s: Chinese, Russians, Americans and, frequently, North Koreans themselves. Pong Choolie was South Korean born, but has lived in the north for five of his 12 years. He is sent to the Manchurian border with a message for the Russian command there (a message about the arrogant demands by the newly arrived Chinese Communist army upon the North Korean People's Militia) and is beset by dangers on every side. Captured by the Chinese, he is forced to spy on American prisoners. In the end he is considered a traitor by every nationality except for some Americans whom he saves from a Communist ambush. YA

910 Dobrin, Arnold. Taro and the Turtles; A Tale of Japan. Ill. by the author. Coward McCann, 1966. The story of a little island boy who deeply longs to earn enough money to rebuild the statue of Amida Buddha in their village temple. E, I

911 Fleming, Elizabeth P. Gift from the Mikado. Ill. by Janet Smalley. Westminster, 1958. A charming, happy story of an American family in turn-of-the-century Japan who own a gift given by the Mikado to their father because of his work as a teacher in the Imperial University. The book is based on experiences of the author, whose father was a teacher in the Imperial University at that time. I

912 Gray, Elizabeth Janet. The Cheerful Heart. Ill. by Kazue Mizumura. Viking, 1959. As soon as "the company" could build a new home for them in ruined Tokyo, the Tamakis moved back from their uncle's big farmhouse in the country where they had stayed during the war. But the new home was little more than a shack, and 11-year-old Tomi dearly wished for a room of her own and a family bath instead of a public one. Post-war life in Tokyo, even for middle-class people, was not easy, but Tomi's cheerful heart carried her through until the city began to recover. I

913 Ishii, Momoko. Dolls' Day for Yoshiko. Ill. by Mamoru Funai. Follett, 1966. A poignant story of a little girl who yearns for a set of O-hina dolls for Girls' Dolls Day. Her great-grandmother's set of

carved ones had been burned during an air raid, and
her widowed mother could not bear to buy the cheap,
mass-produced ones that Yoshiko admired in the department store window. A story about artistic integrity and a lovely mother-daughter relationship.
E, I

914 Johnson, Doris. Su An. Ill. by Leonard Weisgard.
Follett, 1968. A narrative in haiku form about a
little Korean orphan about to be adopted by an American family and her thoughts as she prepares to meet
her new American mother. E, I

915 Kim, Richard. Lost Names: Scenes from a Korean
Boyhood. Praeger, 1970. Seven scenes, each a
self-contained drama, in the life of a Korean family
during the years of Japanese occupation, 1932-45,
when the Koreans were compelled to give up their
own names and language and adopt Japanese names
and speech. A story of terrifying brutality on the
part of the Japanese and heroism on that of the Koreans. YA up

916 Kim Yong-Ik. Blue in the Seed. Ill. by Artur Marokvia. Little Brown, 1964. The story of a Korean
boy who was "different" because of his blue eyes
and how he learned to accept this. I

917 ———. The Happy Days. Ill. by Artur Marokvia.
Little Brown, 1960. Sang Chin, an orphan, comes
to live with his grandfather and uncle in a small
Korean village during the war years in the early
1950s and makes a close friend of his cousin. The
story is about their boyhood pranks and the sacrifices entailed in building a school. E, I

918 Lattimore, Eleanore Frances. Happiness for Kimi.
Ill. by the author. Morrow Jr. Books, 1958. The
story, first, of a little Japanese girl who, when her
family moves to the modern city, is left with her
old-fashioned great-aunt in an old-fashioned village
where the past dominates the present, and second,
how she comes to realize that one can appreciate
and even like old things and old ways but new things
and new ways too. E, I

919 Lewis, Janet. Keiko's Bubble. Ill. by Kazue Mizumura. Doubleday, 1961. A tender little story about
a small girl whose father gives her, instead of the
usual doll for Girls' Doll Day, a beautiful bubble,
the kind fishermen use to make the edges of their
nets stay above water. Keiko lends it to her fisherman father with remarkable consequences. E

Japan and Korea

920 Lewis, Mildred. The Honorable Sword. Ill. by Panos Chikas. Houghton Mifflin, 1960. A historical novel about Taro, the last of the Damai's family (all his Samurai having committed harakiri when their castle was taken by the House of Hari) and how he, with a swordmaker's adopted son, seeks to regain the ancestral blade, "the Honorable Sword," and take revenge on the House of Hari. I

921 Martin, Patricia Miles. The Greedy One. Ill. by Kazue Mizumura. Rand McNally, 1964. The 5th of May in Japan is Boys' Day on which they fly paper fish on bamboo poles along the streets and set out family treasures on shelves in their houses and serve a beautiful big fish for dinner. But alas, Kenji's cormorant swallows the fish planned for his family's dinner, and, fishing having been poor for a while, Kenji cannot afford to buy another. E

922 _____. Little Two and the Peach Tree. Ill. by Joan Berg. Atheneum, 1963. A delicate little story, with delicate drawings, about a little girl too shy to speak, but whose paintings told more than words could. E, I

923 _____. Suzu and the Bride Doll. Ill. by Kazue Mizumura. Rand McNally, 1960. An enchanting story for doll lovers about the Japanese Festival of Dolls, and a little bride doll in search of her doll bridegroom. E

924 Michener, James A. The Bridges of Toko-Ri. Random, 1953. Bantam paperback. A tense, dramatic short novel of the American fliers, the carriers and the Navy in the Korean War. A

925 _____. Sayonara. Random, 1953-4. A novel about the plight of American soldiers and airmen during the Korean war, when, on periods of rest and recreation in Japan, they fell in love with Japanese girls. For some time it was prohibited to take Japanese wives back to the States, and a change in that ruling comes too late for Private Kelly. For Lloyd Gruver, an Air Force officer, the situation is different. Engaged to the General's daughter, he inadvertently falls deeply in love with a beautiful Japanese dancer and is determined to marry her. Everyone, including his own military father and his fiancée's parents try to persuade him not to marry Hana-ogi, and in the end he does not, but it is not because of their pleas. A touching love story of immediate post-War Japan. A

926 Murasaki, Lady. The Tale of Genji, Part One. Tr. from Japanese by Arthur Waley. Houghton Mifflin, 1929 (Anchor Book, 1955). A novel completed at the beginning of the 11th century, probably the world's first novel and one of its greatest. Like Proust's Remembrance of Things Past, it is a work of social and psychological observations, and also, like Remembrance, a book to be read in frequent leisurely sips in order to savor its delicate flavor. Part Two (the original novel is in six parts) is also available in an Anchor Books edition. The cover design of the paperback is by Seong May from a painting by Kitao Shigemasa. A

927 Norris, Faith and Lumn, Peter. Kim of Korea. Ill. by Kurt Wiese. Julian Messner, 1955. An exciting story of a young Korean orphan befriended by an American soldier shortly after the Korean War. The soldier promises to adopt Kim and take him to America, but first he has to go to the hospital for treatment. He fails to return when he said he would, and Kim runs into all sorts of difficulties and dangers in trying to track him down, his search taking him from Seoul to Inchon. There is a diagram of his perilous journey which has some humorous episodes too. I

928 Pak Jong Yong, with Jack Carrol. Korean Boy. Lothrop Lee and Shepard, 1950. A graphic, horrifying first-hand novel about a young Korean who had to flee before the Communist forces with his father who had been a prominent anti-Communist before the war, leaving behind them the mother and five younger children. In constant danger from U.N. bombs as well as Communist troops, they finally make their way to Pusan. When they are able to return home, the Communists having been driven back, they find their village almost entirely destroyed but mercifully the family still alive though weak and worn. A strong indictment of Communism and also of war--any way. I, YA

929 Paterson, Katherine. The Sign of the Chrysanthemum. Ill. by Peter Landa. Thomas Y. Crowell, 1973. A novel set in 12th century Japan, a period of wars between two powerful clans. Muna (which means "no name") is searching for a father he has never known but who, according to his mother just before her death, was a fine tall Samurai with a fine tall sword who was tattooed with a sign of the chrysanthemum.

During Muna's search he becomes involved with a renegade Samurai who claims to be his father and who has the sign of the chrysanthemum on his shoulder to prove it. But is that proof? In any case he pursuades Muna to steal a fine tall sword from the kindly swordmaker who has given the boy a home. Finally Muna discovers who he is and the true meaning of fatherhood. YA

930 Price, Olive. Kim Walk-in-My-Shoes. Ill. by Mamoru Funai. Coward McCann, 1968. The inspiring story of a 12-year-old Korean boy who, as a follower of an American doctor, has learned to care for orphans who need first aid, and then, when the orphans are evacuated to a small island in the straits of Korea, "the Island of Children," helps organize the children into teams for building shelters, sowing crops, and even starting a school. The story is based on actual historical events at the time when the North Koreans had reached Seoul. I

931 Reeder, Col. Red. Clint Lane in Korea. Duell, Sloan and Pearce, 1961. The story of one Lt. Clint Lane, a West Point baseball player familiar to readers of other books about him, and the difficulties he meets in trying to adopt and send to America a Korean orphan who has been badly beaten and nearly starved by his wicked uncle. I, YA

932 Reynolds, Barbara. Emily-San. Ill. by Tack Shigaki. Scribner's, 1955. A warm family story in which 10-year-old Emily Masters and her mother join the father of the family in an American Army village in Japan. At first Emily has difficulty in finding any friends of her own age, Japanese or American, but finally through the help of their maid, Kimi San, and a new Nisei friend of Emily's Mother, she is able to have both Japanese and American friends. An interesting picture of American army life in post-war Japan. I

933 Statler, Oliver. Japanese Inn. Ill. by courtesy of the Art Institute of Chicago (with 8 exceptions). Random House, 1961 (Pyramid paperback, 1962). History in fictional forms of a real inn about 100 miles from Tokyo and of the family that has run it through the generations. The story begins with the Battle of Okitsu in 1569 and ends with the visit to the Inn of the Emperor and Empress of Japan in 1957. The menus served them during their three-day stay are given at the end of the book and also a postscript by

the author drawing the lines between fact and fiction. A

934 Tibbets, Albert. Courage in Korea: Stories of the Korean War. Little Brown, 1962. Ten short stories, seven from The Saturday Evening Post. YA, A

935 Uchida, Yoshiko. The Full Circle. Ill. by the author. Friendship Press, 1957. A fictionalized story of a real Japanese girl and her experiences during and after World War II. Umeko Kagawa is the daughter of Toyohiko Kagawa, one of the world's great Christian leaders, and the story is about her teenage hardships and the adjustment she had to make after the war to the new ideas of democracy and freedom. YA

936 _____. Hisako's Mysteries. Ill. by Susan Bennett. Charles Scribner's Sons, 1969. A modern "young miss," living with her old-fashioned grandparents in Kyoto, dreams of adventure. I

937 _____. In-between Miya. Ill. by Susan Bennett. Scribner's, 1967. The 12-year-old daughter of a poor village priest and teacher, has a chance to live in a rich Tokyo house in exchange for "helping out" an invalid Aunt. She soon finds out that riches don't mean everything, by any means. I

938 _____. Makoto, the Smallest Boy; A Story of Japan. Akihito Shirakama. Thomas Y. Crowell, 1970. How a boy learned that age and size aren't everything when it comes to winning prizes. E

939 _____. Sumi's Prize. Ill. by Kazue Mizumura. Scribner's, 1964. Young Sumi, seven years old, is the only girl to enter a kite-flying contest. The first of three charming stories about Sumi. E

940 _____. Sumi's Special Happening. Ill. by Kazue Mizumura. Scribner's, 1966. A sequel to Sumi's Prize in which she thinks and thinks about what kind of a gift to give her friend Ojii Chan, who is going to be 99. E

941 _____. Sumi & the Goat & the Tokyo Express. Ill. by Kazue Mizumura. Scribner's, 1969. In this third book about seven-year-old Sumi, her 99-year-old friend has just received a new goat, and Sumi takes it a welcoming gift. E

942 _____. Takao and Grandfather's Sword. Ill. by William M. Hutchinson. Harcourt Brace, 1958. How can seven-year-old Takao ever convince his father that he can help in the pottery workshop when his own boasting and a quarrel with his little sister

has caused a disastrous fire there? E
943 Whitney, Phyllis A. Secret of the Samurai Sword.
Westminster, 1958. A mystery story set in colorful, modern Kyoto and also a story of boys and girls of different cultures coming to know and understand each other and themselves. The author's childhood was spent in the Orient--Japan, China, and the Philippines. I, YA
944 Yashima, Taro and Muku, Hatoju. The Golden Footprints. World, 1960. An adaptation by Yashima of an original story by Muku, about a Japanese boy, a captured baby fox, and the devotion of the fox parents to their baby and their gratitude to the boy when he saved their young one from being killed for his valuable fur. E

SOUTHEAST ASIA
(Cambodia, Indonesia, Laos, Malaysia,
the Philippines, Singapore, Thailand, Vietnam)

What a sprawling part of the world this is, one very hard to find clearly presented on a single map. This is particularly true of Indonesia, the world's largest archipelago, comprising about 3,000 islands, the largest being Java, Sumatra, Kalimantan (most of Borneo), Sulawesi (Celebes), and West Irian (the west half of New Guinea). Borneo and New Guinea are treated in this book in Part Four, AUSTRALASIA AND OCEANIA.

Malaysia was created in 1963, from the union of the Malay Peninsula, Singapore Island, and two North Borneo states. Singapore was separated in 1965 to become an independent city republic.

Cambodia declared its independence from France in 1953. Laos became an independent sovereign state by a treaty with France in 1949. Thailand (formerly called Siam) is the only country in Southeast Asia never taken over by a colonial power. In 1946 the Philippines became a republic, independent of the United States, by an act of Congress providing for this that was passed in 1934.

In 1955 Ngo Dinh Diem proclaimed the southern zone

of Vietnam the "Republic of Vietnam." In the north the
"Democratic Republic of Vietnam," in 1959, adopted a constitution based on Marxist-Leninist principles and calling for
reunification of all Vietnam. The events that followed are
all too well known but difficult to understand. Perhaps some
of the books listed here will help to clarify the terribly confused situation.

NON-FICTION

945 Ayer, Margaret. Getting to Know Thailand. Ill. by
 the author. Coward McCann, 1959. A pleasant way
 to become acquainted with Thailand (formerly Siam).
 Appended are a chronology, list of sources, and index. I

946 _____. Made in Thailand; The Story of a Country's
 Arts and Crafts. Ill. by the author and with photographs. Alfred A. Knopf, 1964. History, geography and religion are woven into the arts and crafts
 of this enchanting country. YA up

947 Caldwell, John. Let's Visit Indonesia. Ill. with photographs and a map. John Day, 1960. How little
 most of us know about this part of the world, an independent country now, made up of almost 3000 islands along the equator, the world's largest archipelago and sixth largest nation in population. I

948 _____. Let's Visit Southeast Asia, Hong Kong to
 Indonesia, rev. ed. Ill. with photographs and a
 map. John Day, 1967. It is obviously impossible
 to keep completely up to date with developments in
 the eastern hemisphere, particularly in the war-torn
 regions of Vietnam, Cambodia and Laos, but this
 book provides a good background for a clearer understanding of current events in southeast Asia. A helpful chart of the countries described groups them as
 follows: (1) British-related countries: Malaysia,
 Singapore, Brunei; (2) the Republic of Indonesia;
 (3) the Buddhist nations: Thailand, Cambodia, Laos;
 and (4) the "Chinese Nations": North and South Vietnam. I

949 _____. Let's Visit Thailand. Ill. with photographs
 and a map. John Day, 1967. All about this fairy
 tale country with its 28,000 Buddhist temples--its
 geography, history, peoples, religion, government,
 politics, sports, arts, and so forth. I

950 _____. Let's Visit the Philippines. Ill. with photo-

Southeast Asia

> graphs and a map. John Day, 1961. There have been serious changes in the Philippine government since this book was published, but the history, geography, climate, and, to a large extent the way of life remain the same. And did you realize that there are 7000 islands in the Philippine group? I

951 Clifford, Mary Louise. The Land and People of Malaysia. Ill. with photographs and a map by Donald T. Pitcher. J. B. Lippincott, 1968. This must have been a difficult book to write because Malaysia is not so much a country as a "political arrangement" of what formerly consisted of Malaya and two states on the northern coast of Borneo. This "arrangement," or nation, if you will, came into being in 1963. YA up

952 Conroy, Robert. The Battle of Bataan; America's Greatest Defeat. Ill. with tactical maps by Rafael Palacios and photographs; picture research by Patricia Crum. Macmillan, 1969. An epic of courage and endurance which lasted for three months on Bataan and four on Corregidor, and which delayed the Japanese timetable of conquest long enough to save New Guinea and Australia. YA up

953 _____. The Battle of Manilla Bay. Ill. with photographs. Macmillan, 1968. The story of the 1898 conflict between the United States and Spain in the Philippines, in which Filipino rebel troops joined the Americans, believing that the latter only intended to liberate them from Spain rather than to dominate them for the next fifty years. YA up

954 Cooke, David C. Thailand, the Land of Smiles. Ill. with photographs. W. W. Norton, 1971. A fascinating story of the independent kingdom of Thailand (formerly Siam): its history, customs, religion, natural resources, and its heroes, and emergence into the 20th century. YA

955 Dareff, Hal. The Story of Vietnam; A Background Book for Young People. Parents' Magazine Press, 1966. The emphasis here is on modern times, but the book includes a history of the country from the time when it freed itself from Chinese rule, through its nine centuries of independence before its conquest by the French in the 19th century, by the Japanese for a short period in the 20th, and its final involvement in a long, complicated war. YA

956 Edmonds, I. G. The Khmers of Cambodia; The Story of a Mysterious People. Ill. with photographs by

the author. Bobbs-Merrill, 1970. A book of Cambodian history interwoven with legends, and with a detailed account of recent political developments, in particular the case of Prince Sihanouk and the matter of American intervention in Cambodia. YA up

957 _____. The New Malaysia. Ill. with photographs and maps. Bobbs-Merrill, 1973. Malaysia was formed in 1963 from the union of the Malay Peninsula, Singapore Island and two north Borneo states (Singapore was later expelled). In the author's usual clear and lively style, this is a narration of the history, current nature and continuing problems of a very complex but little-known "country" where there are not only racial conflicts, between Chinese, Indians and Malays, but also political and religious ones. YA up

958 _____. Thailand, the Golden Land. Ill. with photographs and maps. Bobbs-Merrill, 1972. A most enjoyable background book, for, as Edmonds writes, "The Story of Thailand is a fabulous tale of a fabulous people who live in a fabulous land." Of special interest to those who have read Anna and the King of Siam or seen it as a musical or movie, are the chapters on King Mongkut, the husband of 35 wives and father of 82 children, in which he is presented in rather a different light from that of the novel and the shows. Also of current interest is the account of the political situation in Thailand as of 1971. Bibliography and index. YA up

959 Gidal, Sonia and Tim. My Village in Thailand. Ill. with photographs. Pantheon, 1970. Young Chavalit lives just across the river from Bangkok and we learn a great deal about the country of Thailand as we visit him and his family. There is a detailed chart of his village and a map and glossary are appended. I

960 Henderson, Larry. Vietnam and Countries of the Mekong. Ill. with photographs and maps. Thomas Nelson, 1967. The emphasis, of course, is on Vietnam, but there are informative profiles on Laos, Cambodia, Thailand and Burma as well: their cultural backgrounds, their present (as of 1966 or 67) political and economic problems, and sketches of young people growing up in each. Chronology, bibliography and index. YA

961 Keith, Agnes Newton. Bare Feet in the Palace. Ill. by the author's sketches. Little, Brown, 1955. A

Southeast Asia 183

perceptive, informative, entertaining portrait of Manilla during the early days of Philippine independence and the beginning of President Magsaysay's administration, written with humorous understanding, humility, and respect, even love, for the people of the Philippines of various tribes and all classes whom the author met in 1953. A

962 Liss, Howard. The Mighty Mekong. Ill. with photographs and a map. Hawthorne Books, 1967. The Mekong River rises in the Himalayan mountains of Tibet, roars through the western part of China around the border of Burma, and finally empties into the South China Sea from Vietnam, after touching Cambodia, Laos and Thailand. An important river, indeed, especially at its delta. I, YA

963 Matthew, Eunice S. The Land and People of Thailand. Ill. with photographs and map. J. B. Lippincott, 1964 (Portraits of the Nations Series). A comprehensive book about this fascinating, independent and friendly country, with emphasis on its history. YA up

964 Meeker, Oden. The Little World of Laos. Ill. with photographs and a "pictorial essay" by Homer Page. Scribner's, 1959. An entertaining story of Laos and its neighbors, Thailand and Cambodia, written by a man who went there as a representative of CARE and thus had an opportunity to visit isolated parts of the kingdom and to get to know various types of Laotians. YA

965 Poole, Frederick King. Southeast Asia, rev. ed. Ill. with photographs and a map. Franklin Watts, 1972. The ten nations included in the area of this book are: Thailand, Burma, Malaysia, Singapore, North and South Vietnam, Cambodia, Laos, Indonesia and the Philippines. I, YA

966 _____. Thailand. Ill. with photographs and a map by Walter Hortens. Franklin Watts, 1973 (a First Book). A concise, well-organized discussion of the geography, history, religion, culture and people of "the only country in southeast Asia that has never been colonized." I

967 Schloat, G. Warren. Prapan, A Boy of Thailand. Ill. with photographs. Alfred A. Knopf, 1963. A pictorial story of the life of a 13-year-old boy in contemporary Thailand. I

968 Smith, Datus C., Jr. The Land and People of Indonesia. Ill. with photographs and a map. J. B. Lippincott,

1961, 1968 (Portraits of the Nations Series). The Indonesian archipelago is made up of thousands of islands with fragrant, spicy exotic names, many of which are unfamiliar. In this book they are divided into four groups: the Western Islands of Sumatra, Borneo and Java; The Lesser Sunda Islands, a chain running eastward from the end of Java toward Australia; the Eastern Islands including Celebes and the Moluccas group stretching up toward the Philippines; and West Irian, the western part of the island of New Guinea which became Indonesian in 1963. YA up

969 Sully, Francois and Weiner, Marjorie. <u>We, the Vietnamese: Voices from Vietnam.</u> Praeger, 1971. Writings about and by the Vietnamese, including historical matter and a section on both traditional and contemporary protest poetry, with a brief editorial comment preceding each section. A short suggested reading list and index complete a significantly informative book. YA up

970 Taylor, Carl. <u>Getting to Know Indonesia.</u> Ill. by Eleanor Mill. Coward McCann, 1961. A short book about the canoe-shaped chain of more than 3000 islands which make up the Republic of Indonesia. Appended are an outline of Indonesian history, "Say It in Indonesian," and "How to Pronounce Foreign Words in This Book." I

971 Tooze, Ruth. <u>Cambodia, Land of Contrasts.</u> Ill. with photographs and maps. Viking, 1962. A handsome, well organized, readable and richly illustrated book. I, YA

972 Tor, Regina. <u>Getting to Know the Philippines.</u> Ill. by Haris Petie. Coward McCann, 1958. I hope this easy-to-read story of life in the Philippines will soon be updated, but the historical outline is useful as far as it goes. I

973 Vaughan, Josephine Budd. <u>The Land and People of the Philippines.</u> Ill. with photographs. J. B. Lippincott, 1956 (Portraits of the Nations Series). The story of the largest archipelago in the world, consisting of 7000 islands, of which, however, only about 1000 are large enough to have people living on them. YA

974 Watson, Jane Werner. <u>Thailand, Rice Bowl of Asia.</u> Ill. by Payut Ngaokrachang. Endsheet map by James A. Bier. Garrard, 1966. A colorful book about an exotic colorful country, containing a good measure of

Southeast Asia

information along with some little folk tales. I

BIOGRAPHIES

975 Archer, Jules. Ho Chi Minh, Legend of Hanoi. Crowell Collier, 1971. A biography of the man dedicated to the cause of a united independent Vietnam (1890-1969) who was affectionately called "Uncle Ho" by his idolizing countrymen; also a history of the war in Vietnam up to the time of his death. It shows his nationalism, like that of Tito of Yugoslavia, taking priority over international Communism and making him resistant to both the Soviet Union and Red China, and his earnest desire for peace even while forced into war by his devotion to a free united Vietnam. He is presented here as a man of compassion and iron will, and though not without fault, a hero to dissenters against the war. YA up

976 Dooley, Thomas A. Doctor Tom Dooley; My Story. Ill. with photographs. Ariel Books, 1958, 1960. An abridgment for young readers of the books, Deliver Us from Evil, The Edge of Tomorrow, and The Night They Burned the Mountain. It isn't as much a biography as it is the story of Dooley's work and his theory that aid must be given only until the aided can take care of themselves. It also explains the background of the war in Vietnam in the 1960s. An inspiring true story of an incredibly courageous yet humble man. YA

FOLKLORE

977 Courlander, Harold. Kantchil's Lime Pit and Other Stories from Indonesia. Ill. by Robert Kane. Harcourt Brace and World, 1950. A collection of folk tales of great variety, retold with the flavor of the countries and peoples of their origin. I

978 Graham, Gail B. The Beggar in the Blanket and Other Vietnamese Tales. Ill. by Brigitte Bryan. Dial, 1970. Eight fairy-folk tales taken from French language sources and delicately illustrated with black and white drawings. E, I

979 Maugham, W. Somerset. Princess September. Ill. by Jacqueline Ayer. Harcourt Brace and World, 1969. The text of this deliciously amusing fairy tale is

from Gentlemen in the Parlour, by Somerset Maugham (Doubleday, 1930). E, I

980 Robertson, Dorothy Lewis. Fairy Tales from Vietnam. Ill. by W. T. Mars. Dodd Mead, 1968. The folk stories in this book were told by a Vietnamese grandmother, written down by one of her grandsons, and sent in letters from him to his foster mother in the United States. They go back over the centuries to 200 years before Christ, as the author's informative Foreword explains, and embody much Vietnamese history and religious tradition. I up

981 Vo-Dinh. The Toad Is the Emperor's Uncle; Animal Folktales from Vietnam. Ill. by the author. Doubleday, 1970. Eighteen stories of heroic or comical animals told and illustrated by a Vietnamese artist. I, YA

FICTION

982 Appel, Benjamin. We Were There at the Battle for Bataan. Ill. by Irv Doctor; Historical consultant, Maj. Gen. Courtney Whitney. Grosset and Dunlap, 1957. Beginning with the attack upon Pearl Harbor on December 7, 1941, this story moves into the Philippines where a brother and sister and their father take to the hills and become guerrilla fighters along with Filipino soldiers. I

983 Berry, Erick (Allena Best). The Springing of the Rice. Ill. by John Kaufmann. Macmillan, 1966. A story about a small Thai boy and his experiences in the sowing, weeding and harvesting of rice, with the help of a water buffalo; a story of age-old customs and processes still going on. E, I

984 Bothwell, Jean and Sowers, Phyllis Ayer. Golden Letter to Siam. Ill. by Margaret Ayer. Abelard Press, 1953. A mystery novel, set in 17th century Siam, in which a young French boy seeks to find a Siamese boy's father. YA

985 Boulle, Pierre. The Bridge Over the River Kwai. Tr. by Xan Fielding. Vanguard Press, 1954. A novel about a "good" English colonel who, as a prisoner of the Japanese during World War II, built for his captors a fine solid bridge, and about the attempts of other heroic English soldiers to destroy his work. A novel of satire combined with compassion, which was made into a thrilling movie. A

986 Graham, Gail. Cross-Fire; A Vietnam Novel. Ill. by
David Stone Martin. Pantheon, 1972. A short powerful novel about an American non-com, separated
from his unit, and four Vietnamese children whose
village, with all its inhabitants, has been destroyed
by American bombs. Their communication problem,
because of language and mutual distrust and the children's bitter hatred of all Americans, presents a
strong indictment of war in general and foreign intervention in particular, told with tender compassion
and understanding. I up

987 Hámori, László. Adventure in Bangkok. Ill. by Robert
Frankenberg, tr. from Swedish by Annabelle Macmillan. Harcourt Brace and World, 1966. A novel of
espionage in Thailand in the mid-20th century, about
a well-drilling operation of the W.H.O. under the
engineering guidance of a young Austrian engineer who
suddenly and mysteriously disappears. A Swedish
lad, visiting his parents in Bangkok, determines to
get to the root of the mystery--with interesting results. YA

988 Kalish, Betty McKelvey. Siti's Summer. Ill. by Ipe
Maaroef. Macmillan, 1964. Siti is a little city girl
of Djakarta in Java (Indonesia) who, because of her
mother's illness, is obliged to spend the summer with
her great-grandfather out in the country. It is a
charming, warm story of the relationship of old and
young and of Siti's adventures and new friends, including a monkey, with authentic details of Indonesian
life. I

989 Kelsey, Alice Geer. Tino and the Typhoon. Ill. by
Isami Kashiwagi. Longmans Green, 1958. A story
of the oldest son of a lighthouse keeper on the island
of Luzon in the Philippines who has a terrible fear
of heights and always hides when there is a chance
that he might have to climb up the 39 rungs of the
ladder outside the lighthouse. He is crazy about
machinery, especially his father's outboard motor,
but is not allowed to learn to run it because of his
cowardice about the lighthouse ladder. The story of
how he finally conquers his fear and a delightful picture of life in a typical coastal village of northern
Luzon, includes several Philippine legends and the
words and music of the Philippine national anthem,
also a song: "The Fishing Boat." A glossary is
appended. I

990 Landon, Margaret. Anna and the King of Siam. Ill. by

Margaret Ayer. John Day, 1943. A novel, "seventy-five percent fact and twenty-five percent fiction based on fact" (from the author's note) based on two books by a Mrs. Leonowens ("Anna"): The English Governess at the Siamese Court (1870) and The Romance of the Harem" (1872). The book contains a wealth of historical and social background which, of course, could not be presented in the stage and screen productions. A

991 Last, J. and Tisna, U. P. The Bamboo School in Bali. Ill. by Albert Orbaan, tr. from Dutch by Marietta Moskin. John Day, 1969. When the first school is built on the island of Bali in Indonesia, life is quickly changed for four children: one a peasant boy, one a young nobleman, one the son of a witch doctor, and one the daughter of the High Priest. The caste system still exists on the island but is gradually broken down by the events which make up the story. Jef Last spent four years on Bali as a counselor to the government, and Udayana P. Tisna is the son of the last king of Bali. Together they have written this entrancing story of youth on that exotic island in transition. I up

992 Lederer, William J. and Burdick, Eugene. The Ugly American. W. W. Norton, 1958. A novel, based on fact, about American representatives in southeastern Asia in the 1950s, showing the frustrations suffered by those truly trying to understand and communicate with the Asians when their efforts were impeded, or entirely cut off, by bureaucratic fellow Americans (the ugly ones) who made no effort to know the people whom they had been sent to help. A

993 Louden, Claire and George. Far into the Night: A Story of Bali. Ill. by the authors. Scribner's, 1955. The joyful life of little Misi who takes her part in village life as a dancer, is disturbed by her grandfather's compulsive gambling. The slight plot is interwoven with a great deal of interesting information about the enchanting island of Bali, vividly pictured in full-page illustrations. E

994 Minney, R. J. Fanny and the Regent of Siam. Ill. with photographs. World, 1962. An historical novel, largely based on fact, and beginning in 1875, eight years after Anna of The King and I had left Siam. This Fanny's sister married the son of Anna who taught the King's children, and Fanny herself

married a Siamese widower, much against the better judgment of her parents and even more against the will of the powerful Regent who wanted her to marry his son. An absorbing story and study of Siamese politics and intrigue in the late 19th century. A

995 Sherry, Sylvia. Frog in the Coconut Shell. J. B. Lippincott, 1968. Yusof, age 12, living in a little village on the east coast of Malaya, is the object of much teasing by his family and friends because of his extravagant dreams of the great deeds he plans to accomplish with his grandfather's traditional sword. But when the Indonesians invade his village, his dreams become a terrifying reality. An exciting story based on an historic incident in which a Malay boy helped track down the invaders. I

996 Spiegelman, Judith M. Ketut, Boy Woodcarver of Bali. Ill. with photographs by Mallica Vajrathon and Henky Pantoc. Julian Messner, 1971. A story about a young boy learning the art of wood carving and about the way the life and legends of Indonesia are interpreted in wood. E, I

997 Tooze, Ruth. Silver from the Sea. Ill. by Kurt Wiese. Viking, 1962. It is the first "Fish Day" when Dinh is old enough to take an important part in the hauling in of silver fish from a Vietnam beach on the China Sea: he is the Center Boy, who dips the fish out of the center of the great net. The text and illustrations give the reader a sense of participation in the day of the big haul, with the women pulling on the ropes and the boys filling the baskets after Dinh empties his pails into them.

998 Youngberg, Norman. Tiger of Bitter Valley. Ill. by Harold Munson. William Morrow, 1957. A story of "two magics," that of a witch doctor and that of a modern doctor, and the ensuing conflict which drives the chief's son from his village in Sumatra to confront tigers and what is even more dangerous, a madman. I

Part Four

AUSTRALASIA AND OCEANIA
(Australia, Borneo, New Guinea, New Zealand, Tasmania)

Australasia, according to the dictionary, comprises "Australia, New Zealand and neighboring islands in the South Pacific Ocean." However, for the purpose of visualizing geographical areas, I have included New Guinea and Borneo in this section, though parts of them, strictly speaking, belong to Indonesia and Malaysia. As to Oceania, it takes whole books (some of which you will find here) to identify the groups of islands and the political and governmental status of each.

Australia itself includes the states and territories of New South Wales (the setting of much of the fiction), Victoria, Queensland, South Australia, Western Australia, Tasmania, Northern Territory, and Capital Territory, but because there are several good novels set in Tasmania it has received special attention.

NON-FICTION

999 Baker, Eleanor Z. Australian Aboriginals. Ill. with photographs. Steck-Vaughn, 1968. A book about people who seem practically untouched by modern civilization; who are, indeed, living the nomadic tribal life of long-gone centuries. One can't help questioning the efforts to modernize them, and yet their way of life requires space that is gradually, slowly contracting. I, YA

1000 _____. New Guinea; A Journey into Yesterday. Ill. with photographs and a map. Steck-Vaughn, 1968. A book about the second largest island in the world, north of Australia, east of Indonesia and the Philippines, an island divided into three administrative sections: the Territory of New Guinea in the northeast, Papua in the southeast, and West Irian, the western half. It seems hardly credible that there is in the world today a place which is some part of the Stone Age, but such is New Guinea, or at least was in 1968. I, YA

1001 Borden, Charles A. South Sea Islands. Ill. with photographs and jacket and endpaper maps by Guy Fry. Macrae Smith, 1961. A book to make you yearn to travel in the South Seas before they become completely "civilized." Also a book to acquaint you with the main groups of islands: Micronesia, Melanesia and Polynesia. Appended is a summary of basic facts about the islands or groups of islands, who discovered them, and their 1962 status, area and population. YA up

1002 Blunden, Godfrey. The Land and People of Australia, rev. ed. Ill. with photographs. J. B. Lippincott, 1972 (Portraits of the Nations Series). A book of history, geography, economy, culture and people, with a chapter on myth and legend and one on literature. YA

1003 Caldwell, John C. Let's Visit Australia. Ill. with photographs. John Day, 1963. A visit to the last continent to be discovered by Europeans and the only nation to occupy a whole continent. Because it is the oldest continent of all it has unique wild life. I

1004 _____. Let's Visit New Zealand. Ill. with photographs. John Day, 1963. Did you know that the people of New Zealand call themselves "Kiwis" after their unusual national bird (pictured on the jacket by Bob Gray)? This book will tell you many other and more important facts about New Zealand, and, with its photographs, will make you wish you could really visit it, especially if you happen to be a skier. I

1005 Harrington, Lyn. Australia and New Zealand, Pacific Community. Ill. with photographs by Richard Harrington. Thomas Nelson, 1969. Though there are very good maps of Australia, New Zealand, and New Guinea in the book, the reader will find it helpful to keep an atlas open to the whole South Pacific in order to keep before him the relation of one place to another. The book covers history, geography, anthropology, economics and international relations, includes sketches of the lives of young people in various environments, and introduces Australian figures of speech. Appended is a bibliography and a page of "Highlights in Australian history." YA up

Australia, Oceania

1006 Heyerdahl, Thor. Aku-Aku, The Secret of Easter Island. Ill. with 32 pages of full-color photographs and maps and drawings. Rand McNally, 1958 (Pocket Book, 1970-71). About the loneliest island in the world, dotted with house-high statues of long-eared men. How did they come to be carved and raised? Even after Heyerdahl had learned the answers to those questions, he was bewildered by secrets of the island caves. This is the story of a scientific expedition to Easter Island, on which even the scientists had to observe superstitious rites and acknowledge their own "aku-akus" (guardian spirits). A

1007 Hough, Richard. The Battle of Midway; Victory in the Pacific. Ill. with photographs and maps by Rafael Palacios. Macmillan, 1970. Midway Island, more than 1000 miles west of Honolulu, was of great strategic importance in World War II and this is the story of the hard-won victory there in 1942. YA

1008 Johnson, Osa. Last Adventure; The Martin Johnsons in Borneo. Ill. with photographs; ed. by Pascal James Imperato, M.D. William Morrow, 1966. This book of thrilling travel adventures among the headhunters and wild animals of the Borneo jungle was completed by Mrs. Johnson shortly before her death in 1953. It is about an expedition in 1936, backed by the American Museum of Natural History, that was the first to fly over those jungles in their plane, the Spirit of East Africa and Borneo; Osa Johnson was the first white woman ever to reach the then unexplored headwaters of the Kinabatangan River and the first to enter the territory of the Tenggara headhunters. The introduction by Dr. Imperato gives the entire astounding career of the Johnsons in perspective. Animal lovers will particularly enjoy the many fascinating details of Borneo wild life and Osa's love for and patience with some of those they captured and adopted. A

1009 Joy, Charles R. Young People of the Pacific Islands. Ill. with endpaper map and jacket by Bob Ritter. Duell Sloan and Pearce, 1963. After an interesting introduction about the Pacific Ocean, there are nine first-person reports from young people living on the following islands: Hawaii, the Society Islands (Big and Little Tahiti), Cook Islands, Samoa, New Zealand, Fiji, New Caledonia, Guam, and

Okinawa. I
1010 Kaula, Edna Mason. The First Book of Australia.
Ill. by the author. Franklin Watts, 1960. Text
and pictures complement each other in the production of a remarkably concise and readable story of
Australia: its history, government, people and
animals. There are two pages each of drawings
of animals and birds. A list of Australian words
and phrases is appended and an index. I
1011 _____. The First Book of New Zealand. Ill. by
the author. Franklin Watts, 1961. This short,
well organized and attractively illustrated story of
the land of the Maoris, made this reader most
eager to visit the three islands that make up New
Zealand. History, geography, peoples, government, industry are all gone into, and there is a
page of "How to pronounce Maori words." I
1012 _____. The Land and People of New Zealand, rev.
ed. Ill. with photographs and a map. J. B. Lippincott, 1972. The story of a young country with
a short political history and with emphasis on New
Zealand's present economic connection with Britain
and the European Economic Community. The book
also covers New Zealand's scenery, wild life, and
the people at work and play. YA
1013 Keith, Agnes. Land Below the Wind. Michael Joseph,
Ltd. (London), 1939. Labeled a "travel book" this
is truly an adventure book--a book of emotional as
well as physical adventure, by an American woman
married to a British game keeper (and holder of
many other government positions) in Borneo in the
1930s before the war. Her adventures ranged from
adaptation to the tight little white community in the
capital of Sandikan and the problems of housekeeping with a staff of native and even aborigine servants, to expeditions with her husband and his companions (one woman with thirty men) into the depths
of the jungle, all told with quiet humor, understanding, and humility. A
1014 _____. Three Came Home. Ill. by the author.
Little Brown, 1946-7. This is the story of the
nearly four years during which Mrs. Keith and her
son (aged two at the start) were imprisoned by the
Japanese on the island of Borneo, during World
War II, separated from her husband also imprisoned
nearby. It is a story of the senseless cruelty of
their Japanese guards, of filth and illness and near

starvation, of heavy labor and mental and physical torture. Yet she was able to find some kindness in a few of her captors and nobility in many of her fellow prisoners, and to write at the end of her short preface, giving her reasons for writing the book at all, "If there is hate it is for hateful qualities, not nations. If there is love it is because this alone kept me alive and well."

1015 Leckie, Robert. The Battle for Iwo Jima. Ill. with maps by Ted Burwell and photographs. Random House, 1967 (a Landmark Book). It is fearsome even to read about this frightful battle in which 4189 American marines were killed in action, 15,749 men wounded or put out of action, and most of the 21,000 Japanese defenders killed. Appended are: (1) order of events in the invasion of Iwo Jima, (2) a note on unit strength, (3) a list of marines who won the Medal of Honor on Iwo Jima, and (4) a note about the author, and index. I, YA

1016 McGuire, Edna. The Maoris of New Zealand. Ill. with photographs and prints. Macmillan, 1968. A fascinating story of the Polynesians who settled in New Zealand in the 10th century and came to be called Maoris. After the arrival of European colonists in the 1840s there was armed conflict, and it seemed that the Maori culture might not survive. However, a Young Maori Party arose, and now integration is gradually taking place. This is mainly an account of the culture before the arrival of the Europeans, introducing many Maori myths and legends. I, YA

1017 Marsh, Ngaio. New Zealand. Ill. with maps and photographs; Introd. by Keith Holyoake, Prime Minister of New Zealand. Macmillan, 1964. The author, a native-born New Zealander, takes us with her on a trip through cities, bush country sheep stations, and the hot springs of Rotorna, and, with the use of settlers' diaries and stories about her own pioneer grandparents, she relates the history of New Zealand from the time it became a British colony in 1840 until it grew into the present modern welfare state, a member of the British Commonwealth. YA up

1018 May, Charles Paul. Oceania: Polynesia, Melanesia, Micronesia. Ill. with photographs and a map. Thomas Nelson, 1973. A comprehensive, excellently written and organized book about the thousands of islands in the south seas: their main divisions, political status, peoples, geology and ecology, history, present conditions and future expectations. A chronology of historical highlights and list of reading suggestions are appended. YA up

1019 Moorehead, Alan. Cooper's Creek. With 16 pages of illustrations, chapter head drawings and maps. Harper and Row, 1963. A detailed account of the Burke and Wills ill-fated expedition, from August 1860 to June 1861, which, in spite of its lack of proper and adequate preparation and planning, its frequent mistakes, and its unindurable hardships, did achieve its objective: the crossing of Australia from south to north. The personalities of the expedition's members are so fully realized, the terrain they struggled over is so vividly described, and the various routes attempted are so clearly mapped, that the reader can hardly fail to feel a sense of participation in the harrowing adventures and the fascination of the Australian desert--terrible, awesome, and spell binding. A

1020 Parke, Margaret B. Getting to Know Australia. Ill. by Claudine Nankivel. Coward McCann, 1962. A good introduction to the land "down under" where there is winter when we have summer and night when we have day. A history is appended and a guide to pronunciation. I

1021 Place, Marian (Templeton). Gold Down Under; The Story of the Australian Gold Rush. Ill. with historical pictures. Collier-Macmillan, 1969. A colorful character named Edward Hammond Hargrave, having observed the California gold rush of 1848, was convinced that certain parts of the Australian terrain resembled the gold fields of California, persisted in this belief, and finally proved his point. Covering all the facets of those gold fever days and comparing the American and Australian experiences, the book is full of drama and humor. Bibliography and index. YA up

1022 Werstein, Irving. Guadalcanal. Ill. with maps by Ave Morgan. Thomas Y. Crowell, 1963. The battle for the obscure but strategically important island is here presented from both the American and Japanese viewpoints, taken from personal reminiscences, letters and diaries of the men involved. YA up

1023 Wilson, Barbara Ker. Australia, Wonderland Down

Australia, Oceania 197

   Under. Ill. with photographs. Dodd Mead, 1969.
   A fine background, by a (presently) Australian writer, for greater enjoyment of the many excellent novels by outstanding Australian authors. I up

BIOGRAPHIES

1024 Day, A. Grove. <u>Explorers of the Pacific</u>. Ill. with photographs of prints and paintings and with maps. Duell, Sloan and Pearce, 1966. At the beginning of this remarkably concise book is a helpful list of names of places, names which have changed through the years, such as Tasmania which was once called Van Dieman's Land. Sailing dates of the many explorers are given so that, as the author says, "the exciting saga of the sea ... can be followed as part of a connected story." The names of the explorers, with pronunciation, will be found in the index.
   YA
1025 Engle, Eloise. <u>Sea Challenge, The Epic Voyage of Magellan</u>. Ill. by Herb Mott. C. S. Hammond, 1962. A fictional account of Magellan's circumnavigation of the globe, soundly based on the writings of Pigafetta who most fortunately survived with his diaries. Magellan, of course, was not so fortunate. I, YA
1026 Frisbie, Florence (Johnny). <u>Miss Ulysses from Puka Puka; The Autobiography of a South Sea Trader's Daughter</u>. Macmillan, 1948. Edited and translated by her father, Robert Dean Frisbee, whose many books about the south sea islands deserve more attention than they receive these days. Johnny's (Florence's) mother, a native island woman, died of tuberculosis when her four children were all under six, Johnny being the eldest. This book was finished by her when she was 12, and in it she shows her father to have been one of the dearest and best fathers any children could ever have had. Because the family moved about a great deal in the south seas, Johnny grew up with a mixture of languages, which is the reason her father had to translate the writing, but her narrative skill, her powers of description, her keen perceptions of people, native and white, would make this an outstanding book if it had been written by a person of greater years, though in that case it might not have the freshness

and candor that it has. It is rather hard to come
by, but keep hunting. Don't miss it. YA up

1027 Hough, Henry Beetle. Melville in the South Pacific.
Ill. by Frank Nickolas. Houghton Mifflin, 1960.
A beautifully designed and well-written book about
the adventures of Melville in the 1840s; adventures
which provided the material for his south sea novels:
Typee and Omoo. I, YA

1028 Israel, Charles E. Five Ships West; The Story of
Magellan. Ill. with prints and maps. Macmillan,
1966. An excitingly narrated story of Magellan's
life (1480-1522) and particularly of his voyage of
global circumnavigation, 1519-22; of his frustrations,
determination, and ambition to reach the Spice Islands by sailing west instead of east, with interesting sidelights on other characters involved one way
or another in the venture: King Manuel of Portugal who turned Magellan down and Charles of Spain
who supported him, and particularly the writer,
Antonio Pigafetta, who was able to bring back reports of the expedition after Magellan had been
killed almost within sight of his objective. YA

1029 Latham, Jean Lee. Far Voyager: The Story of James
Cook. Ill. with maps by Karl Stueklen. Harper
and Row, 1970. A fine piece of biographical fiction about the life and adventures of Captain Cook
(1728-79) with especially interesting nautical details
in connection with his early days at sea. He was
the first to discover that Australia was a continent
and New Zealand an island (or two islands). I,
YA

1030 MacLean, Alistair. Captain Cook. Ill. with black and
white and color prints and an endcover world map,
showing the latest discoveries of Capt. Cook.
Doubleday, 1972. A handsome book about the man
who wrote, in his last letter to the Earl of Sand-
wich, from Capetown, in 1776, "My endeavor shall
not be wanting to achieve the great object of this
voyage." He was a man either too modest or too
inhibited to write anything about his personal life
but he left over a million words of records of his
"endeavor." A

1031 Pond, Seymour Gates. Ferdinand Magellan, Master
Mariner. Ill. by Jack Coggins. Random, 1957 (a
Landmark Book). A good biography (1480-1521) of
the first circumnavigator of the globe. I

1032 Selsam, Millicent. The Quest of Captain Cook. Ill.

Australia, Oceania   199

       by Lee J. Ames. Doubleday, 1962. A well-organized story of Cook's three voyages (1768, 1772-75, and 1776-78), each with a two-page map. I, YA
1033 Sperry, Armstrong. Captain Cook Explores the South Seas. Ill. by the author. Random House, 1955 (a Landmark Book). The exciting true story, excitingly told, about the self-taught navigator, mapmaker and scientist (1728-1779) who claimed Australia and New Zealand for the British Empire. I
1034 Syme, Ronald. Captain Cook, Pacific Explorer. Ill. by William Stobbs. Morrow, 1960. A biography of the good, peace-loving explorer (1728-79) who charted the New Zealand coastline and the east coast of Australia and some of the Arctic Ocean, before being killed by Hawaiian natives. I
1035   . Magellan, First Around the World. Ill. by William Stobbs. Morrow Jr. Books, 1953. A short biography but giving the essential facts about the man and his mission to prove that it would be possible to sail around the world. I
1036 Warner, Oliver and the Editors of Horizon Magazine. Captain Cook and the South Pacific. Ill. with paintings, drawings and maps; Consultant Dr. J. C. Beaglehole. American Heritage, 1963 (a Horizon Caravel Book). YA
1037 Welch, Ronald. Ferdinand Magellan. Ill. by Ronald Stobbs. Criterion, 1956. A fictionalized biography, by a past-master of historical fiction, of the man whose story well deserves the many biographies written about him. YA

FOLKLORE

1038 Holding, James. The Sky-Eater and Other South Sea Tales. Ill. by Charles Keeping. Abelard Schuman, 1965. Nine folktales gathered from story-tellers in the South Seas where there is no written literature but many fables and legends passed down orally from generation to generation. I
1039 Parker, K. Langlok. Australian Legendary Tales, sel. and ed. by H. Drake-Brockman. Ill. by Elizabeth Durack. Viking, 1966. A collection of fifty stories from the five books of Mrs. Parker (published in 1896). As Catherine Field, she grew up among the aborigines living on her father's sta-

tion and the book should be of special interest to anthropologists, as will the introductions by the editor and illustrator (the illustrations are based on aboriginal art forms). A glossary and a key to pronunciation are appended. I up

1040 Wilson, Barbara Ker. Tales Told to Kabbarli; Aboriginal Legends, collected by Daisy Bates. Ill. by Harold Thomas, an aboriginal artist. Crown, 1972. "Kabbarli" means the "white Grandmother," Daisy Bates, who spent over 40 years from 1899 to 1945 gathering the folklore of the aborigines of Australia. A biography of "Kabbarli" is contained in the Introduction by Elizabeth Salter. The legends, as Barbara Wilson explains in a prefatory note, all belong to the Dreamtime of the race, and the aboriginal words are translated as they occur in the text instead of a glossary at the end, making for easier reading. I up

FICTION

1041 Borden, Charles A. He Sailed with Captain Cook. Ill. by Ralph Ray. Thomas Y. Crowell, 1952. This is not as you might expect another biography of Captain Cook but rather a good sea story about the voyage of the Endeavor. Tobias, too small for his age, suffers persecution by some of the crew, obtains advancement from the captain, is jealously regarded by the men under him and finally accused by them of murder. It is mainly Tobias' story but the character and wisdom of Captain Cook come through clearly, and his achievements toward the building of Britain's South Seas Empire provide the factual background. A sizeable bibliography. I

1042 Brinsmead, H. F. Pastures of the Blue Crane. Coward McCann, 1966. The setting of this novel is the beautiful north coast of Australia, near Brisbane. Amaryllis Merewether has never known her mother and hardly ever her father, who has sent her to boarding schools from the time she was three, while he lived in New Guinea. At his death, when Ryl is 16, she finds that she is to share half his money and half of a run-down farm with an equally run-down grandfather of whose existence she had never been aware. There is a mystery which carries through to the very end, though you may suspect its solution. YA up

1043 _____. Season of the Briar. Coward McCann, 1st American, 1967. A fine novel in every way--a tense story line, skillful characterizations, and above all a setting in the Tasmanian wilderness. A team of oddly assorted young men of college age who are "bush sprayers" for summer work in an isolated valley of Tasmania, meet up with a party of boys and girls who are "bushwalking" during their vacation. The two groups separate but are brought together again in a search for Gisella, a 16-year-old bushwalker who has become lost in the mountains in a heavy fog. And if you don't know exactly what bush sprayers and bushwalkers are here's your chance to find out. YA

1044 Chauncy, Nan. Devil's Hill. Ill. by Geraldine Spence. Franklin Watts, 1960. "Badge" lives with his father and mother in a lonely, hidden, Tasmanian valley and so is thrilled when he hears that his cousin Sam is coming to visit and be his "cobber" (see Glossary). However Sam is accompanied by his little sisters whom he considers pests and is scornful of the rugged pioneer life of Badge's family and the visit begins unhappily. It is only when the whole family takes off on a camping trip in search of a lost cow to take the place of one who has died that Sam pulls his weight and truly becomes Badge's "cobber." I

1045 _____. High and Haunted Island. Ill by Victor Ambrus. W. W. Norton, 1964. An enchanting novel on two time planes: one the period of World War I when two Australian schoolgirls are cast away after a shipwreck near Point Davy on the wild Tasmanian coast, and the other when two teenage boys and their fathers, sailing a private yacht many years later, go ashore at the very same place and find a message in a bottle that sends them to a "high and haunted island." Skillful plotting and characterizations and a perfect conclusion make this a memorable story. YA

1046 _____. Hunted in Their Own Land. Ill. by Victor Ambrus, Introd. and Afterword by Barbara Rader. Seabury, 1973. A tragic novel of the natives of Tasmania, untroubled by white men until the late 18th century, when the English invaded their island, cut down their trees and replaced the people on a barren island. A good map and glossary. YA up

1047 _____. The Secret Friends, 1st Amer. ed. Ill. by Brian Wildsmith. Franklin Watts, 1962. This spell-binding novel of present and past, teaches us about the Tasmanian aborigines through the experience of a little 20th century girl who identifies herself with her great-greataunt in a portrait. It is a portrait of the aunt as the little girl who had played with an aboriginal child. The transitions from present to past and back again are so smooth and natural as to seem quite credible. I, YA

1048 _____. Tiger in the Bush. Ill. by Margaret Horder. Oxford U. Press, 1957 (Franklin Watts, 1961). The glossary of Australian terms is here presented in the front of the book which is helpful for non-Australian readers. It is a grand tale about a family living in an isolated Tasmanian valley and how the youngest son, a bothersome tagalong, discovers and protects a rare Tasmanian tiger. I, YA

1049 Clark, Denis. Boomer: The Life of a Kangaroo. Ill. by C. Gifford Ambler. Viking, 1955. In Australia a baby kangaroo is called a "joey" and when he is full grown, a "boomer," as he becomes a leader of a "mob." This is the story of an endearing joey developing into a courageous boomer, with rich nature descriptions of the Australian bush. YA

1050 Clark, Mavis Thorpe. Blue Above the Trees. Ill. by Genevieve Melrose. Meredith Press, 1968. A warm, pioneering story about an English family trying to make a go of it in Gippsland in Victoria, Australia, in the 1870s, and especially about young Simon who wants to preserve a bit of forest for a family of lyrebirds. YA

1051 _____. Iron Mountain. Macmillan, 1970. Seventeen-year-old Joey Simpson, in serious trouble with the law in the slum district of Melbourne, takes off on foot for western Australia, hoping to find work and a meaningful life. By a lucky pickup on the desert road, he attaches himself to the Rose family en route to join their father in the new mining town of Tom Price in the Pilbara region of West Australia, and there Joey obtains a job as a "trainee driller" in a mine. The novel has strong characterizations and an interesting background of Australian mining operations and the modern pioneers involved in them. A glossary of Australian vernacular is at the beginning. YA

1052 _____. Spark of Opal. Macmillan, 1973 (first pub.

in Australia, 1968). An exciting novel about opal mining in the southern Australian desert and a "dugout" family who are about to give up and move into Adelaide, much against the desires of 13-year-old Bill and his 15-year-old sister, both of whom hate to leave their aboriginal friends, with Bill especially unhappy about leaving his dog. Their secret attempts to find opal nearly cost them their lives. An interesting author's note about Australia's national gem and about the aborigines is an extra dividend. YA

1053 _____. Wildfire. Macmillan, 1973. Victoria, the southeast corner of Australia is particularly susceptible to raging fires as the author explains in her Foreword, but, she adds, "natural causes, such as lightning, are responsible for only one bushfire in a hundred. The other ninety-nine are caused by 'man, woman and child.'" So when Steven, on a "total fire-ban day," tries to learn how to ride a mini-bike, he can't help wondering if he might have struck the spark which set off the deadly wildfire" during drought, dry dams and extreme heat. YA

1054 Cleary, Jon. The Sundowners. Scribner's, 1952 (Young Peoples' Edition). A novel, prepared by the author from a longer adult book, about a migrant family in New South Wales; a warm, loving family of three, consisting of the improvident gambler of a husband and his loyal wife and son, both of whom yearn for a homeplace where they can settle down. The dialogue is spicy with Australian expressions and there is a fine blend of pathos and humor. The characterization of the wife is outstanding as is the portrayal of the harsh country and its dauntless people. Notes and glossary. YA up

1055 Guillot, René. Mountain with a Secret. Ill. by B. L. Driscoll, tr. by John Marshall. D. Van Nostrand, 1965. An engrossing, exotic novel set in the New Guinea bush early in the 20th century. A mystery surrounds the previous owners of the farm where the narrator, Johan, lives with his Uncle Joost, a former sea captain, Johan's search for the solution carries him into "the mountain with a secret," a mountain inhabited by primitive tribes of pygmies. YA up

1056 Holding, James. Poko and the Golden Demon. Ill. by Charles Keeping. Abelard Schuman, 1967. An exciting story of a small Polynesian boy living on the island of Bora Bora before it was exposed to "civilization." His very smallness is the crux of the story. I

1057 Keith, James. The Scuba Buccaneers. Ill. by Nancy Parker. Roy, 1966. Sandy Morgan, flying to join his father on a marine biological expedition, overhears a conversation on the plane which is a clue to the adventures to follow in which Sandy is accompanied by a well educated Australian aborigine, Johnny Daylight. The setting is on the coral reefs of the northern shore of Australia where the waters are crystal clear, and the story is rich in diving and underwater lore as well as the art of survival on a truly desert island (even lacking fresh water), an art in which Johnny Daylight is an expert. YA

1058 Kent, Louise Andrews. He Went with Magellan. Ill. by Paul Quinn. Houghton Mifflin, 1943. This story follows an earlier Kent book, He Went with Vasco da Gama, and may be even more enjoyable if read after it, but it can stand by itself. Here young Vasco Coelo, whose father had voyaged with da Gama at the end of the 15th century accompanies Magellan on his search westward for the Spice Islands on behalf of King Charles of Spain, his venture having been turned down by King Manuel of Portugal. As in Mrs. Kent's other "He Went With" books there is humor, perilous adventures, and even a slight love interest. She has used the accounts of Pigafetta as a sound historical basis. I, YA

1059 Kiddell, John. A Community of Men. Chilton, 1969. A book in which the same three characters as in Euloowirree Walkabout (see next entry) appear in a very different setting and with different objectives as they try to support and take charge of a bankrupt home for boys from broken homes. Here they are again, David, Hamish and Bottle, and in addition a girl, Ann, a young medical student. YA up

1060 _____. Euloowiree Walkabout. Chilton Book Co., 1968. Three 18-year-old youths, David Morgan, Hamish Griffith and 250-lb. Bottle, make a bet with their elders that with a minimum of clothing and equipment, and with one dollar each of unspendable (except for emergency) money, they can make their way 900 miles from Sidney to Adelaide. They may work, but not for money, use horses (or camels), but no modern means of transportation, and they may not hitchhike. It's a hilariously funny book from which, however, the reader gains a real sense of the lonely spaces of the Australian desert and with it a realization of the appeal that that loneliness and some real hardships might have for three ostensibly lighthearted and sophisticated young men. There is an explanation of the strange title at the beginning and a 10-page glossary of Australian expressions. YA up

1061 Kjelgard, Jim. Boomerang Hunter. Ill. by W. T. Mars. Holiday House, 1960. A young Australian aborigine faces thirst, starvation, wild dingo dogs and hostile tribes in order to find food and water for his own desert tribe. As stated on the cover, "this strange story might have taken place a few years ago or a few thousand years ago." I, YA

1062 MacIntyre, Elizabeth. Ninji's Magic. Ill. by Mamoru Funai and with a map. Alfred A. Knopf, 1966. This is a lovely book with a good story line about a very young New Guinea boy, coming out of a primitive stone-age culture into contact with the white man's world. A story of warm humor and interesting information about New Guinea. I

1063 Mark, Polly. Tani. Ill. by Ursula Loering. David McKay, 1964. At the time of this story, the early 1950s, the small state of Sarawak on the island of Borneo was a British Colony, where 10-year-old Tani's father was a native officer aiding the British District Officer in preparing for the day when the independent country of Malaysia should be formed. So Tani, much against her will, is sent to a Mission School to learn new ways and to find out for herself that the evil spirits she has always feared do not exist. A list of unfamiliar words with their pronunciation is given at the beginning of the book. I

1064 Marshall, James Vance. Walkabout. Ill. by Noela Young. Doubleday, 1959. Thirteen-year-old Mary and her brother Peter, age nine, survive a plane crash in the Australian northern desert region and start to walk to find their uncle in Adelaide, South Australia. Near death from thirst and starvation they are saved by a naked aborigine who is on his "walkabout," his tribal survival test for manhood. Prudish Mary is shocked by the boy's nakedness

and he, in turn is shocked by the expression in her
eyes as she shows her feelings, and two cultures
clash. Beautiful detail of the Northern Territory
of Australia. I, YA

1065 Melville, Hermann. Typee: A Peep at Polynesian
Life (1846). There are of course many editions of
this novel, but one published by Dodd Mead in 1924
and illustrated in color by Mead Schaeffer is worth
a hunt, in spite of its size and dark cover. If you
have read Melville in the South Seas you will recognize the source of this plot in which two young men
escape from their ship and wander into the cannibal
valley of Typee where they are captured (but fortunately not eaten) by the Typees. They rather enjoy their captivity but the American regretfully decides to return to civilization and escapes on a
whaler. A

1066 _____. Omoo: A Narrative of Adventures in the
South Seas. This sequel to Typee begins with a
review of the ending of that book, and what a good
idea that is. Here the crew of the whaler on which
the American had made his escape from Typee
mutinies and is imprisoned on the island of Tahiti.
A

1067 Michener, James. Tales of the South Pacific. Macmillan, 1947 (Fawcett Crest paperback, 1973).
Pulitzer prize for fiction in 1948. A war novel
(but not a battle one) composed of short story chapters strung on a chain of characters of young men
who, for the duration of World War II in the Pacific,
lived, loved, and in too many cases, died there.
A

1068 Nordhoff, Charles and Hall, James Norman. Mutiny
on the Bounty. Little Brown, 1932 (Pocket Books,
1972). The first in the Bounty trilogy, based on
the famous mutiny carried out in 1787 by the crew
of the Bounty against their commander, Capt. William Bligh. A

1069 _____. Men Against the Sea. Little, Brown, 1934
(Pocket Books, 1972). The second in the Bounty
trilogy about Capt. Bligh and the loyal members of
his crew after they were cast adrift in an open
boat. A

1070 _____. Pitcairn's Island. Little, Brown, 1934
(Pocket Book, 1972). The last of the trilogy about
the life of the mutineers on a tiny Pacific island.
These three books can also be found in one volume.
A

Australia, Oceania

1071 Nordhoff, Charles. The Pearl Lagoon. Ill. by Anton Otto Fisher. Little, Brown, 1924. A thrilling adventure novel of a young Californian who leaves his father's ranch to go with his uncle in search of a certain bed of gold-lipped oysters, valuable for mother-of-pearl. Aside from the exciting plot concerning a piratical captain of another ship, there is much interesting information about the fish of the southern seas, island boats and houses, divers and pearls. YA up

1072 Norman, Lillian. Climb a Lonely Hill. Henry Z. Walck, 1970. Fourteen-year-old Jack Clarke and his younger sister, Sue, are on a gold hunting trip with their Uncle Bert in the lonely southern Australian bush when an accident occurs. Uncle Bert dies in the wrecked car, and the children must survive on what few provisions they are able to save until help comes (if ever?) or Sue's injured foot is well enough for her to walk with her brother into the unknown distance. Descriptions of the great Australian desert add to the sense of desperation the reader shares with Jack and Sue. I, YA

1073 _____. The Shape of Three. Henry Z. Walck, 1971. Not all novels about Australia are set in the "outback" and this is one of the exceptions where the setting is Sidney and its suburbs. The plot centers on two families caught up together in a strange predicament. I, YA

1074 Ottley, Reginald. The Bates Family. Harcourt Brace and World, 1969. This novel of a large courageous loving family, alone and struggling for survival under the harsh conditions of the Australian outback--drought, flood, bushfire, hunger and accident--is lightened by the rarely expressed but strongly sensed love between the members of the family, especially the 17-year-old twins. YA up

1075 _____. Boy Alone. Ill. by Clyde Pearson. Harcourt Brace and World, 1965. The first of a trilogy by a man who knows whereof he writes, for at 15 he was a "wood and water Joey" on a cattle station at the edge of the Australian desert in the early 1930s as is the boy of this book. The reader thus feels the boy's loneliness, relieved only by his two dogs, one of which he loses, and understands his fears and his courage, and finally shares his discovery of the loneliness of others in the harsh Australian bush. I, YA

1076 _____. The Roan Colt. Ill. by David Parry. Harcourt Brace and World, 1967. A sequel to Boy Alone, this story has the same setting, the Yamboorah cattle station in Central Australia, and the same main characters including Rags, the boy's dog. The boy is never given a name, perhaps because his experiences are, in the main, those of his creator, Reginald Ottley. I, YA

1077 _____. Rain Comes to Yamboorah. Ill. by Robert Hales. Harcourt Brace and World, 1968. The third of the trilogy about the boy on the Yamboorah cattle station in which he becomes aware of the interdependence of all the members of the Yamboorah community and begins to lose his sense of aloneness. I, YA

1078 _____. Brumbie Dust. Harcourt Brace and World, 1969. A selection of short stories about the author's own adventures in the desolate Australian outback. "Brumbies" are wild horses who often fight among themselves, the young stallions trying to establish leadership of the herd by replacing the old ones. The writer carries the reader with him as he "runs brumbies," or even camels, and as he meets up with odd lonely characters in the desert or in pubs. And, for all the desolation of the scene, he communicates to the reader a sense of the wild fascination of the Australian bush. YA up

1079 _____. Giselle. Harcourt Brace and World, 1968. A short, sensitive novel of a young girl's life on the Island of New Caledonia in the south west Pacific; of her religious faith and love of nature and concern about the people close to her. There is her seriously ill uncle who yearns to go to Lourdes for a cure. There is her father who, she fears, may be in trouble with the law. And there is her unhappy mother who suffers from a sense of isolation. But nothing can down Giselle's brave, happy spirit. YA up

1080 _____. Jim Grey of Moonbah. Harcourt Brace and World, 1970. Fifteen-year-old Jim is unhappy and restless after the death of his father, but, devoted to his understanding mother, he tries to carry on the work of the family sheep station. His meeting with a stranger, however, leads to his leaving home and becoming involved in the serious crime of sheep stealing and plans for further criminal activity. The setting of the novel is the Monaro and Snowy

Australia, Oceania

River country, some of the most beautiful in Australia, according to the author's note. I, YA

1081 _____. No More Tomorrow. Harcourt Brace and Jovanovich, 1971. A deeply touching story of a very old man and his dog, wanderers in the Australian outback from one cattle station to another, the old man reminiscing to the dog as they go, of his younger days in that terribly lonely country. Tension grows as the two become separated and desperately try to find each other again. YA up

1082 Phipson, Joan. Birkin, 1st Amer. ed. Ill. by Margaret Horder. Harcourt Brace and World, 1966. Some children in a small country town in southern Australia adopt a motherless black calf which they name Birkin. The story concerns their adventures in trying to keep him fed and shielded from their elders to whom he is nothing but a trial and general nuisance. I

1083 _____. The Boundary Riders. Ill. by Margaret Horder. Harcourt Brace and World, 1962. Jane, age 13, Bobby, age 11 and their 15-year-old cousin, Vincent, are permitted to go off camping for a week in the hills of central New South Wales, with the assignment of checking the boundaries of the Thompson property. Having completed their work in three days they decide to go off on foot for a day to find a beautiful waterfall they have seen from a distance, but they are caught in a storm and fog and become thoroughly lost, cold, hungry and wet until they finally come upon a house. That, however, is far from the end of their adventures. In this book you will again meet the Barker family (see A Family Conspiracy and Threat to the Barkers). I, YA

1084 _____. Cross Currents. Ill. by Janet Duchesne. Harcourt Brace, 1966. This is a sailing story but also one of the generation gap, a universal phenomenon. Seventeen-year-old Jim "borrows" his father's boat to leave the Sidney harbor and sail to a phosphate island where he hopes to find a job. He hasn't counted, however, on his young outback cousin, Charlie, going along and Charlie's presence, plus an exceptionally stormy sea, give Jim second thoughts. It is also Charlie's story as he grows in self confidence through the experience. YA

1085 _____. The Family Conspiracy. Ill. by Margaret Horder. Harcourt Brace and World, 1962. The

six children of the Barker family conspire to raise
money secretly for their mother's needed hospital-
ization, something she keeps putting off because
their sheep farm in west central New South Wales,
never a prosperous one at best, is suffering from
drought. The money-raising ventures of each child
cause their parents, especially the sick mother, untold anxiety, but finally--well this author knows how
to wind up a plot, skillfully, humorously and happily. I, YA

1086 _____. Good Luck to the Rider. Ill. by Margaret
Horder. Harcourt Brace and World, 1968. Barbara, age 12, was timid and unsure of herself and
not very sturdy until she acquired a comical look-
ing motherless colt, named by her brother "Rosin-
ante" as it reminded him of Don Quixote's "bag of
bones." A pleasant family and horse story set in
New South Wales, Australia. I, YA

1087 _____. Peter and Butch. Harcourt Brace and
World, 1969. The story of a curly-headed, rosy-
cheeked boy in his early teens, trying to remake
his image into that of a tough; into "Butch" instead
of over-mothered "Peter." Some good dog characters and a surprising fillip at the end. I, YA

1088 _____. Six and Silver. Ill. by Margaret Horder.
Harcourt Brace Jovanovich, 1971. A novel set
on a sheep station in the mountainous country of
New South Wales, and Silver, you may as well
know, is a remarkable sheepdog (aren't they all?)
and one of the principal characters of the novel.
Of the six who set out to climb the mountain there
is a visiting city girl, Jess, unused to the hardships of country living but bearing them bravely in
the name of "experience." The leader and guide
of the expedition is Ted who owns a string of ponies,
but he does not count as the sixth. Humor, skillful characterizations and vivid landscapes are intrinsic features of all this author's books. I, YA

1089 _____. Threat to the Barkers. Ill. by Margaret
Horder. Harcourt Brace and World, 1963. This
is something of a detective story in which you will
get to know the Barker family if you haven't already
met them in The Family Conspiracy. In this book
Edward Barker and his friend Garry come upon
some clues to sheep stealing which they are afraid
to reveal to Edward's older brother Jack, for fear
of reprisal from the thieves. The dogs in this story

(as in so many of these Australian novels) have as much personality as the two-legged characters, and with the engrossing plot we also may learn much about sheep raising and the training of sheep dogs. I, YA

1090 ———. The Way Home. Atheneum, 1973 (a Margaret K. McElderry Book). A novel of fantasy and mysticism in which three children whose car has been swept over a cliff by a flash flood seek to find their way home through a weird surrealistic world and different periods of time. I up

1091 Price, Willard. Cannibal Adventure. Ill. by Pat Marriott. John Day, 1973. The remarkable Hunt brothers of this author's other "adventure" stories, go to New Guinea with orders from their father (a collector of animals for zoos), for crocodiles, sea cows, tiger sharks, kangaroos, and many other species of wild life and human skulls. As usual there is a villain in the story to add more danger to the perils they face among cannibals and wild animals, the same Kaggs who caused them untold trouble in South Sea Adventure. Also, as is usual in Price's books, there is a wealth of nature lore woven through the wildly improbable action. I, YA

1092 ———. South Sea Adventure. With maps by the author. John Day, 1952. Three white boys, the Hunt brothers, and a native boy are marooned on a desert island in the south seas, with no hope of rescue, though obviously they must be rescued in the end or how could there be any more "Adventure" books as we hope and expect there will be. This one beats Robinson Crusoe and The Swiss Family Robinson and the reader also learns a lot about marine life of the South Pacific. I, YA

1093 Prichard, Katherine Susannah. The Wild Oats of Han, rev. ed. Ill. by Genevieve Melrose. Macmillan, 1968 (first pub. in 1928). A story about the happy childhood of a young girl, Han, in Tasmania in the late 19th century. Her "wild oats" actually were pretty wild for that period, but old Sam, the shingle splitter to whom she turned in joy and sorrow, encouraged her in her misdeeds. I

1094 Roland, Betty. The Forbidden Bridge. Ill. by Geraldine Spence. McGraw-Hill, 1965. An exciting story about a lonely little Australian boy who yearns to play with a family of children who live across the wild river, but the only crossing is a long rail-

road trestle and Jamie is forbidden to cross that
without a grown-up. Of course he disobeys, which
is what makes the story so exciting. E

1095 Southall, Ivan. <u>Ash Road.</u> Ill. by Clem Seale. St.
Martin's Press, 1966. Winner of the Australian
Childrens' Book of the Year Award for 1966, besides two American awards. Warning! Don't start
this book unless you are going to be able to read it
to the end. A bushfire is started by accident by
three teenagers out on a vacation campout, and immediately gets out of control as it is a dangerously
dry season. The reader becomes immediately involved with the terror of the boys responsible for
the fire and all the families on Ash Road, from
the grandparents to the very young. YA up

1096 _____. <u>Chinaman's Reef Is Ours.</u> St. Martin's
Press, 1970. A tense tough novel about a near-
ghost town beside a copper mine and the reaction
of the townspeople when the Pan Pacific Mining Co.
suddenly appears on a Sunday morning in the shape
of a mammoth convoy of bulldozers, trailers and
movers in preparation for digging up the old ruin
of a town so that a new town can be built nearby
for mine workers. Even though the old town of
Chinaman's Reef was a near ruin, it did provide
a certain sense of freedom for children which the
new town, they knew, would never have, and they
put up a good fight for their rights. YA up

1097 _____. <u>The Fox Hole.</u> Ill. by Ian Ribbons. St.
Martin's, 1967. A short novel, best to be read
at one sitting, for the suspense is truly fearsome.
A 10-year-old boy falls into an old mining shaft,
long deserted because of its sinister reputation and
while waiting in terror for his rescue, believes he
sees gold. I, YA

1098 _____. <u>Hill's End.</u> St. Martin's Press, 1963. All
the inhabitants of the little timber town of Hill's
End have gone off to their nearest "big town," 85
miles away, for their annual picnic. All, that is,
except for one man in charge of the mill, and seven
children and their school mistress who are off exploring caves for aboriginal drawings. A sudden
violent story cuts the children off from the outside
world, they lose their teacher in the storm, and
when they finally make it back to Hill's End they
find the town in ruins. With no way to get help
(radio out of commission and telephone lines down),

Australia, Oceania 213

they cope with the situation, each in his individual way. I, YA

1099 _____. Josh. Macmillan, 1971. A Carnegie Medal Book for 1971. An impressionistic novel, almost stream-of-consciousness; the story is told by 14-year-old Josh, a dreamer and poet in constant conflict with his peers as well as with his 73-year-old Aunt Clara (a wonderful character), whom he visits for a miserable week of vacation. YA up

1100 _____. To the Wild Sky. Ill. by Jennifer Tuckwell. St. Martin's, 1967. Australian Children's Book Award for 1968. Six young people (one very young) go off on a private plane for a weekend in New South Wales, but, because of a terrible happening (not a storm) they finally land instead on a deserted island off the coast of Australia, their plane a complete shambles and their possessions swept away by the tide. During their struggle for survival the reader "gets inside" each of the characters, especially the one with aboriginal ancestry. YA

1101 Sperry, Armstrong. The Rain Forest. Ill. by the author. Macmillan, 1947. Chad Powell arrives in New Guinea at a time when a tribal raid has just been carried out in the very district where his orinthologist father is encamped. The plan had been for his father to meet him and fly him into the camp, but his plane is out of commission, so Chad instead accompanies a patrol officer and six native armed constables, on foot and by boat, through the jungle in search of the raiders, the Kuku-kikus. The story takes place in 1940 before the Japanese and Americans were fighting each other in the New Guinea jungle. I

1102 Swenson, Eric. The South Sea Shilling; Voyages of Captain Cook, R.N. Ill. by Charles Michael Daugherty. Viking, 1952. A good suspenseful adventure novel built upon solid, authentic fact. YA

1103 Thiele, Colin. Fire in the Stone. Harper and Row, 1974. A novel set in the opal fields of Australia, about the fierce competition among the miners, working alone and often secretly, trying to find some of the precious color that means opal. Ernie Ryan does find opal and hides the gems from his father but unfortunately not from a thief, and he and his best friend, an Aborigine boy, start on a long and perilous search for the thief and the stolen gem. A story full of adventure, suspense and danger, with an unexpected and touching ending. YA

1104 Woodberry, Joan. Come Back, Peter. Ill. by George Tetlow. T. Y. Crowell, 1972. A sensitive story of three boys of the Australian outback whose lives, quite separate and different in the beginning, are finally drawn together at the end. Paul, 10 years old, sadly misses his brother Peter whose death has left their mother emotionally withdrawn at times, and, at others, over protective of Paul. Johnny Moran, living 25 miles away across the desert, also has a mother problem in that his has become ill in her husband's absence--too ill to care for her new baby and two-year-old daughter. The third boy is an aborigine, wavering between the white and aborigine cultures. And strangely it turns out that his name is Peter. I, YA

1105 Youngberg, Norma R. The Queen's Gold. Ill. by Harold Munson. William Morrow, 1956. What a thriller! The story of a young boy cast away among a tribe of headhunters on the coast of Borneo. His life is saved by a kind Dyak woman and eventually he is accepted by the village tribe and even adopted as a son by the man next in line to the chief. This brings on the bitter hatred of two of the village boys who try more than once to kill him. Because of his writing and pictures in the sand he is considered a witch doctor and, as such, and at the risk of his own life, he saves the villagers from a pirate raid. The time, 1840. I, YA

Part Five

PICTURE BOOKS

In most libraries there is a corner for very little children and picture books of various shapes and sizes, where you are apt to find preschoolers sitting on small chairs, benches, or, most often, the floor, "reading" aloud and expressively from their special favorites among the books. "Why do you want that book again?" a mother asks as her child brings a rather worn volume to the check-out desk. What a silly question. Doesn't she realize that the best stories are those which having been read once or twice to a child can then be read over and over again by him.

First and second graders shy away from this section of the library, but they can certainly enjoy and profit by the books and they can always "save face" by explaining that they are going to read them to younger members of the family. And indeed these are also great read-aloud books for parents, teachers and childrens' librarians.

AFRICA

1106 Adamson, Joy. Elsa. Ill. with photographs. Pantheon, 1961. An album of photographs of the famous lioness and the Adamsons who brought her up from cubhood and taught her to stalk and kill, so that she could be set free in the African jungle; a pick of many fine photographs which could not be included in the book, Born Free. All ages

1107 Bernheim, Mark and Evelyne. In Africa. Ill. with 91 photographs. Atheneum, 1973. A photographic panorama of the "dark continent" especially for very young readers but of interest to all ages. E

1108 Chandler, Edna Walker. Will You Carry Me? Ill. by Meyer Seltzer. Albert Whitman, 1965. A brightly illustrated story of a little Liberian boy who had to carry a pan of coconuts to market and found the load too heavy. The pictures and easy-to-read text convey a great deal of information about the 100-year-old country of Liberia, a country where only Negroes are given citizenship. E

1109 Dayrell, Elphinstone. Why the Sun and the Moon Live in the Sky. Ill. by Blair Lent. Houghton Mifflin, 1968. A logical answer to a logical question. An African folk tale. E

1110 Elkin, Benjamin. Such Is the Way of the World. Ill. by Yoko Mitsuhashi. Parents' Magazine Press, 1968. An amusing story from Ethiopia about a little boy, sent with his pet monkey to watch his father's cattle, who has one mishap after another but philosophically accepts that "such is the way of the world." E

1111 Feelings, Muriel. Moja Means One; A Swahili Counting Book. Ill. by Tom Feelings. Dial Press, 1971. A book primarily addressed to children of African origin, but surely of interest to children of various origins (and their elders). Beautifully illustrated, it also has a map, showing where Swahili is spoken: Somalia, Kenya, Tanzania, Zambia, Mozambique, Uganda, Burundi and the Democratic Republic of the Congo (Zaïre). The introduction explains that it is also used in other parts of Africa. E

1112 _____. Jambo Means Hello: A Swahili Alphabet Book. Ill. by Tom Feelings. Dial, 1974. A good follow-up to the earlier book.

1113 Haley, Gail E. A Story, A Story: An African Folktale Retold. Ill. by the reteller. Atheneum, 1970. An explanatory preface to this African folktale, gives the origin of the many spider stories which abound in African folklore. PB

1114 Lexau, Joan. Crocodile and Hen. Ill. by Joan Sandin. Harper and Row, 1969. An adaptation of the folktale, "Why the Crocodile Does Not Eat the Hen," taken from a book by R. E. Dennet. PB

1115 Lindop, Edmund. Hubert the Traveling Hippopotamus. Ill. by Jane Carlson. Little Brown, 1961. A true story of a hippo whose fame was so great that in 1931 a statue of him was placed in a museum. PB

1116 McDermott, Gerald. The Magic Tree; A Tale from the Congo. Ill. by the author. Holt, Rinehart and Winston, 1973. Adapted from an animated film by Landmark Presentations, this story of twin brothers has such strong African illustrations that one can almost hear the drums. E

1117 Mason, Michael. Clyde of Africa. Ill. with photographs by Ken Heyman. Macmillan, 1963. How Clyde learned that it was not wise to roar until completely grown-up. PB

1118 Merriam, Eve. Epaminondas. Ill. by the author. Follett, 1968. It is good to have this old story back, adapted from Epaminondas and His Auntie: Stories to Tell Children, by Sara Cone Bryant. PB

1119 Phumla. Nomi and the Magic Fish. Ill. by Carole Byard. Doubleday, 1972. A Zulu version of the Cinderella story as told by a 15-year-old girl in Cape Province, South Africa, who entered it in a story contest. John Inglis Hall arranged to have it published. E up

1120 Rockwell, Anne. When the Drums Sang. Ill. by the author. Parents' Magazine Press, 1973. A South African folktale about a little Bantu girl who was captured by wicked zimwis and put into a drum. Delightful water color illustrations. PB

1121 Tworkov, Jack. The Camel Who Took a Walk. Ill. by Roger Duvoisin. Aladdin Books, 1951. The camel began walking in the dark but by the surprising end of the story, the picture shows the sun shining like brass in the sky. PB

1122 Wellman, Alice. Small-Boy Chuku. Ill. by Richard Cuffari. Houghton Mifflin, 1973. This story of Small-Boy beating his father's drum for rain is a little longer than those in most picture books, but its endearing, vivid illustrations place it in this category. E

1123 Wilson, Beth P. The Great Minu. Ill. by Jerry Pinkney. Follett, 1974. It wouldn't be fair to tell any of the story except to say that it is a favorite of West Africans, and is about a poor farmer's journey to the big city of Accra in Ghana, and what befell him on the way. PB, E

AUSTRALIA

1124 Pender, Lydia. Sharpur the Carpet Snake. Ill. by Virginia Smith. Abelard Schuman, 1967. A story from Sidney about a vegetable seller who gets a snake to kill rats, with astonishing results. E

1125 Sasek, M. This Is Australia. Ill. by the author. Macmillan, 1970. Through this colorful big book, the whole family can have an easy and inexpensive trip to Australia. All ages

CHINA AND HONG KONG

1126 Bishop, Claire Huchet. The Five Chinese Brothers. Ill. by Kurt Wiese. Cadmus Books, 1938. The youngest would only have to hear it read once before he could "read" it to himself. PB

1127 Buck, Pearl. The Chinese Children Next Door. Ill. by William A. Smith. John Day, 1942. An American mother tells about her childhood in China and about the family next door. E

1128 ———. The Chinese Story Teller. Ill. by Regina Shekerjian. John Day, 1971. An American grandmother who had lived in China as a child, recalls a story she had heard from a Chinese story teller about why dogs and cats don't get along with each other. A most attractive easy-to-read book. E

1129 Darbois, Dominique. Kai Ming, Boy of Hong Kong. Ill. with photographs by the author and a map. Follett, 1960 (Children of the World Books). E

1130 Handforth, Thomas. Mei Li. Ill. by the author. Doubleday, 1938. The 1939 Caldecott Medal winner. About a little girl at the New Year's Fair in Peking. E

1131 Herrmanns, Ralph. Lee Lau Flies the Dragon Kite. Tr. from Swedish by Annabelle Macmillan. Ill. with color photographs. Harcourt, Brace and World, 19??. Eight-year-old Lee Lau lives with her family aboard a Hong Kong fishing junk and, with her 10-year-old brother, sets out to earn money for schooling. E up

1132 Hoge, Dorothy. The Black Heart of Indri. Ill. by Janina Domanska. Scribner's, 1966. A charming Chinese fairy tale with pictures as delicately drawn as the story, the theme the familiar one of beauty and the beast. E up

1133 Joslin, Sesyle. Baby Elephant Goes to China. Ill. by Leonard Weisgard. Harcourt, Brace and World, 1963. Would you like to know a few Chinese words in case you should ever dig a hole to China? Well, here are some, and a glossary to show you how to pronounce them. E

1134 Kirn, Ann. The Peacock and the Crow. Ill. by the author. Four Winds Press, 1969. An old Chinese fable retold, about how the peacock acquired his brilliant plumage and the crow his black feathers, the moral being to beware of false friendships. E

1135 Littlefield, William. The Whiskers of Ho Ho. Ill. by

Picture Books

Vladimir Bobri. Lothrop, 1958. A Chinese version of the Easter Rabbit's origin, gaily and delicately illustrated. E

1136 Martin, Patricia Miles. The Pointed Brush. Ill. by Roger Duvoisin. Lothrop, Lee and Shepard, 1959. A story about the strength of a man "who knows the written word." E

1137 Mosel, Arlene. Tikki Tikki Tembo. Ill. by Blair Lent. Holt, Rinehart and Winston, 1968. A folktale retold that begs to be read aloud, about why the Chinese give their children short names. PB

1138 Otsuka, Yuzo. Suho and the White Horse; A Legend of Mongolia. Ill. by Suekichi Akaba, tr. by Yasuko Hirawa. Bobbs-Merrill, 1967. The story of how the horsehead fiddle got its name is here so vividly and actively illustrated that it seemed only right to place it in the picture book section, though it might belong as well in the folklore category. PB, E

1139 Sasek, M. This Is Hong Kong. Ill. by the author. Macmillan, 1965. Like the author's other "This Is" books this will interest the whole family, especially if there might be a chance of going to Hong Kong. All ages

1140 Skipper, Mervyn. The Fooling of King Alexander. Ill. by Gaynor Chapman. Atheneum, 1967. A legend of how a little boy foiled the plans of emperor Alexander to conquer China. E

1141 Wolkstein, Diane. 8,000 Stones; A Chinese Folktale. Ill. by Ed Young. Doubleday, 1972. How would you go about it to weigh an elephant? This is how the governor's son, P'ei did it and how he found out that the Satrap of India's present weighed 8000 stones. E

1142 Wyndham, Robert. Chinese Mother Goose Rhymes. Ill. by Ed Young. World, 1968. A book of easy-to-read nonsense verses, humorous poems, riddles and games to play, designed to be read vertically like an Oriental scroll. E

1143 Yen Liang. Happy New Year. Ill. by the author. J. B. Lippincott, 1961. All the happy events as they took place when the author-illustrator was a small boy in China, told and pictured in lively detail. E

1144 Yolen, Jane. The Emperor and the Kite. Ill. by Ed Young. World, 1967. Illustrated in a modern version of Oriental paper-cut style, this is the story of a very little child's devotion to her father who was sadly neglectful. E

INDIA

1145 Gobhai, Mehlli. Usha the Mouse Maiden. Ill. by the author. Hawthorne Books, 1969. A fable about a mouse that fell from the sky and how she chose her husband after she had been turned into a beautiful maiden. E

1146 ———. Lakshmi, the Water Buffalo Who Wouldn't. Ill. by the author. Hawthorne Books, 1969. Lakshmi would let only one person milk her, and when that one person fell ill what was to be done? E

1147 Kipling, Rudyard. The Miracle of the Mountain. Adapted by Aroline Beecher Leach from a much longer story of Kipling's; ill. by Willi Baum. Addison-Wesley, 1969. About a man who gave up riches and honors to become a holy man and make friends with animals high up in the Himalaya mountains. E

1148 Lionni, Leo. Tico and the Golden Wings. Ill. by the author. Pantheon, 1964. A rather subtle fable with equally lovely and subtle illustrations in the Indian tradition. E

1149 Price, Christine. The Valliant Chattee-Maker. Ill. by the author. Frederick Warne, 1965. A very funny, charmingly illustrated story based on an old folktale from a collection by Mary Trere, "Old Deccan Days."

1150 Quigley, Lillian. The Blind Men and the Elephant. Ill. by Janice Holland. Scribner's, 1959. An exquisitely illustrated retelling of the familiar old Indian fable. E

1151 Saxe, John Godfrey. The Blind Men and the Elephant. Ill. by Paul Galdone. Whittlesey House, 1963. Another version in rhyme of the Indian fable about the blind men each of whom had a totally different idea of the elephant. PB

1152 Siddiqui, Ashraf. Bhombal Dass, The Uncle of Lion; A Tale from Pakistan. Ill. by Tom Hamil. Macmillan, 1959. Bhombal Dass was actually a goat, but believing that "wit is mightier than strength" he used his in the face of a tiger. PB

1153 Skurzynski, Gloria. The Magic Pumpkin. Ill. by Rocco Negri. Four Winds Press, 1971. Mother Par-

Picture Books

vati was a wise old woman and a very brave one and did not intend to become the dinner for a tiger or wolf as she traveled through the jungle in her magic pumpkin. E, I

1154 Weiss, Renee Karol. The Bird from the Sea. Ill. by Ed Young. Thomas Y. Crowell, 1970. A humorous story with a serious message about a captured bird that grew sadder and thinner each day as the delightful illustrations show. E

JAPAN

1155 Baruch, Dorothy Walter. Kappa's Tug-of-War with Big Brown Horse: The Story of a Japanese Water Imp. Paintings by Sanryo Sakai. Tuttle, 1962. A read-aloud picture book about a Kappa, a creature who had to have water on the top of his head in order to live. E

1156 Bryant, Sara Cone. The Burning Rice Fields. Ill. by Mamoru Funai. Holt, Rinehart and Winston, 1963 (a Young Owl Book). The pictures tell the story of why the old man in old Japan set fire to the rice fields on the top of the mountain. PB

1157 Hicks, Eleanor B. Circus Day in Japan. Ill. by the author. Tuttle, 1953. An action-packed story of contemporary Japan. E

1158 Hirsh, Marilyn. How the World Got Its Color. Adapted and illustrated by Marilyn Hirsh. Crown, 1972. Beautiful legend and pictures for the very youngest "readers." PB

1159 Ishii, Momoko. Issun Boshi the Inchling; An Old Tale of Japan. Tr. by Yone Mizuta. Ill. by Fuku Akino. Walker, 1965. Small things are always special fun for small people. The illustrations are in the fashion of a traditional scroll. PB

1160 Lifton, Betty Jean. Joji and the Amanojaku. Ill. by Eiichi Mitsui. W. W. Norton, 1965. The story of a famous Japanese scarecrow who made friends with the crows he was set out to scare. PB

1161 _____. The Many Lives of Chio and Goro. Ill. by Yasuo Segawa. W. W. Norton, 1968. Chio and Goro were a Japanese couple who had no children, so they decided that in their next life they would become animals--a chicken and a fox. An original tale in folklore style. PB

1162 _____. The Mud Snail Son. Ill. by Fuku Akino.

Atheneum, 1971. An old tale of kindness and the power of love in which a poor Japanese couple pray for a son and are given a mud snail instead of a baby boy. PB

1163 Matsuno, Masaku. Chie and the Sports Day. Ill. by Kazue Mizumera. World, 1965. A good read-aloud story about the warm relationship of a brother and younger sister. E

1164 _____. Taro and the Bamboo Shoot. Adapted from the Japanese by Alice Low. Ill. by Yasuo Segawa. Pantheon, 1964. Taro grows up with a bamboo shoot and thus finds a way to the sea. Of all things! E

1165 _____. Taro and the Tōfu. Ill. by Kazue Mizumura. World, 1962. What does a boy do when he finds out that the old tōfu seller has given him too much change? E

1166 Matsutani, Miyoko. The Crane Maiden. English version by Alvin Tresselt (tr. from Tsuru no Ongaeshi); ill. by Chihiro Iwasaki. Parents' Press, 1968. A very old legend about an old man who rescues a crane from a trap and how he and his wife were rewarded for this good deed. E, I

1167 _____. How the Withered Trees Blossomed. Ill. by Yasuo Segawa. J. B. Lippincott, 1969. A story-picture book to be read from back to front (as in Japan) with Japanese text as well as English. Interesting for its format. E

1168 _____. The Witch's Magic Cloth. English version by Alvin Tresselt (tr. from Yamanbano Nishiki); ill. by Yasuo Segawa. Parents' Magazine Press, 1969. A weird witchy story with weird witchy pictures. E

1169 Mosel, Arlene. The Funny Little Woman. Ill. by Blair Lent. E. P. Dutton, 1972. A funny little story based on a tale by Lafcadio Hearn, about a little woman who liked to make dumplings and laugh all the time, tee-he-he-he. E

1170 Nakagawa, Ricko. A Blue Seed. Ill. by Yuriko Omura. Hastings House, 1967. How a blue seed produced a blue house which grew and grew and grew. PB

1171 Nakatani, Chiyoko. Fumio and the Dolphins; A Picture Story from Japan. Ill. by the author. World, 1970. How Fumio and his brother Taro rescued some dolphins from fishing nets. E

1172 Slobodkin, Louis. Yasu and the Strangers. Ill. by the author. Macmillan, 1965. A story about a little boy who went on the school bus to visit the great temple of Nara during the Cherry Blossom Festival and got lost, along with a little deer and an American couple, until he remembered what his mother had said before he left. E

1173 Smith, Garry and Vesta. Clickety Cricket. Ill. by Fred Crump, Jr. Steck-Vaughn, 1969. A happy tale with lovely bright pictures. PB

1174 Stamm, Claus. The Very Special Badgers. Ill. by Kazue Mizumura. Viking, 1960. Two rival tribes of badgers have a territorial dispute and each tries to out-cheat, out-guess, and out-magic the other. E

1175 Takeichi, Yasoo. The Mighty Prince. Ill. by Yoshimasa Sejima. Crown, 1971. How a hated prince learned a lesson from a little girl. E

1176 Titus, Eve. The Two Stonecutters. Ill. by Yoko Mitsuhashi. Doubleday, 1967. Adapted from a Japanese folktale this is one of those "wishes" stories, showing that we are usually better off as we are than after getting our wishes to be something else. E

1177 Uchida, Yoshiko. The Forever Christmas Tree. Ill. by Kazue Muzumura. Scribner's, 1963. Two little Japanese children search for a tree to decorate for Christmas, but the only one they find is right in front of the house of a very unfriendly old man. E

1178 Wise, Winifred. The Revolt of the Darumas. Ill. by Beverly Komoda. Parents' Magazine Press, 1970. Did you ever have a roly-poly doll that no matter how you laid it down always sprang up again? Well, such dolls are called darumas and this story is about how they earned their eyes. E

1179 Yashima, Taro. Crow Boy. Ill. by the author. Viking, 1955. A tale of a very small Japanese schoolboy so fearful of the other children and the teacher that he didn't even try to learn from his books, but found his own way of learning. E

1180 ———. The Village Tree. Ill. by the author. Viking, 1953. Memories of childhood summer fun near a river and a huge tree. Pictures and text are filled with action. PB

1181 ——— and Yashima, Mitsu. Plenty to Watch. Ill. by the authors. Viking, 1954. Mostly crayoned pictures with just a few explanatory words about Taro Yashima's childhood on an island far to the

south of Japan. PB
1182 Yoda, Junichi. The Rolling Rice Ball. English version by Alvin Tresselt; ill. by Saburo Watanabe. Parents' Magazine Press, 1969. A story showing clearly that greed never pays. PB
1183 Yolen, Jane. The Seventh Mandarin. Ill. by Ed Young. Seabury, 1970. A beautifully made book with a meaningful story. E

MIDDLE EAST AND BIBLE STORIES

1184 Ambrus, Victor. The Sultan's Bath. Ill. by the author. Harcourt Brace Jovanovich, 1971. This story is based on an old Hungarian folk tale, but since it is about an Arab sultan, why not set it in the Arabian desert, just for fun. E
1185 Bolliger, Max. Noah and the Rainbow, An Ancient Story Retold. Ill. by Helga Aichinger, tr. by Clyde Robert Bulla. Thomas Y. Crowell, 1972. One of children's favorite Bible stories simply told and beautifully illustrated. E
1186 Bulla, Clyde Robert. Jonah and the Big Fish. Ill. by Helga Aichinger. Thomas Y. Crowell, 1970. The ever popular Bible story, handsomely illustrated. PB
1187 ———. Joseph the Dreamer. Ill. by Gordon Laite. Thomas Y. Crowell, 1971. Simply told and dramatically illustrated, the great Bible story of Joseph and his brothers. E, I
1188 DeRegniers, Beatrice Schenk. David and Goliath. Ill. by Richard Powers. Viking, 1965. This retelling of the story of young David and the giant gives in straight narrative form most of the facts about David which are scattered through several books of the Bible. E, I
1189 Economakis, Olga. Oasis of the Stars. Ill. by Blair Lent. Coward McCann, 1965. A Junior Literary Guild selection. An atmospheric story and pictures of desert life and a little boy who dug deep to find stars in the sand. E
1190 Elkin, Benjamin. The Wisest Man in the World; A Legend of Ancient Israel. Ill. by Anita Lobel. Parents' Magazine Press, 1968. Gorgeously illustrated, the legend of King Solomon and the Queen of Sheba and a bee. E
1191 MacBeth, George. Jonah and the Lord. Ill. by Mar-

garet Gordon. Holt, Rinehart and Winston, 1970. How Jonah disobeyed the Lord and suffered for his disobedience but was finally forgiven. E

1192 Saporta, Raphael. A Basket in the Reeds. Ill. by H. Hechtkopf. Lerner Publications, 1968. The story of Moses in the bullrushes, poetically told and illustrated. E

1193 Sasek, M. This Is Israel. Ill. by the author. Macmillan, 1970. A short, comfortable trip to Israel, texts from the Bible along with the colorful pictures. All ages

1194 Spier, Jo. The Creation. Ill. by the author. Doubleday, 1966. The text from Genesis is taken from the Jerusalem Bible and handwritten by Joseph P. Ascherl. All ages

1195 Taylor, Florence M. A Boy Once Lived in Nazareth. Ill. by Len Ebert. Henry Z. Walck, 1969. A description of the place and time setting of Jesus' boyhood, with illustrations of him at work and play and study. E

1196 Weisner, William. The Tower of Babel. Ill. by the author. Viking, 1968. Based on the story in the Book of Genesis and also on Hebrew Myths by Robert Graves and Rafael Patai, this retelling of how people became divided into many nations with different tongues is humorously handled with bright illustrations. Good for story telling. E

1197 Wolcott, Carolyn Muller. At Jesus' House. Ill. by Paul Galdone. Broadman Press, 1959. A simple little story about a real boy who was a carpenter's son. PB

MONGOLIA

1198 Otsuka, Yuzo. Suho and the White Horse, A Legend of Mongolia. Ill. by Suckichi Akaba. Translated by Yasuko Hirawa. Bobbs-Merrill, 1967. The story of how the horsehead fiddle got its name. E

SOUTHEAST ASIA

1199 Arüego, José and Ariane. A Crocodile's Tale; A Philippine Folk Story. Ill. by the authors. Scribner's, 1972. A story about a boy who freed a crocodile after which the croc wanted to eat him.

Is that gratitude? PB

1200 Ayer, Jacqueline. Nu Dang and His Kite; A Tale from Thailand. Ill. by the author. Harcourt Brace, 1959. Pictures and text together tell the story of a little Siamese boy who lost his kite and how he found it again. E

1201 _____. The Paper-Flower Tree; A Tale from Thailand. Ill. by the author. Harcourt Brace and World, 1962. How little Miss Moon tried to raise a paper-flower tree like the one an old peddler had to show. PB

1202 _____. A Wish for a Little Sister. Ill. by the author. Harcourt Brace and World, 1960. The story of a little girl of Bangkok who lived in a house where silk was woven. Not much of a story really but amusing and delightfully illustrated. PB

1203 Darbois, Dominque. Rikka and Rindji, Children of Bali. Photographs by the author and a map. Follett, 1959. A story of childhood on this enchanted island. E

1204 Kaye, Geraldine. The Sea Monkey; A Picture Story from Malaysia. Ill. by Gay Galsworthy. World, 1968. About a little boy living in a fishing village in Malaysia and his monkey, Adek, who is suspected of mischievous acts. E

1205 Taylor, Mark. The Fisherman and the Goblet; A Vietnamese Folktale. Ill. by Taro Yashima. Golden Gates Junior Books, 1971. I

TURKEY

1206 Faulkner, John. Judge Not. Ill. by the author. Albert Whitman, 1968. A Middle East tale, pictured in its Turkish version about an old man who, before leaving on a pilgrimage to Mecca, leaves his savings in what he thought were trustworthy hands. E

1207 Walker, Barbara. Hilili and Dilili, A Turkish Silly Tale. Ill. by Bill Barss. Follett, 1965. A truly funny folktale, delightfully illustrated, about an old couple "with not a whole wit between them." Adapted from a Turkish folk tale translated by Mrs. Neriman Hizir in Ankara, Turkey. E

1208 _____. Just Say Hic. Ill. by Don Bolognese. Follett, 1965. Another Turkish folktale translated by Mrs. Neriman Hizir in Ankara, Turkey. E

1209 _____. Stargazer to the Sultan. (With Mine Sümer.) Ill. by Joseph Low. Parents' Magazine Press, 1967. About a poor woodcutter and his ambitious wife. E

AUTHOR INDEX

Aardema, Verna 63-65, 257, 339
Abrahams, Peter 40, 41
Abrashkin, Raymond 146
Abu-Zahra, Nadia 371
Achebe, Chinua 40, 66, 278
Adamson, Joy 147-149, 1106
Adanson, Michel 41
Addison, John 19
Adu, Omotayo 277
Aitmotov, Chinghis 570
Akeley, Delia 30
Alden, Carella 407
Alexander, Frances 767
Allen, Samuel 20
Alter, Robert Edmond 51
Ambrus, Victor 1184
Ames, Sophia Ripley 251
Anderson, Joy 785
Anderson, Paul 902
Andrews, Mary Evans 16
Andrews, Roy Chapman 786, 787
Appel, Benjamin 711, 842, 982
Apsler, Alfred 611
Archer, Jules 166, 743, 744, 975
Arkell-Hardwick, A. 30
Arkhurst, Joyce Cooper 258
Armstrong, William H. 485
Arnott, Kathleen 67
Arora, Shirley L. 646
Arsenyev, Vladimir 571
Aruego, José and Ariane 1199
Arundel, Jocelyn 176
Ashabranner, Brent 237, 282, 469
Asimov, Isaac 408, 409, 486
Aung, Maung Htin 629
Avidar, Yemima 541
Ayer, Jacqueline 1200-1202
Ayer, Margaret 945, 946

Baba of Karo 40
Bacon, E. 30
Bahar, Hushang 410
Baker, Eleanor Z. 999, 1000
Baker, Nina Brown 745
Baker, Rachel 451
Baldwin, William Charles 30
Balow, Tom 324
Bamboté 311
Banai, Margolit 521
Bang, Garrett 881
Banks, Lynne Reid 522
Barnes, Gregory Allen 279
Barnett, Correlli 80
Barr, Pat 367
Bartos Höppner, B. 572-575
Baruch, Dorothy Walter 1155
Batchelor, Julie Forsyth 647
Battuta Ibn 30
Baumann, Hans 17, 74, 120, 211, 411, 788
Bayliss, John 21
Beaton-Jones, Cynon 768
Beatty, John and Patricia 487
Beebe, B. F. 22
Behn, Harry 843
Beier, Ulli 40
Benét, Laura 52
Benson, Harold 208
Benson, Mary 40
Berger, Terry 340
Bernheim, Marc and Evelyne 23, 230-232, 1107
Berry, Erick (Allena Best) 121, 983
Bertol, Roland 259
Biber, Yehoash 523
Bird, Isabella L. 845
Birch, Cyril 769
Bishop, Claire Huchet 488, 1126
Blatter, Dorothy 395

Bleeker, Sonia 150, 197, 233, 234, 298, 323
Block, Irvin 746
Blunden, Godfrey 1002
Bolliger, Max 489, 1185
Bonham, Frank 648
Booth, Esma Rideout 312, 313
Booz, Elizabeth Benson 649
Borden, Charles A. 1001, 1041
Bothwell, Jean 177, 587, 588, 650-664, 984
Boulle, Pierre 985
Bowles, Cynthis 589
Boyle, Kay 524
Bradley, Duane 139
Braymer, Marjorie 383
Breck, Vivian 903
Breetveld, Jim 412
Brinsmead, H. F. 1042, 1043
Bro, Margueritte Harmon 789, 790
Brooks, Lester 24
Brown, Marcia 467
Brown, William A. 54
Bruckner, Karl 122, 904
Bryan, Ashley 68
Bryant, Chester 665
Bryant, Sara Cone 1156
Bryce, L. Winifred 590
Bryson, Bernarda 468
Buchan, John 343
Buck, Pearl 666, 747, 791-793, 905, 906, 1127, 1128
Buckley, Peter 280
Buehr, Walter 748
Buell, Hal 846
Bulla, Clyde Robert 1186, 1187
Burchell, S. C. 81
Burdick, Eugene 992
Burton, Jane 151
Burton, W. F. P. 314
Byers, Betsy 525
Byrne 794

Cadell, Elizabeth 667
Caillié, René 30
Caldwell, John C. 241, 330, 413, 414, 712, 947-950, 1003, 1004
Camay, Joan 452
Carbonnier, Jeanne 304
Carlson, Dale 315, 795, 796

Carpenter, Allan 152-155, 198, 324, 325
Carpenter, Frances 69, 369, 770, 882, 883
Carr, Rachel 847
Carroll, Jock 928
Cassedy, Sylvia 630
Catherall, Arthur 75, 212, 526, 668
Cavanna, Betty 178, 213, 797, 907
Cervon, Jacqueline 396
Chamberlain, William 934
Chandler, Edna Walker 669, 1108
Chang, Isabelle 771
Channel, A. R. 670
Chapman, Walker (Silverberg) 749
Chase, Francis Jr. 934
Chauncy, Nan 1044-1048
Cheney, Cora 798
Chetin, Helen 70
Chief Kabongo 40
Child, Fay 179
Chisiza, Conduzu 40
Chourou, Bechir 198
Chrisman, Arthur Bowie 772
Christopher, John 180
Chu, Daniel 25
Churchill, Winston Spencer 30
Clair, Andrée 316
Clapperton, Commander 30
Clark, Denis 1049
Clark, Mavis Thorpe 1050-1053
Clark, Roger W. 908
Clauston, A. E. 21
Cleary, Jon 1054
Clifford, Mary Louise 181, 235, 415, 951
Coatsworth, Elizabeth 76, 140, 141, 214, 884, 885
Cocagnac, A. M. 886
Cohen, Daniel 334, 558
Cohen, Joan Lebold 612
Cole, Robert Wellesley 40
Collis, Robert 40
Cone, Molly 527
Conroy, Robert 952, 953
Cooke, David C. 416, 954
Coolidge, Olivia 123, 374, 397, 490, 613

Copeland, Paul W. 82, 417
Cordell, Alexander 799
Costain, Thomas B. 800
Cottrell, Leonard 83, 84, 106, 418
Coughlin, Robert 26
Courlander, Harold 71, 115, 116, 260-262, 370, 977
Cousins, Norman 40
Crane, Louise 53, 299
Cretan, Gladys Yessayan 576
Crockett, Lucy Hernden 909

D'Amelio, Dan 874
Daniel, Anita 305
Darbois, Dominique 236, 1129, 1203
Dareff, Hal 955
Dart, Dr. Raymond A. 30
David, Kurt 801
Davidson, Basil 27, 28
Davis, Jean [pseud.] 107
Davis, Norman 281
Davis, Richard Harding 30
Davis, Russell 237, 282, 469
Day, A. Grove 1024
Dayan, Ruth 453
Dayrell, Elphinstone 1109
DeBeer, Sir Gavin 205
DeBrisson 30
Dejong, Meindert 802
DeKay, Ormonde Jr. 361
DeLany, Milan 152
Denis, Michaela 21
deProrock, Byron Khun 30
DeRegniers, Beatrice Schenk 1188
Dickinson, Peter 398
Dihoff, Gretchen 238
Dilts, Marion M. 848, 849
Dineen, Betty 182
Dinesen, Isak 167, 168
Diqs, Isaac 454
Dobler, Lavinia 54
Dobrin, Arnold 671, 910
Donna, Natalie 183
Dooley, Thomas A. 976
Dorliae, Peter 263
Downey, Glanville 384
Downing, Charles 371
Drewery, Mary 528
DuBois, Theodora 672

Dudman, Helga 453
Duggan, Alfred 375
Dumas, Alexandre 30
Dupuey, Trevor Nevitt 750
Durrell, Gerald 21

Eastwick, Ivy 142
Eaton, Jeanette 55, 614
Eberte, Irmengarde 713
Echezona, W. W. C. 40
Economakis, Olga 1189
Edelman, Lily 850
Edmonds, I. G. 491, 714, 887, 888, 956-958
Edwardes, Michael 615
Edwardson, Cordelia 529
Ekrem, Selma 388
Elkin, Benjamin 1110, 1190
Elkin, Sam 385
Ellis, Harry B. 1, 419
Elting, Mary 317
Engle, Eloise 1025
Engelbert, Victor 85, 239
Ensor, Dorothy 470
Epstein, Beryl 199
Epstein, Sam 199
Equiano, Olandah 41
Eshugboy, Ezekiela 260
Estabrook, Irene 209
Eunson, Roby 751
Evans, M. Fulmer 851
Evarts, Hal G. 673, 803
Exman, Eugene 306

Fafuna, Babs 41
Fairservice, Walter A. Jr. 362, 420, 591
Falls, C. B. 2
Faulkner, John 1206
Fechter, Alyce Shinn 77
Feder-Tal, Karah 530
Feelings, Muriel 1111, 1112
Feelings, Tom 252
Fellows, Lawrence 156
Fenner, Carol 184
Fergar, Mary 371
Fitch, Florence Mary 9, 492
Flack, Marjorie 804
Fleming, Elizabeth P. 318, 911
Fon Eisen, Anthony 18

Forman, Brenda-Lu and Harrison 240
Forman, James 531
Forsberg, Vera 674
Forster, E. M. 675
Franck, Frederick 319
Frankell, Haskell 28
Freville, Nicolas 241
Friend, Morton 559
Frisbee, Florence 1026
Frost, Kelman 215
Fuja, Abayomi 264
Fukei, Arlene 805
Fukuda, Hanako 875
Fullerton, Alexander 21
Fullerton, Garry 40
Fyson, J. G. 512, 513

Gaer, Joseph 631, 632
Garnett, Emmeline 616
Gatheru, R. Mugo 41
Gatti, Attilio 21
Gerson, Mary-Joan 265
Gidal, Sonia and Tim 242, 532, 592, 852, 959
Gillon, Diana and Meir 421
Gilsäter, Robert 422
Gilstrap, Robert 209
Ginsburg, Mirra 565, 566
Gleason, Judith 266
Glubok, Shirley 29, 86, 423, 424, 715, 853
Gobhai, Mehlli 633, 1145, 1146
Godden, Jon 617
Godden, Rumer 617, 676, 677
Godey, John 934
Goetz, Lee Garrett 185
Goldberg, Leah 533
Goldston, Robert 716, 717
Gollomb, Joseph 307
Gorham, Charles 108
Graham, Gail B. 978, 986
Graham, Lorenz 267-270, 283
Grant, Eva 678
Graves, Robert 376
Gray, Elizabeth Janet 912
Gray, J. E. B. 634
Green, Roger Lancelyn 117
Groseclose, Elgin 534
Grousset, René 752
Guillot, René 72, 284-292, 567, 635, 636, 1065

Gunther, John 10, 21, 199
Guthrie, Anne 618
Gutman, Nahum 541

Haggard, Rider 344
Haldane, Charlotte 753
Haley, Gail E. 1113
Hall, Barbara 40
Hall, James Norman 1068-1070
Hallard, Peter 679
Hall-Quest, Olga 56
Hamada, Hirosuke 895
Hámori, László 535, 987
Hampden, John 471
Handforth, Thomas 1130
Hansel, Robert R. 206
Hanser, Richard 493
Han Suyin 754
Hapgood, David 40
Hareff, Hal 955
Harford, John 30
Harmon, Humphrey 171, 186
Harrer, Heinrich 718
Harrington, Lyn 719, 720, 1005
Harris, Rosemary 124-126
Hauff, Wilhelm 472
Haugaard, Christian 514
Haughton, Rosemary 494
Hautzig, Esther 563
Haviland, Virginia 637
Haviv, Yifrach 541
Hawkes, Jacquetta 87
Hay, John 721
Heady, Eleanor 172-174
Helfman, Elizabeth S. 341
Heller, Deane Fons 386
Henderson, Larry 425, 960
Hennessy, Maurice 57, 253, 254
Herodotus 30
Herrmanns, Ralph 680, 1131
Hersey, John 806
Herzog, George 261
Heuer, Kenneth 89
Heyerdahl, Thor 1006
Hicks, Eleanor B. 1157
Hillary, Louise 593
Hinckley, Helen (Jones) 426
Hirsh, Marilyn 1158
Hirschfeld, Burt 722

Author Index

Hitchcock, Patricia 638
Hobart, Alice Tisdale 807, 808
Hodges, Elizabeth Jamison 473, 639, 640
Hodges, Margaret 889
Hoff, Rhoda 30
Hoge, Dorothy 1132
Holding, James 1038, 1056
Holisher, Desider 427
Holland, Cecelia 809
Holland, Janice 773
Honour, Alan 428, 455
Hopkinson, Tom 326
Hornblow, Leonora 109
Hosokawa, Bill 880
Hough, Henry Beetle 1027
Hough, Richard 1007
Houghton, Eric 216
Howard, Alice Woodbury 118
Hsiao, Ellen 810
Hubbard, Wynant E. 21
Huddleston, Father Trevor 40
Huggins, Alice Margaret 811
Hughes, James 153
Hume, Lotta Carswell 774
Hunter, J. A. 21
Hussein, King of Jordan 429
Huxley, Elspeth 169
Huxley, Julian 30
Hyman, Frieda Clark 495

Icenhower, Joseph B. 854
Idewu, Olawale 277
Ingalls, Leonard 157
Iroaganach, John 66
Irving, Clifford 430
Ishii, Momoko 913, 1159
Ish-Kishor, Sulamith 474
Israel, Charles E. 1028
Issa (Kobayashi) 861

Jabavu, Noni 40
Jablow, Alta 271
Jacob, Helen Pierce 681
Jacobs, David 377
Jacobs, William J. 207
James, T. G. H. 90
Jenkins, Sara 496
Jewett, Eleanore M. 890
Jhabvala, R. Prawer 682
Jobson, Richard 30

Johnson, Doris 914
Johnson, E. Harper 110, 187
Johnson, James Ralph 399
Johnson, Osa 1008
Johnson, W. Ryerson 891
Jones, Adrienne 577
Jones, Ruth Fosdick 127
Joslin, Sesyle 1133
Joy, Charles R. 158, 200, 363, 431, 723, 1009

Kabongo, Chief 40
Kalashnikoff, Nicolas 578, 579
Kalish, Betty McKelvey 683, 988
Kamm, Josephine 456, 619
Kandell, Alice 594
Kaufmann, Herbert 217, 218
Kaula, Edna Mason 31, 58, 91, 159, 160, 1010-1012
Kayacan, Feyaz 371
Kaye, Geraldine 1204
Kayira, Legson 40, 41
Keating, Bern 335
Keith, Agnes Newton 92, 961, 1013, 1014
Keith, James 1057
Kelen, Betty 755
Keller, Werner 432
Kellogg, Jean 219
Kelsey, Alice Geer 389, 989
Kennan, George 560, 561
Kent, Louise Andrews 220, 400, 684, 812, 1058
Kenworthy, Leonard 161, 243
Kenyatta, Jomo 30, 40
Kessel, Joseph 188, 595
Kiddell, John 1059, 1060
Kim, Richard 915
Kim, Yong-ik 916, 917
Kimble, George H. T. 32
King, Clive 515
Kinist, Esther 685
Kipling, Rudyard 73, 686-690, 1147
Kingsley, Mary 30
Kirk, Ruth 855
Kirkup, James 892
Kirn, Ann 1134
Kittler, Glen D. 300
Kjelgaard, Jim 1661
Knight, Mary 775

Komroff, Manuel 756
Kotker, Norman 433
Kruger, Paul 30
Krumgold, Joseph 401
Kubie, Nora Benjamin 516, 517
Kublin, Hyman 724
Kuhn, Ferdinand 856
Kume, Genichi 895

Lagus, Charles 21
Lamb, Beatrice Putney 620
Lamb, Bulfinch 30
Lamb, Harold 757, 758
Lampel, Rusia 536
Landon, Margaret 990
Landry, Lionel 596
Lang, Andrew 475
Lang, Robert 597
Lange, Suzanne 537
Lansford, W. Douglas 934
Lansing, Elizabeth 434
Larsen, Peter and Elaine 244, 598
Larson, Jean Russell 476, 477, 776
Laschever, Barnett D. 599, 600
Last, Jef 991
Latham, Jean Lee 1029
Latimer, John 143
Lattimore, Eleanor 813-824, 918
Lauber, Patricia 301
Lavitt, Edward 34
Lavolle, L. N. 580, 691
Laye, Camara 40
Leakey, Louis B. 40
Leckie, Robert 1015
Lederer, William J. 992
Legum, Colin and Margaret 336
Leighton, Margaret 111
L'Engle, Madeleine 221
Lengyel, Emil 3, 387, 621
Lens, Sidney 33
Lerch, Marilyn 645
Leslau, Wolf 115
Levin, Meyer 435
Levine, I. E. 876
Levine, Joseph 43, 729
Levy, Mimi 293
Lewis, Elizabeth Foreman 825, 826
Lewis, Janet 919

Lewis, Mildred 920
Lewis, Richard 725, 857, 858
Lewis, Thomas P. 827
Lexau, Joan M. 1114
Lezia, Giggy 222
Liang, Yen 1143
Lifton, Betty Jean 859, 893, 1160-1162
Lin, Adet 777
Lindop, Edmund 1115
Lindquist, Willis 692
Linevski, A. 581
Lin Yutang 742
Lionni, Leo 1148
Li Shu-fan 759
Liss, Howard 962
Littlefield, William 1135
Liu, Beatrice 828
Lobo, Father Jerome 30
Lobsenz, Norman M. 162
London, Carolyn 78
Long, C. Chaille 30
Louden, Claire and George 693, 993
Lousada, Audrey 189
Lovejoy, Bahija Fattuhi 436-438
Lownsbery, Eloise 128, 704
Lum, Peter 364, 726
Luthuli, Chief Albert 30

McAlpine, Helen and William 894
McBeth, George 1191
McDermott, Gerald 272, 1116
McDowell, Robert E. 34
McGraw, Eloise Jarvis 129, 130
McGregor-Hastie, Roy 35
McGuire, Edna 1016
MacIntyre, Elizabeth 1062
McKown, Robin 36, 255, 302, 303, 308, 327, 345
MacLean, Alistair 457, 1030
Maginnis, Matthew 154, 155
Mahmoud, Zaki Naguib 93
Malraux, André 40
Malvern, Gladys 497-499
Mandel, Oscar 778
Mann, Peggy 458
Manton, Jo 309
Manzi, Alberto 346

Margalith, Yossi 541
Mark, Polly 1063
Marmur, Jacland 934
Marsh, Ngaio 1017
Marshall, Anthony D. 328
Marshall, James Vance 1064
Martin, Dahris 223
Martin, Patricis Miles 921-923, 1136
Masani, Shakuntala 622
Mason, Michael 1117
Masters, John 694
Matsuno, Masaku 1163-1165
Matsutani, Miyako 1166-1168
Matthew, Eunice S. 963
Maugham, W. Somerset 979
May, Charles Paul 1018
Meadowcroft, Enid LaMonte 94
Mears, Helen 860
Meeker, Oden 964
Mehdevi, Anne Sinclair 459, 478, 538
Mehta, Rama 695, 696
Mehta, Ved 623
Melville, Hermann 1065, 1066
Mercer, Charles 11
Merriam, Eve 1118
Merrill, Jean 641, 779
Merrill, Leigh 224, 861
Mertens, Alice 329
Meyer, Edith Patterson 500
Michener, James 539, 924, 925, 1067
Miller, Charles 163
Miller, Shane 460
Minney, R. J. 994
Mirsky, Reba Paeff 347, 348
Mitchison, Naomi 59, 132, 350-352
Modak, Manorama R. 601
Modupe, Prince 30, 41, 256
Moffat, Robert 30
Moorehead, Alan 21, 40, 1019
Morgan, Barbara E. 518, 519
Morrison, Lucile 133
Morton, W. Scott 862
Mosel, Arlene 1137, 1169
Mozley, Charles 119, 479
Mühleweg, Fritz 829
Mukerji, Dhan Gopal 697-699
Muku, Hatoju 944
Mulvey, Mina White 170
Munro, Eleanor 727

Murasaki, Lady 926
Murphy, E. Jefferson 37
Murphy, Eleanor A. 700

Naden, Corinne 95
Nagenda, John 190
Nagenda, Musa 191
Nahmad, H. M. 371
Nakagawa, Ricko 1170
Nakamoto, Hiroko 877
Nakatani, Chiyoko 1171
Nassar, Gamal Abdel 30
Naylor, Penelope 245
Neavles, Janet 134
Neurath, Marie 38, 439, 728, 863
Nevins, Albert J. 624
Newman, Bernard 330
Nickel, Helmut 39
Nirodi, Hira 701
Nkrumah, Kwame 30
Noble, Iris 112, 440, 461
Nolan, Barbara 40
Nordhoff, Charles 1068-1071
Norman, Lilith 1072, 1073
Normand, Marjorie 969
Norris, Faith 927
Nurenberg, Thelma 540
Nyrere, Julius 40

O'Brien, Brian 294
Ochsenschlager, Edward 96
Ofek, Uriel 541
Ojigbo, A. Okion 41
Ojike, Mbonu 40
Olden, Sam 42
Omer, Devorah 542, 543
O'Neill, Mary 501
Oren, Baruch 541
Orrmont, Arthur 113
Osborne, Chester G. 520
Otsuka, Yuzo 1138, 1198
Ottley, Reginald 1074-1081

Pace, Mildred Mastin 97
Pak, Jong-Yong 928
Palmer, Geoffrey 441
Palmer, Myron Tim 135
Palmer, Richard 135
Park, Mungo 30

Parke, Margaret 1020
Parker, K. Langlok 1039
Paterson, Katherine 929
Paton, Alan 331, 353
Patterson, Emma L. 136
Patus, Paul L. 21
Payne, Robert 442
Peare, Catherine Owens 625
Pearlman, Moshe 443
Pender, Lydia 1124
Perkins, Carol and Marlin 332
Perl, Lila 164
Pernoud, Regine 378
Petersham, Maud and Miska 502-504
Philips, Ted 444
Phipson, Joan 1082-1090
Phumla 1119
Picard, Barbara Leonie 480
Pike, E. Roylston 462
Pine, Tillie S. 43, 729
Place, Marion T. 1021
Polatnick, F. T. 337
Polland, Madeleine 830
Pond, Seymour Gates 1031
Poole, Frederick King 965, 966
Portisch, Hugo 562
Potter, Bronson 544, 545
Potter, Jeffrey 702
Powers, Alfred 225
Prechtl, Louise Boylston 864
Prempeh, Albert Kofi 262
Preston, Edna Mitchell 760
Price, Christine 4, 44, 98, 1149
Price, Olive 761, 930
Price, Willard 192-194, 320, 321, 1091, 1092
Prichard, Katherine Susannah 1093
Puleston, Fred 30
Purton, Rowland W. 60
Putnam, Anne 40

Quigley, Lillian 1150

Ragin, Lynn 325
Rama Rau, Santha 602, 603, 703
Rankin, Louise 831
Rappaport, Uriel 445
Rasp-Nuri, Grace 402

Redford, Lora Bryning 604
Reed, David 40
Reed, Philip 481
Reeder, Col. Red 931
Reeves, James 403
Reiss, Malcolm 832
Reusswig, William 365
Reynolds, Barbara 932
Reynolds, Reginald 626
Reynolds, Robert L. 865
Rice, Edward 605
Rice, Justus B. 246
Richard, Adrienne 546
Ridge, Antonia 210
Ripley, Elizabeth 878
Ritchie, Alice 780
Ritchie, Rita 582, 833-835
Rittenhouse, Mignon 12
Roberts, John G. 866
Robertson, Dorothy Lewis 980
Robinson, Adjai 273, 274
Robinson, Charles Alexander, Jr. 13
Rockwell, Anne 1120
Roland, Albert 368
Roland, Betty 1094
Rooke, Daphne 354
Roosevelt, Theodore 30
Ropner, Pamela 355
Rugh, Belle Dorman 547-549
Rugoff, Milton 762
Ruskin, Ariane 5
Russell, Jack 627

Saggs, H. W. 446
Said, Kurban 583
Sakade, Florence 895
Sale, J. Kirk 247
Saleton, A. L. 337
Saporta, Rafael 1192
Sasek, M. 1125, 1139, 1193
Saugnier 30
Sauter, Edwin 57, 253
Savage, Katherine 45
Savory, Phyllis 342
Sawyer, Martha 365
Saxe, John Godfrey 1151
Schatz, Letta 295, 296
Schermann, Li 550
Schlein, Miriam 137
Schloat, G. Warren 248, 379, 606, 730, 867, 967

Schreiner, Olive 30
Schurmacher, Emile 934
Schweitzer, Albert 30
Schwelen, S. 30
Scott, John 731
Scott, Joseph and Lenore 99
Scott, Nancy 40
Scott, Sir Walter 404
Sears, Stephen W. 201
Seed, Jenny 338, 356, 357
Seeger, Elizabeth 366, 642, 643, 732
Selormey, Francis 41
Selsam, Millicent 1032
Senghor, Léopold Sédar 40
Serage, Nancy 644
Serwadda, W. Moses 175
Seufert, Karl Rolf 226
Shaham, Nathan 541
Shakespeare, William 138
Shamir, Moshe 551
Sherer, Mary Huston 836
Sherry, Sylvia 995
Shippen, Katherine B. 6
Sharp, Jean Bowie 733
Siddiqui, Ashraf 645, 1152
Silverberg, Robert 100, 114, 144, 463, 464, 734, 735
Simon, Charlie May 310
Singh, R. Lal 704
Skinner, Elliott 25
Skipper, Mervyn 1140
Skurzynski, Gloria 1153
Slobodkin, Louis 837, 1172
Smith, Datus C. Jr. 968
Smith, Fredrica Shumway 61
Smith, Garry and Vesta 1173
Smith, Noraha 483
Snow, Edgar 736
Snyder, Zilpha Keatley 145
Solberg, S. E. 868
Solzhenitsyn, Alexander 584
Sommerfelt, Aimee 705, 706
Southall, Ivan 1095-1100
Sowers, Phyllis Ayer 984
Speare, Elizabeth George 505
Spencer, Cornelia (Yaukey) 607, 737-739, 763-765, 869
Spencer, Sue 249
Spencer, William 202-204, 380
Sperry, Armstrong 1033, 1101
Spiegelman, Judith 996
Spier, Jo 1194

Spittel, Richard 707
Stamm, Claus 896, 1174
Stanley, Henry 30
Statler, Oliver 933
Steel, Ronald 32
Stein, Mini 333
Stephan, Hanna 372
Sterling, Thomas 46
Stevens, Eden Vale 79
Stevenson, William 195
Stewart, Desmond 7, 381
Stinetorf, Louise 227, 552
Stoutenburg, Adrien 506
Strabo 30
Sturton, Hugh 275
Styles, Showell 708
Sucksdorf, Astrid Bergman 709
Suggs, Robert C. 14
Sugimoto, Etsu Inagaki 879
Sully, Francois 969
Sümer, Mine 1209
Suskind, Richard 8
Sutton, Felix 47
Swenson, Eric 1102
Syme, Ronald 15, 62, 1034, 1035

Takeichi, Yasoo 1175
Talmy, Menahem 541
Tashjian, Virginia A. 568, 569
Taslitt, Israel I. 465
Taylor, Alice 447
Taylor, Carl 970
Taylor, Florence M. 1195
Taylor, Mark 1205
Taylor, Theodore 870
Tchernavin, Tatiana 564
Thampi, Parvathi 630, 710
Thiele, Colin 1103
Thomas, Leslie 781
Thomas, Lowell Jr. 766
Thompson, Elizabeth Bartlett 48
Tibbetts, Albert 934
Tisna, Udayana O. 991
Titus, Eve 1176
Todd, Ruthven 838
Toland, John 740
Tooze, Ruth 373, 971, 997
Tor, Regina 972
Trager, Helen G. 629
Treffinger, Carolyn 782

Trollope, Anthony 30
Trupin, James E. 250
Turnbull, Colin 40, 49
Turner, Philip 507
Tworkov, Jack 1121

Uchida, Yoshiko 897-900, 935-942, 1177
Uris, Leon 553

Van der Post, Laurens 30, 40
Van Stockum, Hilda 196
Vaughan, Josephine Budd 871, 973
Verne, Jules 585
Vining, Elizabeth Gray 872
Vlahos, Olivia 50
Vo-Dinh 981
Von Harff, Arnold 30

Waciumba, Charity 41
Waddell, Helen 508
Wahl, Jan 509, 783
Waldeck, Theodore J. 322, 358
Walden, Amelia Elizabeth 554
Walker, Barbara K. 276, 277, 390-394, 1207-1209
Walker, Warren H. 277
Wallace, John A. 101
Warner, Esther 40
Warner, Oliver 1036
Warren, Ruth 102, 466
Watson, Jane Werner 103, 608, 873, 974
Watson, Sally 555, 556, 557
Weiner, Marjorie 969
Weingarten, Violet 105, 448
Weisner, William 1196
Weiss, Renee Karol 1154
Weiss-Sonnenburg, Hedwig 839
Welch, Ronald 1037
Wellman, Alice 297, 1122
Wenner, Kate 165
Werfel, Franz 405
Werner, Jane 449
Werstein, Irving 741, 1022
Weston, Christine 450
Westwood, Gwen 359
White, Ann Terry 482
Whitney, Phyllis 360, 406, 943

Wibberley, Leonard 510, 609
Wiggin, Kate Douglas 483
Wilbur, Donald 610
Williams, Jay 146, 382
Williamson, Joanne S. 511
Wilson, Barbara Ker 1023, 1040
Wilson, Beth P. 1123
Wise, Winifred 1178
Wolcott, Carolyn Muller 1197
Wolkstein, Diane 1141
Wood, Esther 840
Woodberry, Joan 1104
Worboys, Evelyn 38
Worthington, Marjorie 228
Wren, Percival 229
Wu, K. C. 841
Würthle, Fritz 586
Wyckoff, Charlotte Chandler 669
Wykes, Alan 21
Wyndham, Robert 784, 1142

Yamaguchi, Tohr 901
Yashima, Taro 944, 1179-1181
Yen Liang 1143
Yoda, Junichi 1182
Yolen, Jane 484, 1144, 1183
Yonathan, Nathan 541
Yoshida, Jim 880
Youngberg, Norma 998, 1105

Zinkin, Taya 628

TITLE INDEX

(Locale of story given in parentheses where not evident from title; picture books [see p. 215] are marked with an asterisk; three dots indicate deleted phrase "The Story of ... ")

Abba (Africa, E, I) 79
The Accomplice (Israel, YA) 546
Adventure in Bangkok (Thailand, YA) 987
Adventure in the Desert (Sahara, YA up) 217
Adventure in Tunisia (I) 223
Adventures of Hatim Tai (Persia, I) 470
Adventures of Rama (India, YA) 631
Adventures of So-Hi (China, I) 768
Adventures of Spider (W. Africa, E) 258
Afghanistan (YA up) 450
Africa: Adventures in Eyewitness History (YA up) 30
Africa, Awakening Giant (YA) 33
Africa, Background for Today (YA up) 35
Africa Is People; Firsthand Accounts from Contemporary Africa (YA up) 40
African Adventure (Central Africa, I, YA) 320
African Beginnings (YA up) 50
African Creeks I Have Been Up (A) 249
African Firebrand, Kenyatta of Kenya (YA up) 166
African Herdboy; A Story of the Masai (Kenya, Tanzania, I) 177

African Heroes (YA up) 59
African Kingdoms (YA up) 27
African Lions and Cats (I, YA) 22
African Myths and Legends (I up) 67
African Samson (YA) 186
The Africans Knew (E, I) 43
African Success Story: The Ivory Coast (YA) 230
African Traveler: The Story of Mary Kingsley (I up) 62
African Wonder Tales (I) 69
Africa, Past and Present (YA up) 48
... Africa South of the Sahara (YA) 45
After You, Marco Polo (Venice to Chinese border, A) 733
Agossou, Boy of Africa (W. Africa, E) 236
Air Raid--Pearl Harbor; The Story of December 7, 1941 (I up) 870
Aku-Aku: The Secret of Easter Island (A) 1006
Albert Schweitzer [Manton] (Gabon, I, YA) 309
... Albert Schweitzer [Daniel] (Gabon, I) 305
Albert Schweitzer, Genius in the Jungle (Gabon, YA) 307
Alexander the Great [Gunther] (Asia, Africa, I) 10
Alexander the Great [Mercer] (Asia, Africa, I, YA) 11

Title Index

Alexander the Great, Conqueror and Creator of a New World (Asia, Africa, YA) 13
Alexander the Great, Scientist King (Asia, Africa, I) 14
Ali and Nino; A Novel (Central Asia, A) 583
Allah, the God of Islam-Moslem Life and Worship (Africa, Asia, YA up) 9
All Men Are Brothers: A Portrait of Albert Schweitzer (Gabon, YA) 310
All the Mowgli Stories (India, I) 686
Amrita (India, A) 682
Amuny, Boy of Old Egypt (I) 137
Anansi the Spider: A Tale from the Ashanti (Nigeria, E) 272
Ancient Africa (YA up) 19
Ancient China (YA up) 721
And Perhaps--The Story of Ruth Dayan (Israel, A) 453
The Animal Friends of Peng-U (China, E, I) 789
Animals Mourn for Da Leopard and Other West African Tales (I) 263
Animals of the African Year: The Ecology of East Africa (YA up) 151
Anna and the King of Siam (A) 990
Another Place, Another Spring (Russia, Siberia, YA up) 577
Antony and Cleopatra (Egypt, A) 138
Arabian Nights (I) 475
Arabian Nights' Entertainments (all ages) 4, 83
The Arab Middle East (YA up) 425
The Arabs (Africa, Asia, YA) 1
The Arab World (Africa, Asia, YA up) 7
The Archaeology of Ancient Egypt (YA up) 90
Arms and Armor in Africa (I, YA) 39
The Art of Africa (I up) 29
The Art of Ancient Egypt (I up) 86
The Art of China (I up) 715

The Art of Japan (I up) 853
The Ashanti of Ghana (I) 233
Ash Road (Australia, YA up) 1095
Ataturk, Hero of Modern Turkey (YA up) 386
At Home in India (YA up) 589
At Jesus' House (Palestone, PB) 1197
Australia and New Zealand, Pacific Community (YA up) 1005
Australian Aborigines (I, YA) 999
Australian Legendary Tales (I up) 1039
Australia, Wonderland Down Under (I up) 1023

Baby Elephant Goes to China* 1133
The Bamboo School in Bali (I up) 991
The Bantu Africans (YA up) 31
Bare Feet in the Palace (Philippines, A) 961
The Barque of the Brothers 74
A Basket in the Reeds (Egypt, E)* 1192
The Bates Family (Australia, YA up) 1074
The Battle for Iwo Jima (I, YA) 1015
The Battle of Bataan; America's Greatest Defeat (YA up) 952
The Battle of El Alamein; Decision in the Desert (YA up) 80
The Battle of Jerusalem: The Six-Day War of June, 1967 (YA up) 430
The Battle of Manila Bay (YA up) 953
The Battle of Midway: Victory in the Pacific (YA) 1007
Beau Geste (Algeria, Sahara, A) 229
A Bedouin Boyhood (Palestine, YA up) 454
Before the Buddha Came (Asia, YA up) 362
Before the Sphinx: Early Egypt (YA up) 100

The Beggar in the Blanket and Other Vietnamese Tales (E, I) 978
The Beggar King of China (YA up) 795
Behind the Back of the Mountain: Black Folktales from Southern Africa (E, I) 339
Behind the Silken Curtain: The Story of Townsend Harris (Japan, YA up) 876
Behold Your Queen (Persia, YA) 497
Belisarius, Young General of Byzantium (Turkey, YA) 384
Bemba, An African Adventure (Zaïre, I, YA) 316
Ben-Gurion and the Birth of Israel (YA) 452
Bess and the Sphinx (Egypt, E, I) 140
Bhombal Dass, The Uncle of the Lion: A Tale from Palestine* 1152
The Bible as History (A) 432
The Big Fight (India, E, I) 666
Big Tiger and Christian (Mongolia, YA) 829
The Big Wave (Japan, I up) 905
The Bird from the Sea (India, E)* 1154
Birkin (Australia, I) 1082
Bisha of Burundi (I, YA) 181
The Bitter Choice: Eight South Africans' Resistance to Tyranny (YA up) 336
Black Fairy Tales (S. Africa, I) 340
The Black Heart of Indri (China, E up)* 1132
Black Images: The Art of West Africa (all ages) 245
Black Narcissus (India, A) 676
Black Pilgrimage (Ghana, YA up) 252
The Black Rose (Central Asia, China, A) 800
Black Ships and Rising Sun: The Opening of Japan to the West (YA up) 866
Black Wolf of the Steppes (Mongolia, YA up) 801
The Blind Men and the Elephant [Quigley] (India, E)* 1150
The Blind Men and the Elephant [Saxe] (India)* 1151
Blue Above the Trees (Australia, YA) 1050
Blue in the Seed (Korea, I) 916
A Blue Seed (Japan)* 1170
Bola and the Oba's Drummers (Nigeria, I) 295
Boomer: The Life of a Kangaroo (Australia, YA) 1049
Boomerang Hunter (Australia, I, YA) 1061
Born Free (Kenya, A) 147
Bouboukar, Child of the Sahara (I) 228
The Boundary Riders (Australia, I, YA) 1083
The Boxer Rebellion (China, YA up) 741
Boy Alone (Australia, I, YA) 1075
The Boy: A Novel of Christ's Boyhood (Palestine, I) 501
Boy of Dahomey (E) 244
Boy of Nepal (E, I) 598
Boy of the Masai (Kenya, E, I) 183
Boy of the Pyramids: A Mystery of Ancient Egypt (I) 127
A Boy Once Lived in Nazareth (Palestone, E)* 1195
The Boy Who Woke Up in Madagascar (YA) 345
Brian Wildsmith's Illustrated Bible Stories (I up) 507
The Bridge Over the River Kwai (Thailand, A) 985
The Bridges of Toko-Ri (Korea, A) 924
The Bright and Morning Star (Egypt, YA up) 126
The Bronze Bow (Palestine, YA) 505
Bruce of the Blue Nile (Ethiopia, YA up) 114
Brumbie Dust (Australia, YA up) 1078
Buddha (India, I, YA) 612
Builders of Jerusalem in the Time of Nehemiah (Israel, YA) 495
Burma Boy (I) 692

Burma Rifles (YA) 648
The Burning Rice Fields (Japan)* 1156
The Bushbabies (Kenya, I, YA) 195
The Bushmen and Their Stories (S. Africa, I) 341

Cambodia, Land of Contrasts (I, YA) 971
Camel Caravan (Sahara, I) 212
A Camel for a Throne (Egypt, I, YA) 128
A Camel for Saida (Libya, I) 142
A Camel in the Sea (Somalia, E, I) 185
Camels West (Turkey, YA) 399
The Camel Who Took a Walk (Africa)* 1121
Camera on Africa 85
Camera on Ghana 239
Cannibal Adventure (New Guinea, I, YA) 1091
Cap and Candle (Turkey, YA) 395
A Cap for Mul Chad (India, E, I) 647
Captain Cook (South Seas, A) 1030
Captain Cook and the South Pacific (YA) 1036
Captain Cook Explores the South Seas (I) 1033
Captain Cook, Pacific Explorer (I) 1034
The Caravan (Arabia, I) 472
Caravan from Timbuktu (W. Africa, YA) 293
Caravan in Peril (Sahara, YA up) 226
The Carpenter's Son (Palestine, YA) 494
The Carpet of Solomon, A Hebrew Legend (Israel, I) 474
The Case of the Marble Monster and Other Stories (Japan, I) 887
Castaway from Rhodes (YA) 396
The Cat Who Went to Heaven (Japan, I) 884
Cave of Riches: The Story of the Dead Sea Scrolls (Israel, I) 428
Central Africa; The New World of Tomorrow (YA up) 300
The Centurion (Palestine, A) 510
Chaim Weizman, Builder of a Nation (Israel, YA up) 451
Chaka, King of the Zulus (S. Africa, YA) 335
The Cheerful Heart (Japan, I) 912
Chendru, The Boy and the Tiger (India, I up) 709
Chiang Kai-shek, Generalissimo of Nationalist China (YA up) 763
Chie and the Sports Day (Japan, E)* 1163
Chikka (India, I) 701
The Child, Jesus (Palestine, E) 492
Children of Allah (Libya, A) 92
Children of the Kalahari (S. Africa, E, I) 329
China (YA up) 724
China and the Chinese (YA) 719
China Boat Boy (I, YA) 832
Chinaman's Reef is Our's (Australia, YA up) 1096
China, The Hungry Dragon (YA up) 731
The Chinese Children Next Door (E)* 1127
The Chinese Daughter (E, I) 813
Chinese Gordon, Hero of Khartoum (Sudan, YA up) 113
The Chinese Knew (E, I) 729
Chinese Mother Goose Rhymes (E)* 1142
Chinese Myths and Fantasies (I) 769
The Chinese Story Teller (E)* 1128
The Chinese Way of Life (YA) 742
A Chinese Year (I) 810
Chi Po and the Sorcerer, A Chinese Tale (all ages) 778
Chou En-lai 743
Circus Day in Japan (E)* 1157
City of the Stargazers: The

Title Index

Rise and Fall of Ancient Alexandria (YA up) 89
Cleopatra of Egypt (YA) 109
Cleopatra's Egypt (I, YA) 107
Cleopatra, Sister of the Moon (YA) 111
Clickety Cricket (Japan)* 1173
Climb a Lonely Hill (Australia, I, YA) 1072
Clint Lane in Korea 931
Clive of India (YA up) 627
Clyde of Africa* 117
The Colonial Conquest of Africa (YA) 36
A Coloring Book of Japan (all ages) 844
Come Along to Japan (I) 864
Come Back, Peter (Australia, I, YA) 1104
Commodore Perry and the Opening of Japan (I, YA) 856
Commodore Perry in Japan (YA) 865
A Community of Men (Australia, YA up) 1059
Confucius in Life and Legend (China, YA up) 755
Congo Explorer, Pierre Savorgnan deBrazza (YA up) 304
The Congo, River Into Central Africa (I) 301
The Congo, River of Mystery (YA up) 302
Conqueror of the World; The Life of Ghingis-Khan (Mongolia, A) 752
Conquerors on Horseback: The Nomad Empires of Attila, Ghingis Khan, and Timur (Central Asia, YA up) 558
Constantinople, City on the Golden Horn (Turkey, YA) 377
Cooper's Creek (Australia, A) 1019
The Cossacks (Siberia, YA up) 572
Courage in Korea: Stories of the Korean War (YA up) 934
The Courage of Kazan (Turkey, E) 390
A Cow for Jaya (India, E) 678
The Cow-Tail Switch and Other West African Stories (E, I) 261

The Crane Maiden (Japan, E, I)* 1166
The Creation (Bible, all ages)* 1194
Cricket and the Emperor's Son (Japan, I) 885
Cricket Songs-Japanese Haiku (all ages) 843
Crisis in South Africa (YA) 327
Crocodile and Hen (Africa)* 1114
A Crocodile's Tale; A Philippine Folk Story* 1199
Cross Currents (Australia, I, YA) 1084
Cross-Fire; A Vietnam Novel (I up) 986
Crow Boy (Japan, E)* 1179
A Crown for Thomas Peters (Sierra Leone, YA) 253
The Crusades [Pernoud] (Turkey, Asia Minor, YA up) 378
...the Crusades [Duggan] (Turkey, Asia Minor, YA) 375
Crystal Mountain (Lebanon, I) 547
Cry the Beloved Country (S. Africa, A) 353
A Curious Life for a Lady: The Story of Isabella Bird (Asia, A) 367

Daba's Travels from Ouadda to Banqui (Central Africa, I) 311
Daddyji (India, A) 623
The Dalai Lama (Tibet, YA up) 766
Dance in the Desert (Sahara, I) 221
The Dancing Bear (Turkey, YA up) 398
The Dancing Camel (Arabia, E, I) 525
The Dancing Kettle and Other Japanese Folk Tales (I) 897
The Dancing Palm Tree and Other Nigerian Folk Tales (I) 276
Dancing Princess (India, YA) 650

Daniel (Israel) 489
Danny Dunn and the Swamp Monster (Sudan, I) 146
Daughter of the Mountains (Tibet to India, I) 831
Daughter of the Samurai (Japan, A) 879
David (Israel, E, I) 502
David and Goliath (Israel, E, I)* 1188
David He No Fear (Liberia, E, I) 267
David Livingstone, Foe of Darkness (Africa, YA) 55
The Day of the Bomb (Japan, YA) 904
...the Dead Sea Scrolls (Israel, YA up) 445
The Defender (Siberia) 578
Defiant Bride (India, YA) 651
Desert Fighter: The Story of General Yigael Yodin (Israel, YA up) 460
Desert War in North Africa (YA up) 201
Devil's Hill (Tasmania, I, YA) 1044
Digging in Assyria (YA up) 423
Digging Up Adam: The Story of L. S. B. Leakey (Tanzania, YA up) 170
Discovering the Royal Tombs at Ur (Iraq, YA up) 424
Doctor Livingstone (Africa, I, YA) 60
Doctor Tom Dooley: My Story (Vietnam, YA) 976
Dogs of Fear (Uganda, I, YA) 191
The Dog That Flew and Other Favorite Stories from Israel (I, YA) 541
Dolls' Day for Yoshiko (Japan, E, I) 913
Dom and Va (Tanzania, YA) 180
A Donkey for the King (Palestine, I, YA) 487
The Dragon Kite (Tibet, E) 827
The Drums Speak: The Story of Kofi, A Boy of West Africa (E, I) 231
Duee, A Boy of Liberia (E, I) 248

The Dwarf Pine Tree (Japan, E, I) 893

East Africa (YA up) 156
East Africa--Kenya, Tanzania, Uganda (YA up) 164
Eastern Religions (Asia, YA up) 366
The East in the Middle Ages (Asia, YA up) 361
East to Freedom (China, YA up) 805
Egypt and the Sudan, Countries of the Nile (YA up) 88
Egypt, Child of the Nile (I) 103
The Egypt Game (I, YA) 145
Egyptian Adventures (YA) 123
Egyptian Hieroglyphs for Everyone (YA up) 99
The Egyptian Necklace (I, YA) 135
The Egyptians in the Middle Kingdom (I, YA) 96
Egypt's Queen, Cleopatra (YA) 112
8,000 Stones; A Chinese Folk Tale (E) 1141
Elephant Adventure (Uganda, I, YA) 192
Elephant Bridge (Burma, I) 702
Elephant Road (Sudan, Ivory Coast, YA) 284
The Elephant's Bathtub, Wonder Tales from the Far East (Asia, I) 369
The Elephants of Sargabal (YA) 635
Eleven! Time to Think of Marriage, Farhut (India, I, YA) 683
Elsa (Kenya, all ages)* 1106
The Emerald Clue (India, YA) 652
Emily-San (Japan, I) 932
The Emperor and the Kite (China, E)* 1144
Enchantment of Africa--Botswana (I, YA) 324
Enchantment of Africa--Burundi (I, YA) 154
Enchantment of Africa--Kenya 152

Enchantment of Africa--Rwanda
  (I, YA) 155
Enchantment of Africa--Tunisia
  (I, YA) 198
Enchantment of Africa--Uganda
  (I, YA) 153
Enchantment of Africa--Zambia
  (I, YA) 325
The Endless Steppe: Growing Up
  in Siberia (YA, A) 563
Endless Treasure: Unfamiliar
  Tales from the Arabian Nights
  (I) 471
Epaminondas (Africa)* 1118
The Epics of Everest (Nepal, YA
  up) 609
Ethiopia, Mountain Kingdom (I)
  104
Euloowirree Walkabout (Australia,
  YA up) 1060
Everyday Life in Babylonia and
  Assyria (YA up) 446
Every Man Lay Heart Down (Liberia, E, I) 268
Exiles in the Sahara (YA) 215
Exodus (Israel, A) 553
Exploits in Africa 21
Explorations of Africa (YA) 46
Explorers of the Pacific (YA)
  1024

The Fables of India (I up) 632
Fairy Tales from Viet Nam (I up)
  980
The Family at Kitlabeng (Botswana,
  I, A) 350
The Family Conspiracy (Australia,
  I, YA) 1085
Fanny and the Regent of Siam (A)
  994
Far into the Night, A Story of
  Bali (E) 993
Far Voyager, The Story of James
  Cook (I, YA) 1029
Favorite Childrens' Stories from
  China and Tibet (I) 774
Favorite Fairy Tales Told in
  India (E, I) 637
Fay Gow, A Boy of Hong Kong
  (I) 730
Femi and the Old Grandaddie
  (Sierra Leone, E, I) 273

Ferdinand Magellan (YA) 1037
Ferdinand Magellan, Master
  Mariner (I) 1031
Festivals of Japan (I up) 846
A Few Flies and I: Haiku by
  Issa (Japan, all ages) 861
Fifty-five Days of Terror: The
  Story of the Boxer Rebellion
  (China, YA up) 722
Fighter for Independence,
  Jawaharlal Nehru (India, YA
  up) 611
Fire in the Stone (Australia,
  YA) 1103
The Fire on the Mountain and
  Other Ethiopian Stories (I up)
  115
The First Book of Ancient Araby
  (E, I) 479
The First Book of Australia (I)
  1010
The First Book of East Africa
  (I) 162
The First Book of India (YA up)
  587
The First Book of Japan (E, I)
  860
The First Book of New Zealand
  (I) 1011
The First Book of Pakistan (YA
  up) 588
The First Book of Tales of
  Ancient Egypt (I) 119
The First 3,000 Years (Africa,
  Asia, I, YA) 2
The First Wheel (Sumeria, I)
  520
The Fisherman and the Goblet:
  A Vietnamese Folk Tale (I)*
  1205
The Fisherman's Son (China,
  E, I) 814
The Five Chinese Brothers*
  1126
Five Queens of Ancient Egypt
  (YA up) 106
Five Ships West, The Story of
  Magellan (YA) 1028
The Five Sons of King Pandu
  (India, YA up) 642
The Flame Trees of Thika,
  Memories of an African Childhood (A) 169

Flight to the Promised Land
 (Yemen, Israel, YA up) 535
The Flying Carpet (Arabia, E, I)
 467
The Flying Tigers 740
Fofana (Ivory Coast, YA) 285
Fonabio and the Lion (Ivory
 Coast, YA) 286
The Fooling of King Alexander
 (China)* 1140
The Forbidden Bridge (Australia,
 E) 1094
The Foreigner (Israel, YA) 498
The Forever Christmas Tree
 (Japan, E)* 1177
Forever Free (Kenya, A) 149
The Forty Days of Musa Dagh
 (Turkey, I) 405
Fourteen Hundred Cowries and
 Other African Folk Tales (I)
 264
The Fox Hole (Australia, I, YA)
 1097
The Fox That Wanted Nine Golden
 Tails (China, E, I) 775
Friends and Enemies (Botswana,
 YA) 351
Frog in the Coconut Shell (Malaya,
 I) 995
From Bush to City (Africa, YA
 up) 23
The Full Circle (Japan, YA) 935
Fumio and the Dolphins (Japan)*
 1171
The Funny Little Woman (Japan)*
 1169

Gandhi [Coolidge] (India, YA up)
 613
... Gandhi [Zinkin] (India, YA)
 628
Gandhi, Fighter Without a Sword
 (India, YA) 614
... Gandhi, Man of Peace (India,
 I, YA) 626
A Garland for Gandhi (I) 681
Gassire's Lute: A West African
 Epic (YA up) 271
Gayneck; The Story of a Pigeon
 (India, I, YA) 697
Geeta and the Village School (India, E) 710

Genghis Khan and the Mongol
 Horde (Mongolia, I) 757
Genghis Khan, The Emperor of
 All Men (Mongolia, YA up)
 758
Gertrude Bell, Daughter of the
 Desert (Iraq, Syria, YA up)
 456
Getting to Know Africa's French
 Community (I) 42
Getting to Know Australia 1020
Getting to Know Egypt (I) 101
Getting to Know Hong Kong (I)
 723
Getting to Know India (I) 599
Getting to Know Indonesia (I)
 970
Getting to Know Iran and Iraq
 (I) 410
Getting to Know Israel (I) 431
Getting to Know Kenya (I) 157
Getting to Know Lebanon (I)
 412
Getting to Know Pakistan (I)
 600
Getting to Know Saudi Arabia
 (I) 444
Getting to Know Tanzania (I,
 YA) 158
Getting to Know Thailand (I)
 945
Getting to Know the Central
 Himalayas (I) 604
Getting to Know the Philippines
 (I) 972
Getting to Know the Sahara (I)
 200
Getting to Know the Suez Canal
 (I) 81
Ghost on the Steppe (Mongolia,
 I, YA) 809
The Gideonites (Israel, YA up)
 542
A Gift from the Bride (Armenia,
 E) 576
A Gift from the Mikado (Japan,
 I) 911
Gift of the Forest (India, I)
 704
Gift of the River (Egypt, I)
 94
Gilgamesh, Man's First Story
 (Iraq, YA) 468

Title Index

The Girl Who Loved the Wind (Persia, I) 484
Giselle (New Caledonia, YA up) 1079
The Glass Mountain and Other Arabian Tales (I) 476
A Glorious Age in Africa: The Story of Three African Empires (YA up) 25
Golda, The Life of Israel's Prime Minister (YA up) 458
Gold Down Under; The Story of the Australian Gold Rush (YA up) 1021
The Golden Crane, A Japanese Folktale (I) 901
The Golden Footprints (Japan, E) 944
The Golden Goblet (Egypt, YA) 130
The Golden Hawks of Genghis Khan (Mongolia, YA up) 833
The Golden Impala (S. Africa, I, YA) 355
Golden Letter to Siam (YA) 894
The Golden Pharaoh (Egypt, YA up) 122
The Golden Slippers (Syria, I) 550
The Good Earth (A) 791
Good Luck to the Rider (Australia, I, YA) 1086
Gorilla Adventure (E. Africa, I, YA) 321
Gorilla, Gorilla (E. Africa, all ages) 184
Gozo's Wonderful Kite (Japan, E) 891
The Grand Canal of China (YA) 720
Great Civilizations of Ancient Africa (YA up) 24
Great Day in China: The Holiday Moon (E) 726
Great Day in Israel (E) 551
The Great Minu (W. Africa, E)* 1123
Great Rulers of the African Past (I) 54
The Greedy One (Japan, E) 921
Grishka and the Bear (Siberia, I) 567
Growing Up in Israel (I, YA) 427

The Growth of Civilization in East Asia (YA up) 364
Guadalcanal (YA up) 1022
A Guide to African History (I up) 28

Hadassah; Esther the Orphan Queen (Persia, I, YA) 485
Hamid and the Palm Sunday Donkey (Palestine, I) 528
Hand of the King (Mesopotamia, YA) 518
Hannibal, An African Hero (Carthage, YA up) 207
Hannibal: Challenging Rome's Supremacy (Carthage, A) 205
Hannibal's Elephants (Carthage, YA) 225
Happiness for Kimi (Japan, E, I) 918
The Happy Days (Korea, E, I) 917
Happy New Year (China, P.B.) 1143
Haran's Journey (Palestine, YA) 506
Hari the Jungle Lad (India, I, YA) 699
The Hat-Shaking Dance and Other Tales from the Gold Coast (I) 261
Henry M. Stanley, The Man from Africa (I, YA) 51
He Sailed with Captain Cook (I) 1041
He Went with Hannibal (Carthage, YA) 220
He Went with Magellan (South Seas, I, YA) 1058
He Went with Marco Polo (China, I, YA) 812
He Went with Vasco da Gama (India, I, YA) 684
High and Haunted Island (Tasmania, YA) 1045
Hilili and Kilili, A Turkish Silly Tale (E)* 1207
Hill's End (Australia, I, YA) 1098
Hisako's Mysteries (Japan, I) 936

Hittite Warrior (Israel, YA up) 511
Ho Chi Minh, Legend of Hanoi (YA up) 975
Ho Fills the Rice Barrel (Taiwan, I) 836
Hokusai; A Biography (Japan, I) 878
The Holy Land in the Time of Jesus (Palestine, YA up) 433
Home to India (A) 602
Honey of the Nile (Egypt, YA) 121
Hong Kong Surgeon (YA up) 759
Hongry Catch the Foolish Boy (Liberia, E, I) 269
The Honorable Sword (Japan, I) 920
Hostage to Alexander (Africa, Asia, I) 16
The House in the Tree; A Story of Israel (E) 527
The House of Sixty Fathers (China, I up) 802
How the Leopard Got His Claws (Africa, E) 66
How the Withered Trees Blossomed (Japan, E)* 1167
How the World Got Its Color (Japan)* 1158
Hubert the Traveling Hippopotamus (Africa)* 1115
The Human Apes (Central Africa, YA) 315
Hunted in Their Own Land (Tasmania, YA up) 1046
Hunters of Siberia (YA) 573

The Ibo of Biafra (I) 234
Ifrit and the Magic Gifts (Turkey, E) 391
The Illustrated Book About Africa (all ages) 47
The Illustrated Book About the Far East (all ages) 363
I Marched with Hannibal (Carthage, YA) 211
I, Momolu (Liberia, I) 283
In Africa (E)* 1107
In-Between Miya (Japan, I) 937
India (YA up) 591
India, Land of Rivers (YA up) 590
India, Old Land, New Nation (I) 608
India's Tales and Legends 634
In Search of the Abominable Snowman: A Story from Nepal (I) 680
In the Land of Ur (Mesopotamia, YA up) 411
Iran (I up) 447
Iran, Crossroads of Caravans (I) 449
Iron Mountain (Australia, YA) 1051
I Saw You from Afar: A Visit to the Bushmen of the Kalihari Desert (I) 332
Isfendiar and the Bears of Mazandaran (Iran, I, YA) 545
Isfendiar and the Wild Donkeys (Iran, I, YA) 544
...Israel (YA up) 435
Israel, One Land Two Peoples (YA) 419
Israel's Golda Meir; Pioneer to Prime Minister (I up) 461
Issun Boshi, The Inchling, An Old Tale of Japan* 1159
Ivory, Apes and Jimibel (French Equatorial Africa, I, YA) 294
I Was a Savage (Nigeria, A) 256

The Jade Gate (Central Asia, YA) 580
Jamba the Elephant (Belgian Congo, I) 322
Jambo Means Hello, A Swahili Alphabet Book (E)* 1112
Jambo Sungura; Tales from East Africa (E, I) 172
Japan, Crossroads of East and West (YA up) 855
Japanese Children's Stories (E, I) 895
The Japanese: How They Live and Work (YA up) 862
Japanese Inn (A) 933
Japanese Tales and Legends (I, YA) 894
Japan in Story and Pictures (E,

Title Index

I) 850
Japan, Islands of the Rising Sun (I) 873
Jesus, "What Manner of Man Is This?" (Palestine, YA up) 493
Jim Grey of Moonbah (Australia, I, YA) 1089
Joel of the Hanging Gardens (Mesopotamia, YA) 491
Joji and the Amanojaku (Japan)* 1160
Jonah and the Big Fish (Israel)* 1186
Jonah and the Lord (Israel, E)* 1191
Jordan, River of the Promised Land (I, YA) 448
Joseph the Dreamer (Israel, E, I)* 1187
Josh (Australia, YA up) 1099
Journey for Tobiyah (Israel, YA) 519
Journey of Ching Lai (China, E) 815
The Journey of the Eldest Son (Mesopotamia, YA) 513
Judge Not (Turkey, P.B.) 1206
Junichi, A Boy of Japan (I) 867
The Jungle Book (India, I) 688
Just Say Hic (Turkey, E)* 1208
Just So Stories (Africa, E, I) 73

The Kaha Bird: Tales from the Steppes of Central Asia (E, I) 565
Kai Ming, Boy of Hong Kong (E)* 1129
Kalena (Zaïre, YA) 312
Kalena and Sana (Zaïre, YA) 313
Kalu and the Wild Boar (India, I, YA) 679
Kantchil's Lime Pit and Other Stories from Indonesia (I) 977
Kappa's Tug-of-War with Big Brown Horse: The Story of a Japanese Water Imp 1155
Kari the Elephant (India, I, YA) 698
Katsina, Profile of a Nigerian City (YA up) 238

Keoko's Bubble (Japan, E) 919
Kenny (Uganda, I) 187
Ketut, Boy Woodcarver of Bali (E, I) 996
The Khmers of Cambodia (YA up) 956
Kim (India, YA up) 689
Kim of Korea 927
Kim Walk-in-My-Shoes (Korea, I) 930
A Kingdom Lost for a Drop of Honey and Other Burmese Folktales (I up) 629
Kingfishers Catch Fire (India, A) 677
The King's Drum and Other African Stories (I up) 71
King Solomon's Horses (Israel, I, YA) 516
King Solomon's Mines (S. Africa, YA, A) 344
King Solomon's Navy (Israel, YA) 517
The King Who Rides a Tiger and Other Folk Tales from Nepal (I) 638
Knights of the Crusades (Turkey, Asia Minor, I, YA) 382
Korean Boy (I, YA) 928
Korolu the Singing Bandit (Turkey, I) 392
Kublai Khan, Lord of Xanadu (China, YA) 749
Kumar (India, I, YA) 669
Kuwait, Miracle on the Desert (YA up) 416

Lakshmi, the Water Buffalo Who Wouldn't (India, E)* 1146
The Lament of the Deer 66
The Land and People of Afghanistan (YA) 415
The Land and People of Algeria (YA) 202
The Land and People of Australia (YA) 1002
The Land and People of Burma (YA) 596
The Land and People of Ceylon (YA) 610
The Land and People of China

(YA) 737
The Land and People of Egypt (YA) 93
The Land and People of Ethiopia (YA) 91
The Land and People of Ghana (YA) 247
The Land and People of India (YA) 601
The Land and People of Indonesia (YA) 968
The Land and People of Iran (YA) 426
The Land and People of Iraq (YA) 436
The Land and People of Japan (YA) 871
The Land and People of Kenya (YA) 159
The Land and People of Korea [Evans] (YA) 851
The Land and People of Korea [Solberg] (Ya up) 868
The Land and People of Liberia (YA) 235
The Land and People of Libya (YA) 82
The Land and People of Malaysia (YA) 951
The Land and People of Morocco (YA) 203
The Land and People of New Zealand (YA) 1012
The Land and People of Nigeria (YA) 240
The Land and People of Pakistan (YA) 597
The Land and People of South Africa (YA) 331
The Land and People of Syria (YA) 417
The Land and People of Tanzania (YA) 160
The Land and People of Thailand 963
The Land and People of the Congo (YA) 299
The Land and People of the Philippines (YA) 973
The Land and People of Tunisia (YA) 204
The Land and People of Turkey (YA) 380

Land Below the Wind (Borneo, A) 1013
Land in the Sun: The Story of West Africa (I) 237
Land of Canaan (YA) 408
Land of the Pharaohs (Egypt, YA up) 83
Land of the Two Rivers (Mesopotamia, YA up) 418
The Lane of Eternal Stability (China, A) 841
Last Adventure: The Martin Johnsons in Borneo (A) 1008
The Last Great Empress of China (A) 753
The Last Pharaoh (Egypt, YA) 143
Lawrence of Arabia (YA) 457
Leaders of the New Africa (YA up) 58
Lee Lau Flies the Dragon Kite (Hong Kong, E up)* 1131
The Legend of the Orange Princess (India, E up) 633
Let's Visit Afghanistan (I, YA) 413
Let's Visit Australia (I) 1003
Let's Visit Formosa (I) 712
Let's Visit Indonesia (I) 947
Let's Visit New Zealand (I) 1004
Let's Visit Nigeria (I) 241
Let's Visit South Africa (I, YA) 330
Let's Visit Southeast Asia (I) 948
Let's Visit Thailand (I) 949
Let's Visit the Middle East (I) 414
Let's Visit the Philippines (I) 950
The Life of Keshav (India, YA up) 695
Li Lun, Lad of Courage (China, I) 782
The Lion (Kenya, YA, A) 188
Lion Adventure (Tanzania, I, YA) 193
The Lion of Judah: A Life of Haile Selassie I, Emperor of Ethiopia (YA up) 108
Lions on the Hunt (S. Africa, YA) 358

Little Boat Boy (Kashmir, E, I) 655
Little Pear (China, E, I) 816
Little Pear and His Friends (China, E, I) 817
Little Pear and the Rabbits (China, E) 818
Little Queen of Sheba: A Story of the New Immigrant Children in Israel (I) 533
The Little Tumbler (China, E, I) 819
Little Two and the Peach Tree (Japan, E, I) 922
The Little World of Laos (YA) 964
Little Wu and the Watermelons (China, E, I) 828
The Lives of Pearl Buck (China, YA up) 746
Living Free: The Story of Elsa and Her Cubs (Kenya, A) 148
Lo Chau of Hong Kong (I) 797
The Long March, 1934-1935 (China, YA up) 716
The Long Rampart: The Story of the Great Wall of China (YA up) 734
The Lost Kingdom (India, I, YA) 665
Lost Names; Scenes from a Korean Boyhood (YA up) 915
The Lost Queen of Egypt (YA up) 133
The Lost Sahara Trail (YA) 218
The Lost Waters (Lebanon, I, YA) 548
Lumumba (Congo, YA up) 308
The Lunatic Express (Kenya to Uganda, A) 163
A Lurk of Leopards (Kenya, I, YA) 182

Madame Ambassador: The Life of Vijaya Lakshmi Pandit (India, YA up) 618
Madame Prime Minister: The Story of Indira Gandhi (India, YA up) 616
Made in Ancient Egypt (YA up) 98
Made in China (YA up) 738
Made in India (YA) 607
Made in Japan (I, YA) 869
Made in Thailand (YA up) 946
Magellan, First Around the World (I) 1035
The Magic Drum (Japan, I) 892
The Magic Drum: Tales from Central Africa (I) 314
The Magic Listening Cap: More Folk Tales from Japan (E, I) 898
The Magic Pumpkin (India, E, I)* 1153
The Magic Tree; A Tale from the Congo (P. B.) 1116
Mahatma Gandhi (India, YA up) 625
Mahatma Gandhi, Great Soul (India, YA) 621
Majola, A Zulu Boy (S. Africa, E, I) 333
Makoto, The Smallest Boy; A Story of Japan (E) 939
The Malagasy Republic (I up) 328
Malaria Ross, A Story Biography (India, YA up) 619
The Man Who Changed China: The Story of Sun Yat-sen (China, I) 747
The Man Who Found Nineveh (Iraq, YA up) 463
The Many Lives of Chio and Goro (Japan)* 1161
The Maoris of New Zealand (I, YA) 1016
Mao Tse-tung (China, YA up) 744
Mao Tse-tung, The Man Who Conquered China (YA up) 751
Mara, Daughter of the Nile (Egypt, YA up) 129
Marco Polo [Komroff] (China, YA) 756
... Marco Polo [Price] (China, I) 761
Marco Polo; A Story of the Middle Ages (China, I, YA) 760
Marco Polo's Adventures in China (I up) 762

The Masai, Herders of East Africa (Kenya, I) 150
The Mask of Akhnaten (Egypt, I, YA) 144
The Master of the Winds and Other Tales from Siberia (I up) 565
Matthew, Mark, Luke and John (Korea, I) 906
Mechido, Aziza and Ahmed (Morocco, I) 222
Meeting with a Stranger (Ethiopia, I, YA) 139
Meet North Africa (YA up) 199
Mei Li (China, P.B.) 1130
Melville in the South Pacific (I, YA) 1027
Men Against the Sea (South Seas, A) 1069
Men from the Village Deep in the Mountains and Other Japanese Folk Tales (E, I) 881
Mesopotamia, The Civilization that Rose Out of Clay (YA) 420
Messer Marco Polo (China, A) 794
Michael Strogoff, Courier of the Czar (Siberia, YA) 585
The Mighty Mekong (S.E. Asia, I, YA) 962
The Mighty Prince (Japan, E)* 1175
The Military Life of Genghis Khan, Khan of Khans (Mongolia, YA) 750
The Milky Way and Other Chinese Folk Tales (I) 777
The Miracle of the Mountain (India, E)* 1147
Miriam Lives in a Kibbutz (Israel, E) 529
The Missing Violin (India, I) 654
Mission to Cathay (China, I, YA) 830
Mission to Tibet (YA up) 803
Miss Ulysses of Puka Puka (S. Pacific, YA up) 1026
Mogo's Flute (Kenya, I) 196
Mohammed, Prophet of the Religion of Islam (Arabia, YA up) 462
Moja Means One; A Swahili Counting Book (Africa, E)* 1111
Mokokambo, The Lost Land (Sudan, I) 287
The Moment of Wonder: ... Chinese and Japanese Poetry (all ages) 725, 857
A Mongo Homecoming (Zaïre, I) 318
Moon Blossom and the Golden Penny (China, E) 837
The Moon in the Cloud (Egypt, YA up) 124
Moon-Uncle, Moon-Uncle: Rhymes from India (E) 630
More About Little Pear (China, E, I) 820
A Mortal Flower (China, A) 754
Moses (Israel, E, I) 503
... Moslem Art (Africa, Asia, YA) 4
The Most Terrible Turk (Turkey, E, I) 401
Mother India's Children: Meeting Today's Generation (YA up) 605
The Mountain of Truth (Tibet, YA) 796
Mountain with a Secret (New Guinea, YA up) 1055
Ms. Africa: Portraits of Modern African Women (YA up) 53
M'Toto; The Adventures of a Baby Elephant (Africa, E, I) 77
The Mud Snail Son (Japan)* 1162
Muhammad the Prophet (Arabia, YA) 466
Mukasa (Uganda, I up) 190
The Mukhtar's Children (Israel, YA) 555
Musa the Shoemaker (Algeria, I) 227
Mutiny on the Bounty (South Seas, A) 1068
My Childhood in Siberia (I up) 564
My Cousin the Arab (Israel, YA up) 540
My Enemy, My Brother (Palestine, YA up) 531
My Friend in Africa (Gabon, E) 319

My Friend Yakub (Siberia, I) 579
My Japan (YA) 877
My Number Two Wife (West Africa, A) 246
Mystery in Marracech (Morocco, YA) 213
Mystery of the Golden Horn (Turkey, I, YA) 406
Mystery of the Pharaoh's Treasure (Egypt, I, YA) 134
Mystery on Safari (East Africa, YA) 178
My Village in Ghana (I) 242
My Village in India (I) 592
My Village in Korea (I) 852
My Village in Thailand (I) 959
My War with Israel (Jordan, YA up) 429

Naim, A Boy of Turkey (E, I) 379
The Na of Wa (Nigeria, E) 257
Narni of the Desert (S. Africa, E) 359
The Near East: 10,000 Years of History (YA up) 409
Nehru, A Pictorial Biography (India, YA up) 615
The Nehrus of India (YA up) 620
Nehru's Story (India, E, I) 622
Never Run from a Lion and Another Story (Algeria, I) 210
New Guinea; A Journey Into Yesterday (I, YA) 1000
The New Malaysia (YA up) 957
New Zealand (YA up) 1017
Nhoti, Son of India (I, YA) 691
Nigerian Folk Tales (A) 277
Nightrunners of Bengal (A) 694
Nihal (Ceylon, I up) 700
The Nile (YA up) 102
The Nile, Lifeline of Egypt (I) 105
The Nile River (I up) 95
Ninji's Magic (New Guinea, I) 1062
Nkrumah, A Biography (Ghana, YA up) 255
Nkrumah of Ghana (YA up) 251
Noah and the Rainbow (Israel, E)* 1185
Noko of Japan (I) 907
Nomi and the Magic Fish; A Story from Africa (P.B.) 1119
No More Tomorrow (Australia, YA up) 1081
Nomusa and the New Magic (Natal, I, YA) 349
Nu Dang and His Kite; A Tale from Thailand (E)* 1200

Oasis of the Stars (Arabia, E)* 1189
Oceania: Polynesia, Melonesia, Micronesia (YA up) 1018
The Oil Countries of the Middle East (Africa, Asia, YA up) 3
Oil for the Lamps of China (A) 807
Okolo of Nigeria (I) 280
An Old Tale Carved Out of Stone (Siberia, YA up) 581
Olode the Hunter and Other Tales from Nigeria (I up) 260
Omen for a Princess (India, YA) 655
Omoo: A Narrative of Adventures in the South Seas (Tahiti, A) 1066
Once the Hodja (Turkey, E, I) 389
Once There Was and Twice There Wasn't (Turkey, E, I) 393
Once There Was and Was Not: Armenian Tales (I) 568
One Day in the Life of Ivan Denisovich (Siberia, A) 584
One More River (Israel, YA up) 522
Orisha: The Gods of Yorubaland (Nigeria, YA up) 266
Other Bible Lands (Near East, YA) 437
Other Sandals (Israel, I, YA) 556
Otwe (Africa, E) 63
Out of Africa (A) 167
The Ox of the Wonderful Horns and Other African Folktales (E, I) 68

The Pageant of Chinese History (YA up) 732
The Pageant of Japanese History (YA up) 848
The Pai-Pai Pig (Formosa, E, I) 785
Paji (Ceylon, E) 685
Palace in Bagdad: Seven Tales from Arabia (I) 477
Pandas Live Here (China, Tibet, Nepal, all ages) 713
The Paper-Flower Tree; A Tale from Thailand* 1201
Parveen (Persia, YA) 538
Pascal and the Lioness (Ivory Coast, E, I) 288
Passage to India (A) 675
Pastures of the Blue Crane (Australia, YA up) 1042
The Path Above the Pines (Lebanon, I) 549
Path Beneath the Sea (Israel, YA) 543
Peachblossom (China, E, I) 821
The Peacock and the Crow (China, E)* 1134
The Pearl Lagoon (South Seas, YA up) 1071
The Peasant and the Donkey: Tales of the Near and Middle East (Asia, I up) 371
Pebbles from a Broken Jar: Fables and Hero Stories from Old China (E, I) 767
People from the Sky: Ainu Tales from Northern Japan (I) 882
People in Palestine (YA up) 490
The Peoples of Africa (YA up) 49
Perry and the Open Door to Japan (I up) 854
Persian Adventure (A) 459
Persian Folk and Fairy Tales (I up) 478
Peter and Butch (Australia, I, YA) 1087
Pharaohs of Egypt (YA) 87
Piankhy the Great (Ethiopia, YA) 110
Pia's Journey to the Holy Land (E up) 422
Picken's Great Adventure (Nigeria, YA) 281

Picture Story of Japan (I up) 847
Pirates of Samarkand (Central Asia, I, YA) 582
Pitcairn's Island (South Seas, A) 1070
Plenty to Watch (Japan) 1181
Plum-Blossom and Kai Lin (China, YA) 839
Poachers in the Serengeti (Tanzania, I) 189
Poems from Africa (YA up) 20
The Pointed Brush (China, E)* 1136
Poko and the Golden Demon (S. Pacific, I) 1056
Pong Choolie, You Rascal (Korea, YA) 909
Portals to the Past: The Story of Archaeology (Africa, Asia, I, YA) 6
The Possible Impossibles of Ikkyu the Wise (Japan, I) 888
Prapan, A Boy of Thailand (I) 967
Prehistoric Art and Ancient Art of the Near East (Africa, Asia, I, YA) 5
Prester John (S. Africa, A) 343
The Prince of Fergana (Turkestan, YA) 586
The Prince of Omeya (Africa, Asia, YA) 18
The Princess and the Lion (Ethiopia, I) 141
Princess September (Siam, E, I) 979
The Prince Who Gave Up a Throne: A Story of the Buddha (India, I) 644
Prisoners of Hannibal (Carthage, YA) 224
Profile of Kenya (I, YA) 161
Profile of Nigeria (I) 243
Profiles from the New Asia (YA up) 368
Promise in the East: The New Siberia (YA up) 562
The Promise of the Rose (India, YA) 656
The Pygmies, Africans of the

Congo Forest (I) 298

The Queen's Gold (Borneo, I, YA) 1105
The Quest (Asia, I, YA) 372
Quest for the Dead Sea Scrolls (Israel, I, YA) 441
Quest in the Desert (Mongolia, YA) 786
The Questions of Lifu (China, E) 822
The Quest of Captain Cook (South Seas, I, YA) 1032
Quest of the Snow Leopard (China, Tibet, YA) 787

Rain Comes to Yamboorah (Australia, I, YA) 1077
The Rain Forest (New Guinea, I) 1109
Rain in the Winds: A Story of India (E) 693
Rakubei and the Thousand Rice Bowls (Japan, E) 899
The Ramayana (India, YA up) 643
Ramu, A Story of India (I) 696
The Red Chair Waits (China, YA) 811
The Red Scarf (India, YA) 657
Red Sea Rescue (Saudi Arabia, I) 526
Red Star Over China (A) 736
Remember the House (India, A) 703
René Guillot's African Folk Tales (I) 72
Return to Hiroshima (Japan, I up) 859
The Revolt of the Darumas (Japan, E)* 1178
The Rider and His Horse (Palestine, YA up) 514
Riders of the Wind (Ivory Coast, YA up) 289
Ride the White Tiger (Korea, I, YA) 908
Ride, Zarina, Ride (India, YA) 658
Rikka and Rindji, Children of Bali (E)* 1203

Ring of Fate (India, YA up) 658
The Rise of Red China (YA up) 717
The River Boy of Kashmir (I) 660
A Road Down in the Sea (Liberia, E, I) 270
The Road to Agra (India, I, YA) 705
The Roan Colt (Australia, I, YA) 1076
The Rod and the Rose (N. Africa, A) 219
Rogue Elephant (Burma, I, YA) 670
The Rolling Rice Ball (Japan)* 1182
Ronnie and the Chief's Son (Africa, I) 76
Royal Persia: Tales and Art from Iran (I up) 407
Runaway Jonah and Other Tales (Israel, E) 509
Ruth,[Petersham] (Israel, E, I) 504
...Ruth [Asimov] (Israel, YA) 486

Safari Adventure (Kenya, I, YA) 194
Safiri the Singer, East African Folk Tales (I) 173
Saint Augustine [The Life of] (N. Africa, YA up) 206
St. Francis of the Seven Seas (India, YA) 624
Salima Lives in Kashmir (E) 674
Sama (Ivory Coast, YA) 290
The Sand and the Stars: The Story of the Jewish People (Israel, YA) 421
Saul's Daughter (Israel, YA) 499
...Saul the King (Israel, I up) 508
Savage Island (Ceylon, I, YA) 707
Save the Khan (Siberia, YA) 574
Sayonara (Japan, A) 925

Scarab for Luck (Egypt, I, YA) 131
The Scimiter of Saladin (Iran, YA) 534
The Scuba Buccaneers (Australia, YA) 1057
Sea Challenge; The Epic Voyage of Magellan (I, YA) 1025
The Seal of Jai (India, Sikkim, Bhutan, YA) 649
The Sea Monkey, A Picture Story From Malaysia (E)* 1204
The Sea of Gold and Other Tales from Japan (I) 900
Search for a Golden Bird (India, YA) 661
Search for a Lost City: The Quest of Heinrich Schliemann (Turkey, I) 385
Season of the Briar (Tasmania, YA) 1043
Secret Beyond the Mountains (Mongolia, YA up) 834
The Secret Friends (Tasmania, I, YA) 1047
The Secret of the Himalayas (Nepal, YA) 673
Secret of the Samurai Sword (Japan, I, YA) 943
Secret of the Tiger's Eye (S. Africa, I, YA) 360
The Secrets of Tutankhamen's Tomb (Egypt, YA) 84
Serendipity Tales (Ceylon, I, YA) 639
Seven Grandmothers (S. Africa, I, YA) 348
The Seventh Mandarin (Japan, E)* 1183
The Seven Voyages of Sinbad the Sailor (Arabia, I up) 481
Seven Women Explorers (Africa, Asia, YA up) 12
Seven Years in Tibet (A) 718
The Shadow on the Sun (Egypt, YA up) 125
Shadows on the Grass (Kenya, A) 168
Shaka, King of the Zulus (YA up) 334
Shamba Letu: An American Girl's Adventures in a Communal Village in Tanzania (YA up) 165

Shan's Lucky Knife; A Burmese Folk Tale (E, I) 641
The Shape of Three (Australia, I, YA) 1073
Sharpur the Carpet Snake (Australia, E)* 1124
Shen of the Sea: Chinese Stories for Children (I) 772
The Shepard of Abu Kush (Palestine, YA) 552
Sherpa Adventure (Nepal, YA) 708
Siberia and the Exile System (A) 560
The Siege and Fall of Troy (Turkey, YA) 376
The Sign of the Chrysanthemum (Japan, YA) 929
Sikkim, The Hidden Kingdom (I up) 594
Silk and Satin Lane (China, E) 840
The Silk Spinners (China, E, I) 776
Silver from the Sea (Vietnam, E) 997
The Silver Mango Tree (India, YA up) 662
Simba of the White Mane (Tanzania, I) 176
Singing Tales of Africa (E, I) 274
A Single Pebble (China, A) 806
Sirga, Queen of the African Bush (W. Africa, YA) 291
Siti's Summer (Java, I) 988
Six and Silver (Australia, I, YA) 1088
The Sky-Eater and Other South Sea Tales (I) 1038
Small-Boy, Chuku (Africa, E)* 1122
Sokar and the Crocodile 118
Soldier of Africa (Nigeria, YA) 57
Soldier of Israel: The Story of General Moshe Dayan (I, YA) 465
A Song for Gilgamesh (Sumeria, YA up) 473
The Song of Deborah (Israel, YA) 496

Title Index

Songs and Stories from Uganda 175
Son of the Leopard (N. Africa, I, YA) 116
Sons of the Desert (Upper Sinai, I) 532
Sons of the Steppes (Mongolia, YA up) 788
The Source (Israel, A) 539
South Africa (YA up) 326
Southeast Asia (I, YA) 965
South Sea Adventure (I, YA) 1092
South Sea Islands (YA up) 1001
South Sea Shilling (YA) 1102
Spark of Opal (Australia, YA) 1052
The Splendor of Persia (YA up) 442
The Springing of the Rice (Thailand, E, I) 983
The Spy Who Talked Too Much (Kuwait, A) 554
Stanley, African Explorer (I, YA) 61
Stanley, Invincible Explorer (Africa, YA up) 52
Stargazer to the Sultan (Turkey, E)* 1209
The Stolen Fire, Legends of Heroes and Rebels from Around the World (I, YA) 17
The Stone of Peace (Israel, I, YA) 530
Storm Over the Caucasus (Central Asia, YA up) 575
A Story, A Story: An African Folk Tale Retold* 1113
The Story about Ping (China, E) 804
The Story on the Willow Plate (China, E, I) 781
Strangers in Africa (Nigeria, YA) 282
Su-An (Korea, E, I) 914
Such Is the Way of the World (Ethiopia, E)* 1110
Suho and the White Horse; A Legend of Mongolia (E)* 1138, 1198
The Sultan's Bath (Arabia, P. B.) 1184
The Sultan's Fool and Other North African Tales (E, I) 209
Su-Mei's Golden Year (China, I) 790
The Sumerians, Inventers and Builders (Iraq, YA up) 434
Sumi and the Goat and the Tokyo Express (E) 941
Sumi's Prize (Japan, E) 939
Sumi's Special Happening (Japan, E) 940
Sun and Moon (Egypt, E, I) 132
Sundiata; The Epic of the Lion King (Mali, YA) 259
The Sundowners (Australia, YA up) 1054
Sun in the Morning (India, YA) 667
Sun-Queen, Nefertiti (Egypt, YA) 136
Sunrise Tomorrow; A Story of Botswana (YA up) 352
Sun Yat-sen (China, YA) 745
Sun Yat-sen, Founder of the Chinese Republic (YA) 764
The Superlative Horse; A Tale of Ancient China (I) 779
Suzu and the Bride Doll (Japan, E) 923
Sword of the Hausas (Nigeria, YA up) 254
The Sword of the Prophet; The Story of the Moslem Empire (Africa, Asia, YA up) 8

Taiwan, The Other China (YA up) 714
Taiwo and Her Twin (Nigeria, I) 296
Takao and Grandfather's Sword (Japan, E) 942
The Takula Tree (The Congo, I, YA) 318
The Tale of Gengi (Japan, A) 926
Tales for the Third Ear from Equatorial Africa (E, I) 64
Tales from an African Drum (I) 70
Tales from Old China 771
Tales from the Story Hat, African Folk Tales (E, I) 65
Tales of a Chinese Grandmother

Title Index

(I, YA) 770
Tales of a Korean Grandmother
  (I, YA) 883
Tales of Ancient Egypt (I up) 117
Tales of Ancient Persia (YA up)
  480
Tales of the Crusades (Turkey,
  Asia Minor, YA) 397
Tales of the South Pacific (A)
  1067
Tales the People Tell in China
  (I up) 784
Tales Told Near a Crocodile;
  Stories from Nyanza (I) 171
Tales Told to Kabbarli; Aboriginal
  Legends (Australia, I up) 1040
The Talisman (Turkey, Asia
  Minor, A) 404
Talking Drums of Africa (I) 44
Taller than Bandai Mountain;
  The Story of Hideyo Noguchi
  (Japan, I, YA) 874
Tani (Borneo, I) 1063
Tan's Fish (China, E) 838
Taro and the Bamboo Shoot
  (Japan, E)* 1164
Taro and the Tōfu (Japan, E)*
  1165
Taro and the Turtles (Japan,
  E, I) 910
Tatu and the Honey Bird (W.
  Africa, E, I) 297
Ten Thousand Desert Swords;
  The Epic Story of a Great
  Bedouin Tribe (Arabia, YA)
  469
Tent Life in Siberia (A) 561
Thailand (I, YA) 966
Thailand, The Golden Land (YA
  up) 958
Thailand, The Land of Smiles
  (YA) 954
Thailand, Rice Bowl of Asia (I)
  974
That Summer with Ora (Israel,
  I, YA) 536
They Called Him Ataturk (YA up)
  387
They Lived Like This in Ancient
  Africa (E, I) 38
They Lived Like This in Ancient
  China (E, I) 728
They Lived Like This in Ancient
  Palestine (I) 439
They Lived Like This in Old
  Japan (I) 863
Things Fall Apart (Nigeria, A)
  278
Third World Voices for Children
  (I up) 34
The Thirteenth Stone (India, YA)
  663
Thirty-one Brothers and Sisters
  (Natal, I, YA) 347
This Is Australia (all ages)*
  1125
This Is India (A) 603
This Is Israel (all ages)* 1193
This Is Hong Kong (all ages)*
  1139
Threat to the Barkers (Australia,
  I, YA) 1089
Three Apples Fell from Heaven;
  Armenian Tales Retold (I)
  569
The Three Brothers of Ur (Meso-
  potamia, I, YA) 512
Three Came Home (Borneo, A)
  1014
The Three Daughters of Madame
  Liang (China, A) 792
The Three Guardsmen (Israel,
  I, YA) 500
The 397th White Elephant (India,
  E, I) 636
The Three Little Chinese Girls
  (E) 823
The Three Princes of Serendip
  (Ceylon, I, YA) 640
Three Sisters; The Story of the
  Soong Family (China, YA up)
  765
Three Strong Women (Japan,
  E, I) 896
Three Tales of Monkey; Ancient
  Folk Tales from the Far East
  (Asia, E) 373
The Three Trees of the Samurai
  (Japan, E up) 886
Through the Vermilion Gate, A
  Journey into China's Past (YA
  up) 727
Thunder Dam (Burma, YA) 668
Tico and the Golden Wings (India,
  E)* 1148
Tiger Burning Bright (India, I,

YA) 672
Tiger in the Bush (Tasmania, I, YA) 1048
Tiger of Bitter Valley (Sumatra, I) 998
The Tiger's Whisker and Other Tales from Asia and the Pacific (I) 370
Tikki Tikki Tembo (China)* 1137
Tino and the Typhoon (Philippines, I) 989
The Toad Is the Emperor's Uncle; Animal Tales from Vietnam (I, YA) 981
To Beat a Tiger (China, YA) 825
To Build a Land (Israel, YA) 557
To Katmandu, A Story of Nepal (E, I) 671
Tombi's Song (S. Africa, E) 356
Tom-Toms in Kotokro (Ivory Coast, YA) 292
Toontoony Pie and Other Tales from Pakistan (E, I) 645
To the Rock of Darius; The Story of Henry Rawlinson (Persia, YA up) 464
To the Wild Sky (Australia, YA) 1100
The Tower of Babel (Israel, E)* 1196
The Traiter Within (China, YA) 799
The Treasure of Li-Po (I) 780
The Treasure of the Caves; The Story of the Dead Sea Scrolls (Israel, YA up) 440
The Treasure of the Turkish Pasha (The Negev, YA) 523
The Treasures of Lin Li-Ti (Taiwan, I, YA) 798
Treasure Under the Sand; Woolley's Finds at Ur (Iraq, YA up) 455
The Trojan Horse (Turkey, E, I) 403
The Trojan War (Turkey, YA) 374
Tropical Africa (I up) 26
Tropical Africa Today (YA up) 32

The Tuareg, Nomads and Warriors of the Sahara (I) 197
Turkey (YA up) 381
Turkish Fairy Tales (I) 388
The Twenty-Two Letters (Phoenicia, YA up) 515
Twins in South Africa (I, YA) 354
Two Arabian Tales: Sinbad the Seaman and the Ebony Horse (I) 482
Two Boys of Baghdad (Iraq, I) 438
Two Children of Troy (Turkey, I, YA) 400
Two Japans (YA up) 849
The Two Stonecutters (Japan, E)* 1176
Two Under the Indian Sun (A) 617
The Two Worlds of Jim Yoshida (Japan, YA up) 880
The Two Worlds of Noriko (Japan, YA up) 903
Typee; A Peep at Polynesian Life (S. Pacific, A) 1065

The Ugly American (S.E. Asia, A) 992
Unbeaten Tracks in Japan (A) 845
Understanding Africa (YA up) 37
Usha, The Mouse Maiden (India, E)* 1145
Uttam, A Boy of India (I) 606

The Valley of Rubies (Burma, A) 595
The Valliant Chattee-Maker (India)* 1149
The Vanishing Tungus (Siberia, YA up) 559
Vasco da Gama, Sailor Toward the Sunrise (Africa, Asia, I) 15
Vengeance of the Zulu King (S. Africa, YA) 357
The Very Special Badgers (Japan, E)* 1174
...Vietnam (YA) 955

Title Index

Vietnam and Countries of the Mekong (YA) 960
The Village Tree (Japan)* 1180
The Voice of the Great Elephant (S. Africa, I up) 338

Wacheera, Child of Africa (Kenya, I, YA) 179
Walkabout (Australia, I up) 1064
The Walls of Windy Troy (Turkey, YA) 383
The Water Buffalo Children (China, E, I) 793
Watermelons, Walnuts and the Wisdom of Allah (Turkey, E, I) 394
The Wave (Japan, I) 889
The Way Home (Australia, I up) 1090
The Way of Silence (I up) 858
A Week in Aya's World (Ivory Coast, E) 232
Wee Willie Winkie and Other Stories (India, A) 690
West Africa from Ancient Kingdoms to Modern Times (YA up) 250
We, the Vietnamese: Voices from Vietnam (YA up) 969
We Were There at the Battle for Bataan (I) 982
What It Means to Be Young and Black in Africa (YA up) 41
What Then, Ramon? (India, I, YA) 646
When the Drums Sang; An African Folk Tale* 1120
When the Stones Were Soft; East African Fireside Tales (I) 174
Which Was Witch? (Korea, I, YA) 890
The Whiskers of HoHo (China, E)* 1135
White Boy (Swaziland, YA) 346
The White Bungalow (India, I, YA) 706
White Fawn of Phalera (India, YA) 664
The White Horse (Morocco, I) 214
The White Ship (USSR, YA up) 570

The White Wall (N. Africa, YA) 216
Why the Chinese Are as They Are (YA) 711
Why the Jackal Won't Speak to the Hedgehog; A Tunisian Folk Tale (E) 208
Why the Japanese Are as They Are (YA) 842
Why the Sky Is Far Away; A Folk Tale from Nigeria (E, I) 265
Why the Sun and the Moon Live in the Sky; An African Folk Tale (E)* 1109
Wildfire (Australia, YA) 1053
The Wild Oats of Han (Tasmania, I) 1093
Willow Tree Village (China, E) 824
Will You Carry Me? (Liberia, E)* 1108
Wind in My Hand; The Story of Issa, Japanese Haiku Poet (I up) 875
A Wind of Change (Nigeria, YA) 279
Windows for the Crown Prince (A) 872
The Wisest Man in the World (Israel, E)* 1190
A Wish for a Little Sister (Thailand)* 1202
The Witch's Magic Cloth (Japan, E)* 1168
With Dersu the Hunter (Siberia, YA) 571
With Stanley in Africa (I, YA) 56
The Wonderful Kite (China, E, I) 783
Wonders of Ancient Chinese Science (I, YA) 735
The World of Albert Schweitzer (Gabon, I up) 306
The World of Marco Polo (China, E, I) 748
The World of the Pharaohs (I, YA) 120
Wrapped for Eternity (I up) 97

Yael and the Queen of Goats

(Israel, I) 521
A Yak for Christmas (Nepal, A) 593
Yang and Yin (China, A) 808
Yangtze, China's River Highway (I) 739
Yasu and the Strangers (Japan, E)* 1172
The Year: Life on an Israel Kibbutz (YA) 537
The Year of the Horse (Mongolia, YA up) 835
Yeshua, Called Jesus (Palestine, I) 488
Yong Kee of Korea (E) 902
You Never Can Tell (China, E) 773
The Youngest Camel (Arabia, E up) 524
Young Fu of the Upper Yangtze (China, I, YA) 826
Young People of South Asia (I) 363
Young People of the Pacific Islands (I) 1009
Yusuf, Boy of Cyprus (I, YA) 402

Zaïre (The Republic of) (YA up) 303
Zambia's President, Kenneth Kaunda 337
Zarga's Shadow, An African Adventure (I, YA) 78
The Zealots of Masada: Story of a Dig (Israel, YA up) 443
A Zebra Came to Drink (Africa, I) 75
Zomo the Rabbit (Nigeria, I) 275
Zulu Fireside Tales (S. Africa, I up) 342
The Zulu of South Africa (I) 323

ILLUSTRATOR INDEX

Aas, Ulf 705, 706
Adamson, Joy (photo) 147-149, 1106
Afework 103
Aichinger, Helga 1185, 1186
Akaba, Suekichi 1138, 1198
Akino, Fuku 893, 1159, 1162
Allen, J. E. 698
Almelkar, A. A. 608
Ambler, Clifford 1049
Ambrus, Victor 195, 285, 512, 513, 526, 572, 574, 799, 1045, 1046, 1184
Ames, Lee J. 1032
Anderson, Erica (photo) 306, 310
Ariel, J. P. 286
Arno, Enrico 8, 71, 260, 262, 370, 566, 777
Artzybasheff, Boris 697
Aruego, José and Ariane 1199
Ayer, Jacqueline 979
Ayer, Margaret 653, 660, 665, 945, 946, 984, 990, 1200-1202

Baldridge, Leroy 812
Baltzer, Hans 801
Banbery, Fred 874
Bang, Garrett 881
Barberis, Juan Carlos 544
Barbour, Margaret 277
Barnett, Isa 10
Barnett, Moneta 25, 317
Barss, Bill 1207
Baum, Willi 1147
Baxter, Sylvia 342
Baynes, Pauline 470
Bayrack, Liba 388
Beaton, Cecil 168
Bennett, Susan 937

Benson, Harold 208
Beorden, Romare 20
Berg, Joan 640, 922
Bernardi, Anita 421
Bernheim, Marc and Evelyne (photo) 230, 232, 1107
Bernstein, Ted 1051
Berry, Erick 121
Berson, Harold 394, 525
Besunder, Marvin 735, 798
Biggers, John 283
Bird, Isabella L. 845
Bjorklund, Lorence 833, 835
Bobri, Vladimir 1135
Bock, Vera 499
Bolognese, Don 488, 495, 1208
Brand, Pippa 721
Brown, James, Jr. 269
Brown, Marcia 467
Browning, Colleen 268
Bryan, Ashley 68
Bryan, Brigitte 775, 978
Bryson, Bernarda 468
Buctel, George (photo) 36
Buehr, Walter 748
Burges, Albert 120
Busoni, Rafaello 447, 829
Buttfield, Helen (photo) 858
Byard, Carole 1119
Byfield, Barbara 485
Byrd, Robert 888

Carlson, Al 315
Carlson, Jane 1115
Carrick, Donald 717
Cassel, Lili 557
Castellon, Fred 747
Cellini, Joseph 178
Chapman, Frederick T. 293
Chapman, Gaynor 1140
Chastain, Madye Lee 261

Illustrator Index

Chen, Tony 771
Christianson, Per 66
Cirlin, Edgard 756
Cizik, Milka 445
Coggins, Jack 1031
Colabella, Vincent 482
Cooke, Donald E. 476
Cooley, Lydia 875
Corwin, June Atkin 639
Coughlin, Mildred 667
Crockett, Lucy Hernden 909
Crump, Fred, Jr. 1173
Cruz, Raymond 84
Cuffari, Richard 341, 565, 809, 1122

Darbois, Dominique (photo) 236, 1129, 1203
Daugherty, Charles Michael 1102
Dave, Shanti 608
Davis, Omar 668
DeFoll, Alain 886
Delessert, Etienne 73
Dempster, William 475
DeMuth, Flora 223
Dennis, Wesley 176
Dewey, Katherine 94
Dillon, Corinne 647
Dillon, Leo and Dianne 175, 271, 339, 514
Dinesen, Isac 168
Dobias, Frank 389
Dobrin, Arnold 671, 910
Doctor, Irv 982
Domanska, Janina 1132
Dotzenko, Grisha 294
Douthwaite, A. 292
Driscoll, B. L. 287, 1055
Duchesne, Janet 1084
Dupays, Thea 137
Durack, Elizabeth 1039
Duvoisin, Roger 1121, 1136

Ebert, Len 1195
Edmonds, I. G. (photo) 714, 956
Elgin, Kathleen 431, 599, 860
Ellis, John 728
Escourido, Joseph 69
Evans, M. Fulmer (photo) 851

Evers, Alie 530

Fairfield, Helen Nixon 446
Fairservice, Jan 362, 420, 645
Falls, C. B. 2, 794
Faulkner, John 1206
Fax, Elton 63, 65, 257, 296, 757
Feelings, Tom 174, 295, 302, 1111, 1112
Fegis, Rita Fava 576
Fisher, Anton Otto 1071
Fisher, Leonard Everett 1, 14, 442, 469
Flora, Paul 586
Forberg, Ati 391
Ford, George 171
Forster, Peter 441
Fortnum, Peggy 142
Franck, Frederick 319
Frank, Mary 612
Frankenberg, Robert 172, 987
Frazer, Betty 882
Friedel 521
Frost, George 560, 561
Funai, Mamoru 666, 906, 913, 1062, 1156

Galdone, Paul 185, 1151, 1197
Galsworthy, Gay 1204
Garbutt, Bernard 77
Gentz, Frank 133
Ghikas, Panos 920
Gidal, Tim (photo) 242, 532, 592, 852, 959
Gilham, Alan 60
Gobhai, Mehlli 633, 1145, 1146
Gordon, Margaret 1191
Gorsline, Douglas 228
Gray, Reginald 528
Greaves, Duncan G. (photo) 333
Greco, Robert 209
Greenwood, Marion 836
Gretzer, John 795
Grifalconi, Ann 43, 267, 351
Grimble, Rosemary 256
Grisha 199
Guggenheim, Hans 369, 646

Illustrator Index

Hales, Robert 628, 1077
Haley, Gail E. 1113
Hamil, Tom 1152
Hampshire, Michael 81, 401, 678
Handforth, Thomas 1130
Harrington, Richard (photo) 719, 720, 1005
Harrison, George Russell (photo) 797
Hassanein, Samiha 103
Hasselriis, Else 772
Hasselriis, Malthe 770
Hayashi, Yoshio 895
Hechtkopf, H. 1192
Helms, Georgeann 406
Herrmanns, Ralph (photo) 680, 1131
Heyman, Ken 1117
Hicks, Eleanor B. 1157
Higgins, Don 284
Hinds, Robert William 237
Hiroshige 905
Hirsh, Marilyn 1158
Hodges, C. Walter 375, 376
Hoeker, Hazel 410
Hoffmann, Felix 635
Hogrogian, Nanny 568, 569
Hokusai 878, 905
Holisher, Desider (photo) 427
Holland, Janice 773, 1150
Holzing, Herbert 17
Horder, Margaret 1048, 1083, 1085, 1086, 1088, 1089
Hortens, Walter (photo) 419
Horwitz, Richard 360
Hosoe, Eikoh (photo) 859
Hsiao, Ellen 810
Huffmann, Tom 97
Hutchinson, P. A. 428
Hutchinson, William M. 942

Isaac, Barbara Kohn 34
Ishii, Tekesin 879
Iwasaki, Chihiro 1166

James, Harold 173
Jaques, Robin 28, 196, 216, 582, 669
Jefferson, Louise 37
Jefferson, Robert L. 318
Johnson, Avery 16
Johnson, E. Harper 110, 187, 188, 227, 312, 313
Johnson, James Ralph 22, 399
Johnson, Yvonne 54
Jones, Richard C. 897
Jones, Robert A. 437

Kalantari, Parviz 449
Kandell, Alice (photo) 594
Kane, Robert 115, 977
Karlin, Eugene 217
Kashiwagi, Isami 989
Kaufmann, John 983
Kaula, Edna Mason 58, 1010, 1011
Kaye, J. Graham 856
Keats, Ezra Jack 700, 729
Keeping, Charles 1038, 1056
Keith, Agnes 92, 961
Kelk, Narredin Zarrin 449
Kennedy, Paul 478, 649
Kennedy, Richard 289, 515
Kibbee, Gordon 393
Kiddell-Monroe, Joan 290, 291, 567, 634, 769, 894
Kim 908
Kim Yong Hwan 902
Kipling, J. Lockwood 688
Kirn, Ann 1134
Koering, Ursula 1063
Komoda, Beverly 1178
Kubie, Nora Benjamin 517
Kubinyi, Laszlo 506, 559
Kubinyi, Coleman 118

Laite, Gordon 642, 643, 1187
Lambo, Don 157
Landa, Peter 830, 929
Larson, Peter (photo) 183, 244, 598
Lattimore, Eleanor Frances 813-824, 918
Lazzaro, Victor 102
Leatham, Moyra 636
LeCain, Errol 827
LeFoil, Alain 886
Legueret, J. P. 691
Leight, Edward 760
Lent, Blair 637, 889, 1109, 1137, 1169, 1189
Levin, Eli 435

Lewis, Allen 607
Lewis, Richard 179
Lieberman, Archie (photo) 435
Lignell, Lois 891
Lilly, Charles 190
Linton, Anne 215, 619
Lionni, Leo 1148
Little, Lisa 245
Lobel, Anita 1190
Loewenstein, Bernice 140
Loering, Ursula 1063
Lo-Koon-Chiu 774, 778
Lonette, Reisie 661
Lorraine, W. 354
Louden, Claire and George 578, 693, 993
Low, Joseph 123, 1209

Maaroef, Ipe 988
McCrea, James and Ruth 390
McDermott, Gerald 272, 1116
MacDougal, Dugald 356
McMillan, Constance 701
Maitland, Antony V. 372
Malvern, Corinne 497, 498
Marokvia, Artur 654, 916
Marriott, Pat 1091
Mars, W. T. 109, 220, 347, 349, 519, 679, 696, 870, 980, 1061
Martin, David Stone 986
Martin, Stefan 76
Masani, Shakuntala 622
May, Seong 789
Melrose, Genevieve 1050, 1093
Merriam, Eve 1118
Meryman, Hope 265
Mill, Eleanor 970
Miller, Shane 96
Mitsuhashi, Yoko 1110, 1176
Mitsui, Eiichi 1160
Mizumura, Kazue 644, 847, 896, 898, 899, 912, 919, 921, 939, 940, 941, 1163, 1165, 1174, 1177
Molina, Charles 346
Monk, Randy 631, 632
Mordvinoff, Nicolas 692
Morse, Dorothy Bailey 127, 548, 549
Moser, Charles 61
Mott, Herb 1025

Moyler, Alan 534
Moynihan, Roberta H. 702
Mozley, Charles 119, 479
Munson, Harold 998, 1105
Myers, Jack 129

Nairac, Rosamonde 90, 721
Nakatani, Chiyoko 1171
Nankivel, Claudine 723, 1020
Negri, Rocco 116, 1153
Ness, Evaline 141
Ngaokrachang, Payut 974
Nicholas, Frank 1027
Nickel, Helmut 39
Nodjaumi, Nickzad 392

Ohlsson, Ib 64
Olorisa, Aduni 266
Olugebefola, Ademola 264
Omura, Yuriko 1170
Onishi, Toyojiro 848
Orbaan, Albert 991
Osborne, Richard G. 520
Owens, Carl 177

Page, Homer 964
Palmer, Juliette 885
Palmer, Myron Tim 135
Pantoc, Henky 996
Papin, Joseph A. 212
Pappas, William 72, 371
Parker, Bob 491
Parker, Nancy 1057
Parrish, Maxfield 483
Parry, David 1076
Payson, Dale 297
Pearson, Clyde 1075
Peck, Graham 828
Petersham, Maud and Miska 502, 503, 504
Petie, Haris 42, 101, 200, 412, 444, 972
Petrash, Rosalie 373
Philips, W. F. 286
Pinkney, Jerry 258, 273, 1123
Pitchford, D. Watkins 670
Powers, Richard 83, 418, 591, 869, 1188
Prabha, B. 608
Prassano, Bani 608

Illustrator Index

Prechtl, James Rovert (photo) 864
Prestopino, Gregorio 259, 270
Price, Christine 4, 44, 98, 274, 1149
Price, Harold 685

Quackenbush, Robert 345
Quinn, Paul 684, 812, 1058

Rafael, Elaine 117
Raible, Alton 145, 683
Ray, Ralph 55, 614, 1041
Reed, Philip 481
Reid, James 225
Renner, Hans Peter 120
Ribbons, Ian 1097
Richter, M. 218
Ridge, Antonia 210
Ritchie, T. 780
Riwkin-Brick, Anna (photo) 529, 533, 674
Roberts, Doreen 508
Robinson, Charles 70, 182, 796
Rockwell, Anne 1120
Roedelius, Hildegard 550
Rojansky, Fedor 579
Roselli, Luciana 134
Rousseau, P. 580
Russell, George (photo) 907
Rutherfoord, William deJ. 600

Sader, Lillian 638, 681
Sadighian, Parvia 626
Sagsoorian, Paul 146
Sakai, Sanryo 1155
Sandin, Joan 1114
Sandoz, Eduard 374
Santosh, G. R. 608
Sasaki, Kisa 150, 197, 323
Sasek, M. 1125, 1139, 1193
Satorsky, Cyril 551
Sawyer, Martha 365
Schaeffer, Mead 1065, 1066
Schloat, G. Warren 248, 379, 606, 730, 867, 967
Schnidler, Edith 489
Schoenherr, John 75
Schramm, Ulrich 74, 211
Schroeder, Ted 301
Seale, Clem 1095

Segawa, Yasuo 1161, 1164, 1167
Sejima, Yoshimasa 1175
Seligsohn, Nancy 222
Seltzer, Meyer 1108
Sendak, Maurice 802
Sewell, Helen 214
Shekerjian, Regina 1128
Shepard, Ernest H. 547
Sherman, Theresa 838
Shigaki, Tack 932
Shimin, Symeon 184, 221, 527
Shirakama, Akihito 938
Shore, Robert 556
Shulevitz, Uri 474, 509, 523, 776, 783
Siberell, Anne 487
Siegl, Helen 276
Silverman, Burt 472
Silverman, Mel 6, 535
Simon, Howard 500, 518
Singer, Edith 233, 234, 298
Slobodkin, Louis 837, 1172
Smalley, Janet 911
Smee, John 398
Smith, Virginia 1124
Smith, William A. 793, 1127
Solbert, Ronni 105, 524, 641, 710, 779, 861
Sowell, Floyd 191
Spence, Geraldine 1044, 1094
Sperry, Armstrong 1033, 1101
Spier, Jo 1194
Spring, Bob and Ira (photo) 855
Stevens, Anthony 79
Stinemetz, Morgan 699
Stirnweis, Shannon 158
Stobbs, William 13, 59, 1034, 1035, 1037
Stubley, Trevor 181
Suba, Suzanne 630
Sucksdorf, Astrid Bergman (photo) 709

Tamarin, Alfred (photo) 29, 424, 853
Tekle 103
Tetlow, George 1104
Thet Pau Oo 629
Thomas, Hans 122
Thomas, Harold 1040
Thomas, Leslie 781

Thompson, Peter 726
Thompson, Ralph 314, 355
Tohani, Mohammad 103
Tomes, Jacqueline 62
Tong, Wallace 103
Tresilian, Stuart 189
Tuckwell, Jennifer 1100
Turska, Kristyna 403

Uchida, Yoshiko 935

Vajrathon, Mallica (photo) 996
Vaughan, Anne 704
Vaughan-Jackson, Genevieve 609
Vestal, H. B. 47
Vo-Dinh 892, 981

Wafi, Abdel Maquid 103
Walford, Astrid 309
Walker, Gil 457
Wangbaje, Irein 263
Ward, John 768
Ward, Lynd 884
Warner, Peter 275, 359
Watanabe, Saburo 1182
Watkins, Bernard 732
Weisgard, Leonard 131, 492, 914, 1133
Weisner, William 1196
Weiss-Sonnenburg, Hedwig 839
Werth, Kurt 471
Weston, Christine (photo) 450
White, David Omar 340, 473, 545
Whitear, A. R. 344
Wiese, Kurt 322, 358, 686, 738, 739, 782, 786, 787, 790, 804, 826, 831, 840, 927, 997, 1126
Wildsmith, Brian 507, 1047
Wilkinson, Barry 132, 288
Wilson, George 78
Winslade 281
Wolcott, Elizabeth Tyler 128, 400
Wong, Jeanyee 745, 811, 832
Worboys, Evelyn 38, 439, 863
Wright, Matvyn 708
Wyath, N. C. 585

Yamaguchi, Marianne 900, 901
Yamaguchi, Taro 477, 944
Yamazaki, Sanae 887
Yang, Jan 784, 785
Yashima, Mitsu 1181
Yashima, Taro 890, 1179, 1180, 1181, 1205
Yen, Liang 1143
Young, Ed 484, 1142, 1144, 1154, 1183
Young, Noela 1064

Zacks, Lewis 604
Zamani, Zaman 449

BIOGRAPHICAL INDEX*

Alexander the Great 10, 11, 13, 14
Allah 9
Ataturk 386, 387
Augustine, Saint 206

Belisarius 384
Bell, Gertrude 456
Ben-Gurion, David 452
Bird, Isabella 367
Brazza, Pierre Savorgnan de 304
Bruce, James 114
Buck, Pearl 746
Buddha 612

Chaka [also, Shaka] King of the Zulus 334, 335, 338
Chiang Kai-shek 763
Chou En-lai 743
Cleopatra 107, 109, 111, 112
Clive, Robert 627
Confucius 755
Cook, Captain James 1030, 1032, 1033, 1034, 1036

Dalai Lama 766
Dayan, Moshe 465
Dayan, Ruth 453

Dinesen, Isak 167, 168
Diqs, Isaac 454
Dooley, Dr. Tom 976

Feelings, Tom 252
Francis Xavier, St. 624
Frisbee, Florence (Johnny) 1026

Gama, Vasco da 15
Gandhi, Indira 616
Gandhi, Mohandas 613, 614, 621, 625, 626, 628
Genghis Khan 750, 752, 757, 758
Glover, John Hawley 254
Godden, Jon and Rumer 617
Gordon, Charles George (Chinese) 113

Haile Selassie 108
Hannibal 205, 207
Han Suyin 754
Harris, Townsend 876
Hautzig, Esther 563
Ho Chi Minh 975
Hokusai 878
Huxley, Elspeth 169

---

*The following, by title, are books containing multiple biographies: African Heroes 59; The Bitter Choice: Eight South Africans' Resistance to Tyranny 336; Explorers of the Pacific 1024; Five Queens of Ancient Egypt 106; Great Rulers of the African Past 54; Leaders of the New Africa 58; Ms. Africa: Profiles of Modern African Women 53; The Nehrus of India 620; Profiles from the New Asia 368; Seven Women Explorers 12; Three Sisters; The Story of the Soong Family 765.

Biographical Index

Issa 875

Kaunda, Kenneth 337
Kenyatta, Jomo 166
Kingsley, Mary 62
Kublai Khan 749

Lawrence ["of Arabia"], T. E. 457
Layard, Austin Henry 463
Leakey, L. S. B. 170
Li Shu-Fan [Hong Kong Surgeon] 759
Livingstone, David 55, 60
Lumumba, Patrice 308

Magellan, Ferdinand 1025, 1028, 1031, 1035, 1037
Maigumeri, Charley 57
Mao Tse-tung 744, 751
Marco Polo 748, 756, 760, 761, 762
Mehdevi, Anne Sinclair 459
Mehta, Amolak Ram 623
Meir, Golda 458, 461
Melville, Hermann 1027
Modupe, Prince 256
Mohammed 462, 466

Nakamoto, Hiroko 877
Nehru, Jawaharlal 611, 615, 622
Nkrumah, Kwame 251, 255
Noguchi, Hideyo 874

Pandit, Vijaya Lakshmi 618
Peters, Thomas 253
Piankhy the Great 110

Rawlinson, Henry 464
Ross (Malaria) Ronald 619

Schliemann, Heinrich 383, 385
Schweitzer, Albert 305, 306, 307, 309, 310
Shaka see Chaka

Stanley, Henry M. 51, 52, 56, 61
Sugimoto, Etsu Inagaki 879
Sun Yat-sen 745, 747, 764

Tchernavin, Tatiana 564
Vasco Da Gama 15
Weizmann, Chaim 451
Woolley, Sir Leonard 455
Xavier see Francis

Yadin, Yigael 460
Yehonala, or Tzu Hsi (Chinese Empress) 753
Yoshida, Jim 880